Original illisible

NF Z 43-120-10

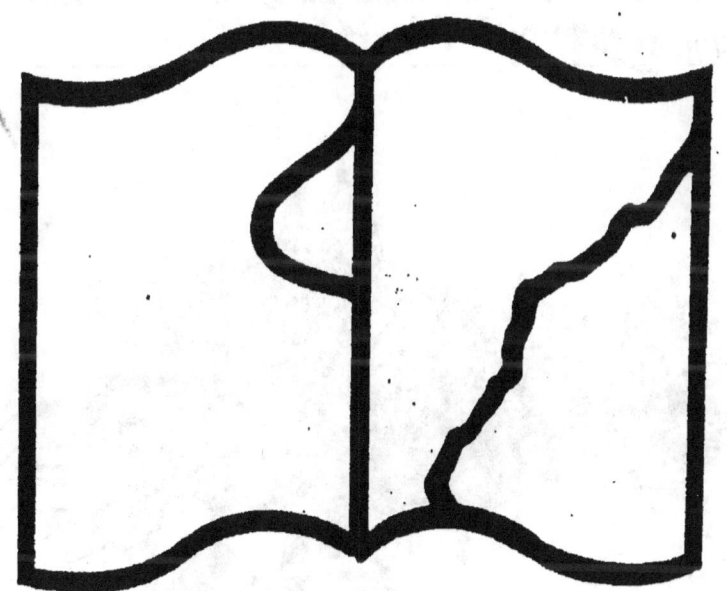

Texte détérioré — reliure défectueuse

NF Z 43-120-11

"VALABLE POUR TOUT OU PARTIE DU DOCUMENT REPRODUIT".

THE SAÔNE

A Summer Voyage

BY

Philip Gilbert Hamerton

AUTHOR OF "A PAINTER'S CAMP," "ROUND MY HOUSE,"
"THE UNKNOWN RIVER," ETC., ETC.

With a hundred and forty-eight Illustrations by JOSEPH PENNELL
and the AUTHOR, and four Maps.

Gray from the west

LONDON
SEELEY & CO., 46, 47 & 48 ESSEX STREET, STRAND
1887

RICHARD CLAY AND SONS,
LONDON AND BUNGAY.

TO THE MEMORY OF

FRANÇOIS FRÉDÉRIC GINDRIEZ,

FORMERLY

PREFECT OF THE DEPARTMENT OF THE DOUBS,

AND

DEPUTY FOR SAÔNE-ET-LOIRE,

ONE OF THE KINDEST, MOST UPRIGHT, AND MOST

DISINTERESTED OF MEN,

THIS DESCRIPTION OF A RIVER THAT HE FIRST MADE KNOWN

TO THE AUTHOR,

Is affectionately Inscribed,

BY HIS FRIEND AND SON-IN-LAW.

PREFACE.

This account of a voyage on the Saône includes the whole of that river which is navigable, and the navigable Saône has been increased in length of late years by the engineering works that now make it accessible for sixty miles above the beautiful little town of Gray.

A clear understanding of the fluvial character of the Saône may be gained by dividing it into three parts.

The first part is from its source at Vioménil in the Vosges to the junction with the river Coney at Corre. This is the young Saône, and it is not navigable unless possibly in an interrupted manner for canoes.

From the junction with the Coney to that with the Doubs at Verdun we have the Upper Saône, which is navigable naturally for very considerable distances, and yet, as a whole, only open in consequence of great engineering works. It was, however, open from Auxonne downwards in the times of the Crusades.

The addition of the waters of the Doubs at Verdun greatly increases the importance of the Saône, which is navigable from Verdun to Lyons for small sailing yachts. Here the river is broad and has a current, the extreme slowness of which was noticed long ago by Cæsar. What little speed it had in ancient days has been still further diminished by the five weirs between Verdun and Lyons, which convert the river into a series of very long ponds, except when the sluices are opened and the current flows naturally, according to the quantity of water.

From the Coney to the Doubs the Saône is a good river for oarsmen, but the locks are too numerous for their taste. From the mouth of the Doubs to Neuville, above Lyons, it is the best river to sail upon in Europe, and probably in the world. This quality is not owing simply to the extreme slowness of the current, but also to a general sufficiency of depth, and to the good exposure of the surface of the water to the action of different winds.

The scenery of the navigable Saône is never so hilly anywhere as it is between Trévoux and Lyons, but in the upper river the ground is pleasantly diversified by the kind of hill that the French call *collines*, and there are many beautiful woods. From Verdun to Ormes, a village a few miles above Tournus, the scenery is almost Dutch in its flatness, but not without a strong character and a peculiar beauty of its own. Afterwards it remains generally open, with fine distances, till the distances become more mountainous as we travel south, and finally the hills approach the borders of the river just below Trévoux, which is rather more than fourteen miles above Lyons.

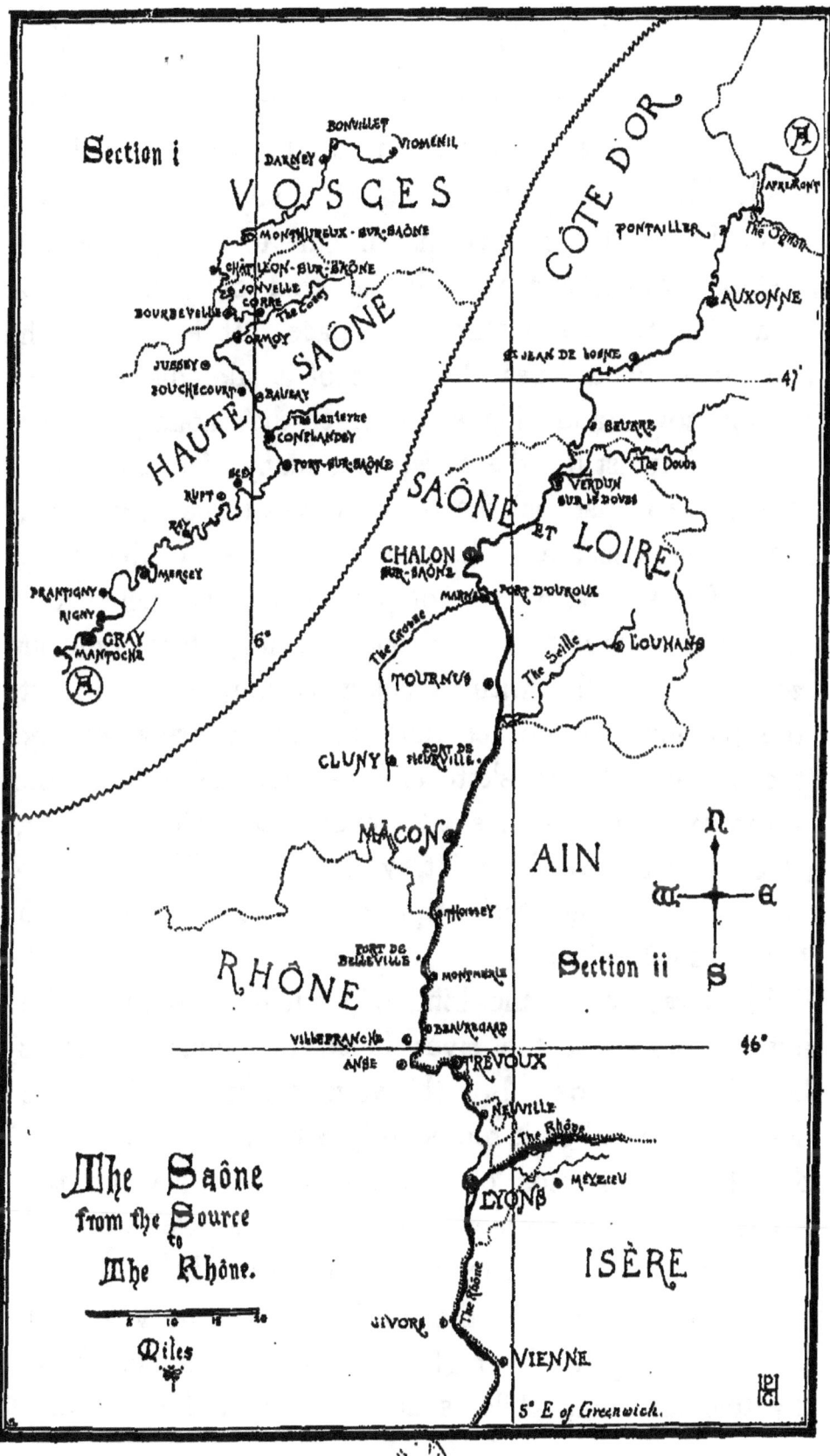

The landscape of the Saône is alternately beautiful or dull (the dull parts giving the voyager a renewed appetite for the beauty that is sure to follow), but it is seldom grand, except with the kind of grandeur that may be due to vastness of space. It has more the character of the sea than that of a lake district.

The towns and villages by which the Saône passes are rich in interest for the artist, and many of them also for the archæologist, but the reader ought to be warned that sketching is scarcely tolerated. The arrest of the author and of the artist who accompanied him was believed in England to have been a mistake resulting from officious zeal in combination with ridiculous ignorance; but, in fact, the *gendarmes* acted according to their instructions, and the release of the sketchers was due entirely to the authority of a distinguished General, an artillery officer, who commanded the military district of Dijon. Even after this incident efficient protection was obtained with the greatest difficulty.

With regard to the kind of travelling adopted, the author preferred the river itself, as being the most beautiful of roads. For the voyage above Chalon he used a long canal-boat, temporarily converted into a house-boat by the erection of a camp inside it, and for the Lower Saône he employed a sailing-boat well adapted to those waters. The reason for this difference of navigation was that on the northern river the voyagers had often to pass the night at a great distance from any tolerable inn, whilst south of Chalon the inns are sufficiently frequent to make the necessity for sleeping on board a boat no more than an occasional little hardship. Besides this the Lower Saône is so favourable to sailing that the temptation was not to be resisted, and a lover of aquatic amusements finds his patience rather too severely tested by a month on a canal-boat.

The form of narrative adopted is that of familiar letters, addressed to the author's friend and publisher, Mr. Richmond Seeley. His practice was to write these letters as far as possible on board the boat, and to take ample notes for those which the work of the voyage itself did not leave him time to write at the moment. The letters were really addressed to Mr. Seeley in the first place, and written in a more especial sense for him, though it would be a false pretence to say that the writer had not, at the same time, an eye to a more numerous public. It was the author's own idea that letters of an informal kind, addressed to one who had taken from the first a most friendly interest in the expedition, would naturally permit the introduction of many not insignificant details that must have been eliminated from a more formal narrative. What seems most desirable is to make the reader feel himself one of the party, and this object may be attained more completely by letters conveying accurately the impressions received from day to day than by a colder *résumé* written out long afterwards. For the same reason the earlier projects and impressions are retained in their own place even when later ones have subsequently corrected or superseded them.

With regard to the freshness of the material, it is believed that no Englishman or American ever before made the voyage of the navigable Saône. Many, no doubt, have descended in the public steamer from Chalon to Lyons, but to ascend the river from Chalon to Corre (a much longer distance) is to pass through regions in which there is no accommodation for tourists. In fact, the voyage would have been impossible without an arrangement for living entirely on board the boat. In this case the expedition was planned so as to give both author and artist every convenience for their work. The author had his private study at hand in all places and in all weathers, with books for reference and every convenience for writing; the artist worked from nature with the knowledge that he was never more than a mile from his lodging, his luggage, and his dinner, in fact, he had not to give a thought to any material consideration. Every member of the expedition had his appointed duties, which were performed with a very near approach to the strictest regularity, and a degree of order was maintained that would have done credit to a much more fashionable vessel. In all attempts at independent travel there are sure to be some causes of vexation. Those which occurred in this voyage are told quite frankly in the following pages.

LIST OF ILLUSTRATIONS.

Of the illustrations in the following list a hundred and two are original pen-drawings by Mr. Pennell, nineteen are original pen-drawings by Mr. Hamerton, twenty-four are drawings in ink by Mr. Pennell from originals in lead-pencil by Mr. Hamerton, and three are done in ink by Mr. Hamerton from originals in aquatint, etching, and pencil by M. Jules Chevrier and Mr. J. P. Pettitt. Auxonne and Lyons, being fortified towns, are not illustrated.

By J. Pennell.

	PAGE
Gray from the West	*Title Page.*
The *Boussemroum* Moored	11
Above Chalon	13
The Galley Stove	17
A Sketch	19
A River Train	20
The Tents from La Cour Pennell . . . *To face page*	22
St. Jean de Losne	27
Gray, the Bridge and Weir	30
The Lock at Corre	40
The *Boussemroum* at Corre . . . *To face page*	44
The Church at Corre	45
The Land Gipsies at Corre	46
Corre, the Main Street . . . *To face page*	50
Franki and Zoulou	52
Ormoy in the distance	53
Ormoy from the Canal	59
Ormoy, the Public Fountain	60
A House in Ormoy	61

List of Illustrations.

	PAGE
Richecourt from Ormoy	62
Richecourt	62
A Country House near Ranzevelle	63
A Street at Cendrecourt	65
Cendrecourt from the Fields	66
A Barn at Cendrecourt	67
Ferry near Jussey	69
Wood near Jussey	72
A Curve of the Upper Saône	75
Fouchécourt	75
Conflandey, the Village	78
Conflandey, the Towing Path	79
Port-sur-Saône	81
Port-sur-Saône, the Little Bridge	82
Port-sur-Saône, the Channel between the Islands	84
The *Boussemroum* in the Canal at Chemilly	85
The Bridge at Chemilly	87
The River Durgeon at Chemilly	88
From the Terrace, Chemilly	90
Canal between Scey and Chemilly	92
The *Boussemroum* in the Basin at Scey	*To face page* 92
A House in Scey	*To face page* 94
Tunnel below Scey	97
Ovanches—the Cross	100
A House at Ovanches	101
Rupt, the Church	*To face page* 102
Rupt, the Round Tower	104
The Saône near Ray	107
Lock on the Ray Canal	108

By P. G. Hamerton.

Ray	109

By J. Pennell.

The River Bank near Ray	111
On the Canal near Savoyeux	*To face page* 116

List of Illustrations.

Ferry at Prantigny	119
Gray from the North East	124
Gray from the North . . . . *To face page*	124
Old Shop in Gray	125
Courtyard at Gray	126
A Little Bridge at Gray	129
Near Gray	131
Mantoche	132
In the Woodland	138
Pontailler, from the Second Bridge	140
Pontailler, on the Old Saône	142
Old House at Pontailler	147
A Sketch	149
Coming down behind Steamer	154
Our Quarterdeck	159
Sunset on the Broad Saône	161
A Sketch	164
The Church at St. Jean de Losne	166
The Main Street at St. Jean de Losne . . . . *To face page*	168
Steam Tug at St. Jean de Losne . . . . *To face page*	170
On board a Péniche	175
A House Boat	177
A Sketch	178
A Sketch	179
Écuelles	179
A Sketch, Evening	180
A Sketch, Evening	180
Verdun, the Ferry from the Island	183
Verdun, from the Island in the Doubs	184
Verdun, the Foot-bridge . . . . *To face page*	184
A Corner in Verdun	186
The Bridge at Verdun	189
A Sketch	194
A Sketch	195
A Haystack	196
Gergy	197

	PAGE
A Village in the Plain	197
Allériot	199

By P. G. Hamerton.

Zoulou's Farewell	202
Chalon, the Bridge from the North	207

By P. G. Hamerton after J. Chevrier.[1]

Chalon, the Bridge, A.D. 1600	212

By P. G. Hamerton.

Place du Châtelet, Chalon	213
Chalon, the Deanery Tower	215

By P. G. Hamerton after J. Chevrier.

Rue St. Vincent, Chalon	219

By P. G. Hamerton.

Chalon, Place de l'Hôtel de Ville, flooded	*To face page*	216
Chalon, from the Little Creusot		220
Chalon, the Hospital		222
The *Arar*, Deck View		230

By J. Pennell.

Port d'Ouroux, North End	234
Port d'Ouroux, South End	235

---

[1] M. Chevrier's etching, of which the drawing is a copy, was itself done from a picture contemporary with the state of the bridge which it represents.

By P. G. Hamerton.

	PAGE
The *Arar* under sail	237

By J. Pennell.

Tournus, the Bridge	249
On the Quay at Tournus	250
Ruelle at Tournus	251
The Market-place at Tournus	252
The Towers of Tournus . . . *To face page*	256
Tournus, the Big Parasol	260
A Sketch	261
Villars	262
A Landing-stage	264

By P. G. Hamerton.

The *Arar*, with Tents	266

By J. Pennell after P. G. Hamerton.

Island of Fleurville from the Inn	271
Mâcon, from St. Laurent	273

By P. G. Hamerton.

Mâcon, the Hotel du Sauvage	275

By J. Pennell.

The Bridge at Mâcon	281

By P. G. Hamerton.

	PAGE
Mâcon, St. Laurent	282
Mâcon, Towers of St. Vincent and Prefecture	283

By J. Pennell after P. G. Hamerton.

Mâcon from the Railway Bridge	287
The Cliffs of Solutré	288
A House at Port d'Arciat	291

By J. Pennell.

A Sketch	293

By J. Pennell after P. G. Hamerton.

The Beaujolais Hills from Thoissey	295
Where we slept at Port de Thoissey	297
Near Thoissey	298
Montmerle from Port de Belleville	302
Montmerle from the South	304

By P. G. Hamerton.

Beauregard from the South	308
Beauregard from the West	309
The *Arar*, with a fair wind	310

By J. Pennell after P. G. Hamerton.

Riottier from the North	311
Riottier from the South	312
Trévoux from the North	313

The Quay at Trévoux . . . . *To face page* 314
Trévoux, Rue du Port 316
Trévoux, the Bridge 318

By J. Pennell after P. G. Hamerton.

St. Germain au Mont d'Or 322

By P. G. Hamerton.

Petite Amie in a Light Breeze 324
Petite Amie in a Gust 327

By J. Pennell after P. G. Hamerton.

In the Basin above Neuville 328
Cliff of Quarry at Couzon 329
Couzon Church and Hills 330
Île Barbe, North End 333
Île Barbe, from the East . . . . *To face page* 336
St. Rambert, Île Barbe to the Right . . . . *To face page* 338

By P. G. Hamerton after J. P. Pettitt.

Confluence of Saône and Rhône 343

By J. Pennell after P. G. Hamerton.

The Mont d'Or from Île Bène 346

LIST OF MAPS.

        PAGE

1. The Saône, from the Source to the Confluence with the Rhône (in Preface)

  To face page viii

2. The Saône, from the Source to the Confluence with the Ognon. *To face page* 42

3. The Saône, from the Confluence with the Ognon, to the Confluence with the Seille . . . . *To face page* 140

4. The Saône, from the Confluence with the Seille, to the Confluence with the Rhône . . . . *To face page* 262

THE SAÔNE

LETTER I.

AUTUN, *April 20th*, 1886.

My projected voyage on the Saône presents many practical difficulties. I am familiar with the Lower Saône from many different sailing voyages, and therefore know the peculiarities of the river travel that it affords, but the case of the Upper Saône is entirely different. It would evidently be a great error to think of *sailing* there, except, perhaps, for an occasional reach of river with little current, well-exposed water, and a wind that happened to be agreeable, so I propose to hire a steam-launch for the Upper Saône, and only take the *Arar* (my sailing-boat) from Chalon down to Lyons. I have a particular steamer in view, a new boat that has attained a high speed and excelled good rivals in the last Chalon regatta. This seems the most rational plan, as with a steamer I can run up the 150 miles from Chalon rapidly and come down again at leisure making sketches. The steamer in question has a saloon that will hold two comfortable berths, a kitchen, and a rather commodious forecastle for the men. By setting up a small tent on the roof at night an additional berth might be gained, so there would be accommodation for three gentlemen and the sailors. These last would consist of the engineer, the pilot (who is quite indispensable), and a cook. The gentlemen would be an artist (I should not have time to illustrate the river adequately myself), a military friend, and your correspondent. If I were lucky in the choice of an artist and of the crew the expedition would be pleasant and probably successful. The military friend that I have in view is to be thoroughly relied upon as a travelling companion, and I have but one anxiety about him, which is, that possibly some engagement may prevent him from joining me.

LETTER II.

(An Extract.)   AUTUN, *April 26th.*

I have applied for the steamer, but as the owner is also the builder he declines to let because he is anxious to sell, and after an excursion of this kind the boat might be considered no longer perfectly new. An application elsewhere for another steamer has met with exactly the same response. The difficulty about hiring appears to be practically insurmountable. There are a certain number of private steam-yachts on the river, but their owners are rich men who would not be tempted to deprive themselves of their vessels during the summer season, and builders only want to sell. I have not the least desire to encumber myself permanently with a steam-yacht, even if I could afford the luxury. The oily smells, the smoke, and the vibration, are to my taste insuperable objections in a machine intended for pleasure. There is one sailing-yacht on the river with fair cabin accommodation, but she is only useful on the tranquil reaches of the Lower Saône. Just at present I hardly see what is to be done.

LETTER III.

(Extract.)   AUTUN, *May 1st.*

All hopes of a steamer are finally at an end, and I am devising another plan. My sailing-boat, the *Arar*, might be treated as a canal-boat on the Upper Saône, and drawn by a horse on the towing-path. I have a deck-tent to sleep under at night, and when a rain-storm comes on. This, of course, we should take, and though the accommodation is narrow for three it is just sufficient. The present plan would be to sleep in the inns when they were available, and in the boat tent when an inn happened to be too far from the river. The scheme is feasible, though I foresee difficulties, nevertheless it is the only plan that suggests itself at present. The greatest objection is the narrowness of the accommodation for three persons on board my boat. This is endurable in a short excursion, but would be felt as a serious inconvenience in a voyage extending over several weeks.

LETTER IV.

(Extract.)   AUTUN, *May 8th.*

I have found a man and horse, and asked a friend at Chalon to engage them definitively, so the manner of the voyage is quite settled. The man's charge is reasonable, and he is a perfectly respectable character, well-known to some friends of mine. We shall work up the river as quickly as possible.

LETTER V.

AUTUN, *May 10th.*

My friend at Chalon, just before engaging the man and horse, happened to meet with a contractor for water transport and mentioned my scheme to him. The contractor immediately said, "The scheme looks attractive, but it will not work. The defect of it is, that the man with the horse will be separated from the boat every evening, when he will have to seek for a lodging for himself and his beast. He will therefore always have a good excuse, towards evening, for leaving everything and riding off in search of a village. The gentlemen will either be left with their boat and its small accommodation, having to dine as they can, or else they, too, will have to leave the boat and all it contains without any one to guard it, whilst they seek for some village inn. They may possibly find the village, but it is not certain that they will always find an inn fit to receive them, and they may have to come back to their boat late, after seeking in vain. The practical inconveniences of this might, at times, be rather serious — meals missed, and the narrow lodging on the boat after all, besides the frequent and unavoidable absences of the man just at a time when he would be particularly useful. *Ce serait un cas de force majeure.*

"Now what I should suggest," the contractor went on to say, "is that Mr. Hamerton should rent a *berrichon*[1] and take its owner and a pilot for his crew. Every berrichon has a donkey on board in its own stable, which is a regular part of the boat, and although at first sight it may appear that the donkey would be slow, the fact is that the horse would only go at a walking pace, and the difference would not be so great as it might appear. The men, too, could tow the boat at times if the donkey were tired, and a considerable distance might be quietly got over each day. Then, in descending the Saône, and especially the Upper Saône, the current would be some advantage. The men would always sleep on the berrichon, and could be found when wanted at all hours of the day and night."

Another suggestion has grown out of this, which is, that I should take a *coursi*. This kind of boat has much more beam than a berrichon, and is not so long. It has the great advantage of possessing two good permanent rooms, and there is stabling for a pair of horses on board. The coursi would cost me more, but the temptation of the permanent rooms is considerable. They look rough from the outside, but might be made sufficiently comfortable within.

Here is a practicable idea! The notion of the floating

---

[1] An extremely long and narrow canal boat, built expressly for the canals in the Berri country, where the locks used to be very narrow. Since the widening of the locks it is not unlikely that this curious type of boat may become extinct.

habitation on the coursi has suggested a combination of camp and berrichon. I have preserved as relics of my camp life in Scotland three of my best tents. Two of these are the regular Edgington porch tent in good condition, the third is a studio tent that served me in Scotland for painting from nature at a distance from my hut. I should have nothing to do but set up this camp on the berrichon, and it might be pitched far more perfectly than a camp that has to be removed every day.

A berrichon is such a very long boat—eighty feet at least—that the camp could be set up with ease, and there would be spaces between the tents, an immense convenience. The carrying power of a berrichon being about eighty tons, one is free to take luggage without limit.

LETTER VI.

AUTUN, *May 15th.*

Too busy to go to the Saône to select a berrichon myself, I have intrusted the commission to a friend. He writes that he has considerable difficulty in finding what I want, as I do not desire to have women and children on board, and almost all these boats are family residences. He tranquilly inquires if I have any objection to a bigamist, as there is a very suitable berrichon with a man and two wives. This I suspect to be an invention of his own; probably the man's wife has her sister with her or some other relation, as I know that whole families live together on the water. My objection to children is, that they would generally be in the way and make noise; as for the sex that we all adore, I should like to know the woman personally before intrusting my peace to her for many weeks. She might possibly be a talker, or even a scold, she might be dirty and slovenly in her habits, all which would spoil the pleasure of my trip completely, and there would be no remedy against a woman who was established in her own house, under the protection of her own husband.

In any case I shall require what is called, on the Saône, a "marinier," in addition to the owner of the boat. I may explain here that a "marinier" is a professional river boatman, whereas the men on the berrichons are often simply canal boatmen belonging to central France, and unaccustomed to the great rivers. A "marinier" of the first rank would probably be classed as a pilot and expect high wages, but it may be necessary to take a pilot as I know nothing about the Upper Saône. The river below Chalon is familiar to me in detail, and I could take a small sailing-yacht over it without help, but I feel no desire to accept the management of an eighty-ton canal-boat even there. The art of managing those long heavy boats is peculiar, and a profession of itself. The navigation of such a thing would not be a pleasure to me. I look upon it simply as a convenience for having the camp afloat.

LETTER VII.

AUTUN, *May 20th.*

My friend has engaged a berrichon on the recommendation of the contractor. The owner is described as *un brave homme*, which in French, as you know, means a trustworthy, straightforward sort of fellow.

What a good thing it is to be very strict and precise about measurements! The exact *interior* measure of the berrichon is seven feet two and a half inches, and it is impossible to squeeze my studio tent, by any artifice, into that dimension on account of its pole framework. With the pyramidal tents the case is different. They can be set up with a narrower base and a steeper inclination of roof. I have decided at once to use the side walls only of the studio tent, and have light wooden ends made, so that it will be a combination of hut and tent, which is more convenient than either and combines the merits of both. I can have a window in one end and a door in the other, with ventilating doors in the two gables. The length of the hut is determined by that of the canvas walls, a little over twelve feet. Such is the advantage of knowing exactly what you want in all its details that the mechanical drawing for this hut, complete to scale, occupied me only an hour. This comes of old experience in hutting. It was simply necessary to remember what was good in my Scotch hut and retain it, whilst remembering at the same time what was defective, to improve it.[1]

---

[1] In practice this hut turned out to be exactly what I desired. Its dimensions were a little over twelve feet by six feet six. The height to the top of the walls was seven feet six, and to the top of the gable ten feet nine inches. The roof was simply composed of a couple of rick-cloths, one upon the other. These dimensions gave space and air. Small and low huts are unendurable in hot weather.

LETTER VIII.

CHALON-SUR-SAÔNE, *May 31st.*

At last I have seen the berrichon. It was lying in the canal (the *Canal du Centre*), just opposite the church of St. Côme. As I was looking at the boat a little old man came along the canal bank with a basket on his arm, saluted me, and said that he was the owner of the boat and at my service. I was pleased with his appearance. He wore a straw hat, a blue summer coat, and a pair of nankeen trousers, all perfectly clean. His eyes were as blue as his coat, but much paler. We immediately went on board the odd-looking craft that is to be my home for several weeks. My first anxiety was about the state of its floor. A berrichon in good condition has a floor in thick boards of excellent oak, level from end to end, but a berrichon in bad condition is likely to have a very defective floor. Had this boat been out of repair I should have been compelled to have a new floor for each of the tents, but it luckily happens that this is excellent and nearly new. The bottom of the boat is quite flat, the sides are perpendicular walls of stout oak, breast high. The interior would be a long open corridor were it not divided at intervals by cross-beams, and in the middle of its length by the donkey's house, which crosses from bulwark to bulwark, as the Bridge of Sighs at Venice crosses its narrow canal. The donkey's house is a complete interruption internally, and the most awkward thing in the boat, and near it is a place for hay. At the stern is a poop cabin with two berths for the men, and at the opposite end of the boat there is a small but very necessary forecastle deck, with a sort of cramped cabin under it that is used as a cellar.

The boat is simply blackened with coal-tar (perfectly clean and dry), but the prow is sparingly adorned with white and red paint, and there is some attempt at decoration at the stern. There, by diligent investigation close at hand, or with a glass at a little distance, the name of the vessel may be made out. I print it more plainly here:—

BOUSSEMROUM.
(*pronounced Boossemmrroomm.*)

It was a most unpractical notion, in such a country as France where nobody can learn a strange name, to give this extraordinary one to a canal boat, but the owner tells me that he took it from a place in Algeria, where there is a sacred mosque, and which is connected with his own experience as a soldier.

Vernet, the owner of the *Boussemroum*, showed me the inside of his private cabin, which is clean and orderly. His cooking apparatus is a stove with the conveniences of a small kitchen range, which he keeps outside in the galley. An inspection of his few and simple cooking utensils leads me to hope that his services may be occasionally acceptable when we are at a distance from an inn.

The contrast between the Patron (the owner of a boat is called *le patron* here) and the Pilot is the most striking that could be imagined. If the Patron is a small man, even for France, the Pilot would be considered a big and powerful man in England, or anywhere. He is reputed to be one of the best pilots on the Saône. Besides this he is a splendid swimmer, has rescued no less than fourteen people from drowning, and has received four medals for his bravery. He always wears a little bit of riband belonging to one of these medals. I like his manners, which are plain and straightforward, without either rudeness or any excess of deference. His swimming powers may perhaps be useful, as the patron cannot swim a stroke.

Decidedly there is an African character about the *Boussemroum!* the donkey is called "Zoulou." He is a handsome and lively beast of a dark-brown colour, with fine intelligent eyes.

The "Boussemroum" moored.

The Patron is proud of Zoulou, and bought him for three hundred francs.

The mention of this great sum of money reminds me that perhaps you may be curious to know how much the *Boussemroum* is to cost me. Answer, ten francs a day for boat, Patron, and donkey, and six francs a day for the Pilot. The Patron is to keep himself and Zoulou, the Pilot is to provide his own food and drink.

This does not seem expensive, but to change a berrichon into a comfortable house-boat would have been a costly operation if I had not already possessed the camp, and even as it is there has been an appreciable outlay in adapting the camp to its present employment. There are the two new ends to the hut, with a skeleton to carry the canvas walls and roof. In the tents the poles would have been in the way, so I have replaced them by chevrons,[1] three to each tent, besides which there are washboards round the bottom of the tents to keep them well pitched, as the space is too narrow for correct pitching. There will also be a good deal of joiner's work in the shape of a small quarter-deck, some companion-ladders, shelves, and other trifles that may, however, be useful after the present voyage.

The charge for one man and horse to tow my own sailing-boat was twelve francs a day, if I took him for a month, so I have now only four francs a day in excess of that and I get the boat into the bargain. The expense of setting up the camp divided by the number of days out and added to this sum of four francs a day will give the exact daily cost of the boat considered as lodgings for three gentlemen. But, in addition to the convenience of lodging on board, I shall have two servants always with me and always at my service, instead of one man frequently leaving me to go in search of bed and stable. On the whole, therefore, it seems up to the present time as if I had not made a foolish bargain about the berrichon.[2]

---

[1] Pieces of wood in pairs, opening like pairs of compasses.

[2] These little practical and economical details are left in their place from a belief that they may possibly be interesting, or even useful, to readers who have themselves a turn for independent travel. From the literary point of view they are fully authorised by Defoe, and other examples.

LETTER IX.

RACONNAY, *June 1st, Evening.*

We have already done some miles on the river, and the boat is at rest opposite a little village called Raconnay, below Verdun.

As we shall have to pass all these places in coming down, I do not wish to trouble you with any descriptions of the

Above Chalon.

scenery or the localities during the ascending voyage. I shall confine myself for the present quite strictly to the circumstances and events (if any) of the voyage itself.

Yesterday, after writing my letter, I had the berrichon taken up to a basin in the *Canal du Centre,* above a lock, and there she was fastened to the shore at a pleasant spot, where a green lawny bank goes down to the water, and there is a path in the grass under shady trees. There the dray brought all the camp apparatus from the railway station, which is very near, and a clever joiner set up the woodwork of the saloon. All the rest of the luggage was put on board in a confused way, but with some regard to future convenience.

I then went to inquire at different offices about steam-tugs ascending the river, and learned that a tug was to start for Gray this morning, early, and that there would be no other for four days. One could not hesitate about the proper course to pursue. Everything was on board, though in confusion. It was plain, therefore, that we must start as we were, and try to get our habitations in order whilst the boat was in motion.

The berrichon had to be brought down from the canal to the river. The canal bridges at Chalon are remarkably low. The Pilot had the foresight to go and measure the height of the lowest above the water exactly with a piece of string. He found that it gave about three inches clear above the gable of the saloon. This bit of carefulness promises well; no really careless man would have taken such a precaution without orders.

In the canal the Pilot was ostentatiously submissive, asking the Patron for his orders and obeying them with such phrases as this, "It is your business to command, mine to obey." The length of the voyage on the canal is nine hundred English yards. We had no sooner got through the last bridge, and out into the river, than the Pilot gave an order in a stentorian voice, and as the Patron seemed rather taken aback the new commander curtly explained the state of affairs, "On the canal you are master, on the river I am master. You have no authority on the river." It is easy to be submissive during some hundreds of yards when you are to be master for hundreds of miles!

According to the laws of inland navigation the Pilot is quite right. He is a registered Saône pilot and commands the working of the ship. It remains to be seen how the old Patron, who has never been on the river before, will submit to a master on his own boat which he has commanded ever since she was launched, now eleven years ago.

Considering that we were obliged to start in a hurry on account of the tug, it was fortunate that my friend and guest, Captain Kornprobst, had joined me already at Chalon instead of coming to join me three days later, when I expected to leave that place. I knew that he would be of great use during the preparations, and had begged him to meet me early yesterday morning on that account. This he did with his usual punctuality, that is, to the minute.

The Captain began his intercourse with our family by being the friend of my eldest son, who had, and still preserves, the warmest affection for him, notwithstanding the disparity of their ages, and who was very anxious that I should make his acquaintance. He has now for some years been a friend of my own, and I owe great thanks to my boy for his discernment. The Captain has all the qualities that are most rare and most valuable in a travelling companion on an expedition such as this. To begin with, I never in my life knew any human being who excelled him in equality of good humour. In the most vexatious circumstances he remains perfectly cool, perfectly serene, perfectly well able to see how to make the best of the situation thus freshly created for him, and, having rapidly decided what to do, he is as cheerful as before, with a mind completely disengaged and ready to pay attention to any other matter. His long military experience makes him look upon the small hardships of my river expeditions as nothing more than a variety of amusement. He has a most robust constitution, and has enjoyed finer health, on the whole, than any man I ever knew intimately enough to be acquainted with the details of his life; and this in spite of the long hardships of the Crimean war, and also of the terrible winter in the Franco-German war, and in spite of a wound in that war which caused long and severe suffering. The ball then received has never been extracted, but it now gives no more than occasional trouble. The Captain tells me that the most obvious result of his wound was to age him considerably. His hair and beard became rapidly grey, and are now almost white. He maintains his health by regular exercise, walking in ordinary times twelve or thirteen miles a day, as a rule, and as much more as any pedestrian companion may desire. He has often made excursions with my eldest son, who is a good walker, and has youth on his side.

The Captain is an ingenious amateur workman in various ways. He can do joiner's work neatly enough for boat-building, and can make sails. On board the *Boussemroum* he will always be ready to lend a hand, and I know that whatever he does will be executed dexterously and tidily. I like a gentleman to be able to use his hands, and I hold a private opinion that a gentleman ought naturally to be a neater workman than another, as he is more refined. The Captain is as steady as he is accurate. He has been working most patiently with me the whole of the day in setting up the saloon and getting it into order, in spite of the intense heat.

The saloon being too much crowded with boxes and other matters we dined in the court between it and the poop cabin,

The Galley Stove.

a court that I intend henceforth to call the galley. Our table consisted of two boxes, one upon another, our chairs were two camp-stools. The natural heat, already more than sufficient, was increased by the proximity of the Patron's stove. The disorder about us was of that absolutely complete kind that paralyses one for the time being, and seems to say, "You may conquer me in time by patience, industry, and skill, but for the present you have to put up with me as if I were a bailiff in possession."

Oh, wonderful and delightful discovery! The Patron is not only a cook, but a good one! He made us a *déjeûner* and a dinner to day that would have done credit to a well-kept private house. The Patron's cookery is not elaborately artful, but he knows the plainer French dishes, and knows them well. You get little now of the old homely French cookery in the hotels, but it has the two great merits of being agreeable whilst you dine, and digestible afterwards. This is more than can always be said of experimental mixtures. Very likely you think I am a sybarite for paying any attention to cookery, and that a philosopher might dine very well with a biscuit and a slice of tinned beef from Chicago. Being, however, neither sybarite nor philosopher, but at the present time simply a practical traveller, I rejoice in the Patron's talent for the most practical reasons. For us it is an emancipation. It at once delivers us from all trouble about seeking our meals in the inns, from the waste of time that such seeking always involves, and from the constant inconvenience of having to adjust our travelling arrangements so as to bring us to inns at meal-times.

I find that the Patron began his culinary career long ago as assistant cook to General Lamoricière, and that since then he has been servant to more than one officer of rank. Before finding out this we observed that he waited well. In a word, instead of a rough donkey driver, which was all I had expected, I have an experienced servant, who is cook and butler in one.

The speed attained to-day has been very slow, though the tug is a powerful boat, but she had a heavy train, consisting of two great laden barges, two great empty ones, and a berrichon of the same size as our own boat laden with coals down to the water's edge. The steamer is perfectly new, and this is her first voyage. She is a screw-boat, intended for the narrow Upper Saône, between Gray and Corre. Not being as yet accustomed to manage her with a train of barges, the sailors got the train at one time into confusion across the whole breadth of the river, and we all drifted together. It was a long time before order was re-established. This gave me an opportunity for admiring the extreme readiness and skill of the bargemen, who ran along the edges of the boats with the sureness of acrobats, and jumped from one to another. Such agility comes from years of practice, beginning generally with early youth, and it would be madness to attempt to imitate it. Our Pilot was conspicuous in this; he seemed to be everywhere at the same time, and was always full of hearty willingness and good temper.

The decision to avail myself of the tug was all my own. The Pilot declared that we should ascend the river quite as rapidly with our own donkey, Zoulou. With all due deference to his experience, I declined to believe this. Besides, it is not clear that he has had any experience with donkeys. The Saône barges are usually drawn by a pair of horses. The *Boussemroum* is simply a canal boat, intended for the very narrowest canals. Even river-boats are towed, and the other berrichon that is with us has her donkey in its stable on board, being towed exactly like ourselves.

It is a remarkably odd position this of having a crew that one has never seen before. I have been studying the two men with anxious interest since we started, as the whole expedition will fall through if they do not work well. This evening both the men worked most willingly on board as house servants. The tents not being set up yet, the saloon is for the present a double-bedded room at night. The men set up the bedsteads

and made the beds very cleverly, whilst I looked in through the window giving directions. If they go on as they have begun it will be a successful expedition.

The weather to-day has been windy, beginning with a light breeze against us, that increased to a strong breeze in the afternoon. The saloon is well set up, and watertight, I hope, in case of rain.

Evidently our Patron is an economical man. I told him to go on shore and buy some candles and some strawberries. He returned with the candles, and said he had found strawberries, very fine ones, but too dear, so he left them. The price was quite ordinary, even for France. The Patron seems so decided that I shall not easily induce him to permit me a little extravagance in strawberries. He appears to think that he is *in loco parentis*, and that I am a young boy who ought not to be allowed to spend his pocket-money on fruit.

LETTER X.

IN MOTION, BEYOND SEURRE, *June 3rd.*

The night we spent at Raconnay was peaceful enough as the train of boats slept on the star-reflecting waters, but I cannot say so much for last night, which we spent in the Trugny Canal below Seurre.

It is one of the peculiarities of voyaging behind a tug that you have no idea where you will pass the night. That depends on circumstances, and on the will of the tug's captain, who comes to anchor exactly where he pleases, quite independently of the towns and villages on the shore. A passenger steamer invariably stops at a town ; a tug may stop in the country where there is not a roof in sight.

We had got the tents up before night came on working in a fearful heat. The inside of a berrichon, under a blazing Burgundy sun, is one of the hottest places in my experience. The black walls are high enough to concentrate the heat, and almost to double it. However, the Captain and I worked cheerfully enough inside this oven, getting out of it now and then to be in the cooler river breeze, and the consequence of our labours is that both the tents are set up exactly as they ought to be, and ready for a gale of wind.

What a happy thing it is to travel with a man who has no false notions about luxury! When the Captain's tent was set up and furnished, with its Japanese matting on the oak floor, its little iron bedstead and table, its single camp chair, and its fresh-looking ewer and basin,[1] he remarked that in all his experience he had never encamped so comfortably before. The other tent, which is reserved for the American artist, is exactly like the Captain's, but smaller. I used this tent myself during the night, and a very wild night it was.

We had a great thunderstorm, with violent gusts of wind and a deluge of rain. In the midst of this, about two o'clock in the morning, it suddenly occurred to my recollection that the boxes containing my books were outside in the galley, and that as they were wooden boxes, and had not tin covers, the rain would probably get in. There is no material thing that I care for with as much

---

[1] These are made of paper and are quite satisfactory, being light and unbreakable as well as perfectly watertight. The ewers are of a rational cone-like shape, not easy to upset, and they hold a good supply of water.

The Tents from "La Cour Pennell."

solicitude as my books, so I immediately got up and went to house them in the saloon. Then it successively occurred to me that a number of other things were out in the rain, and I found much occupation in sheltering them, so the night was a very disturbed night for me, and the less agreeable that we have no companion ladders yet to go up and down, and there is no communication between the parts of the boat except by walking along the gunwale. As the wood became slippery from the rain I was likely enough to get a fall, and could not help laughing by myself in the midst of the lightning and rain at this original way of passing the night. Would you believe that I took a pleasure in it? For one thing, I like to hear rain pattering heavily into water, and it is grand to see a dark landscape suddenly illuminated by lightning. Besides, a night of this kind recalls past experiences in old camping and boating times.

Whilst occupied in this way I remarked that the boat inclined towards the port side, and attributed it to unequal loading, the inequality being afterwards increased by the rain-water, which, in a flat-bottomed boat, would flow to the lower angle. Having quieted myself with this explanation, and not being able to sleep, I had taken a chair and a book in the saloon when I heard a sudden commotion at the stern of the *Boussem-roum.* The Pilot had got up, and so had the bargeman alongside, and for a minute they were evidently in a great hurry about something. Luckily the Pilot had noticed the heeling of the boat and immediately guessed the true cause. When night fell we were tied to the other berrichon, which, as you know, is laden with coal almost to the water's edge. The ropes that fastened us to this boat had been shortened by the rain, and had acted with irresistible force, lifting up the starboard side of the coal-boat and depressing our port side. They had done more, they had depressed the port side of the coal-boat at the same time, and as it was already close to the water, the least additional depression was perilous in the extreme. The man on the coal-boat had taken the alarm just when our Pilot did, and by a great effort, not one minute too soon, they together succeeded in disengaging her. Now, what would have happened if the men had remained asleep a little longer? The berrichon would certainly have sunk to the bottom, and its master and his wife would have been drowned in their cabin. The ropes that bound our boat to the other would have capsized ours, and our men also might have been drowned in their cabin, as well as the Captain in his tent, and your present correspondent in the saloon.[1]

So you perceive that in the same night we have had a thunderstorm and imminent risk of shipwreck with loss of life.

LETTER XI.

GRAY, *June 5th.*

We have arrived at Gray in such a downpour of rain that we are waiting till it clears before landing. This gives me an opportunity for writing a letter, the great convenience of

---

[1] I felt very much dissatisfied with myself for not having perceived the danger and given the alarm, but as I am not a bargeman, and as the heeling of our vessel was slight, the true cause did not occur to me. Bargemen are watchful from hard experience. The Pilot tells me that accidents often happen, and that the overladen boats not infrequently sink. A berrichon, in particular, has very little stability.

this voyage being that when there is any delay I can open my desk and find myself in my study at once.

The berrichon laden with coal that nearly sank in the canal is inhabited by a young couple, whom I have been watching with much interest since we started. The man is lively and very intelligent with the most frank and pleasant manners, besides which he is a fine strong-looking fellow; the woman is pretty and graceful, and as clean in her dress and surroundings as a young lady. As soon as her husband found we were suffering considerable inconvenience from the want of companion-ladders he said they could very soon be made, as he had wood on board his boat that was at our disposal and also a set of joiner's tools. He and the Pilot, therefore, set to work at once, and in little more than an hour we possessed rough ladders that answered the purpose. People like yourself who have staircases can hardly imagine what an immense acquisition a rough ladder is when one has no staircase at all.

The strangest coincidences happen in real life. When we got near St. Jean de Losne and were about to part company, as the laden berrichon was going to Dijon by the Burgundy canal, the young bargeman told me that he had offered himself and his boat to my friend at Chalon for our voyage. It was a matter of deep regret, to him, not to have been accepted. He had a liking for long voyages and wished to know the whole of the River Saône, instead of being always sent along the same tiresome canals. When telling me this he added that my friend had declared I would have "neither women, nor children, nor fleas, nor bugs." Observe the powerful effect of concentration in verbal expression! It is true that I had objected to these four kinds of living things, but separately; my friend had brought them together, only too effectively, in a single phrase. "I could not drown my wife, could I?" said the happy husband. "Some wives," I answered, "might be improved by drowning, especially such as are scolds, but you ought not to make a personal application of my objections. I had never seen your wife and had no notion that she would be so *comme il faut;* I had thought it well to protect myself against a possible slattern or scold. I felt well able to order men about, but was destitute of authority over women, and their exclusion was a general measure of prudence to which there might have been an exception." Just before we separated the young woman cooked her husband's dinner in the little open space before their cabin, and I noticed the perfect cleanliness of everything.

At St. Jean de Losne I landed for the first time since our departure, having been fifty-seven hours on board without liberty but certainly not without exercise. The waking hours had been passed in manual labour. I like manual labour, especially if constructive, better than any sports or games, and find that it does me more good. Will it be unseemly boasting if I tell you that I am a fairly decent sort of joiner for plain work? I am slow but accurate, like the Captain, and between us we are worth perhaps fivepence an hour.

During our evening walk at St. Jean de Losne we happened to be close behind a bourgeois of that little town, who was taking his two young daughters out for a walk and giving them some paternal advice. The thesis of the discourse was that every human being has a right to our respect until he has done something to forfeit it, and this quite independently of his position in society. "Therefore," said the father, "you ought never to treat any one haughtily or contemptuously, but you should be civil and polite to every human being, and really respect him, however humble may be his station." This is merely an abridgment, the kernel of the doctrine. It is the good side of French equality, and excessively French. The family were very *comme il faut* in appearance, and belonged to the upper middle class.

The curious independence of our present kind of life is felt in nothing more than in the morning departures. There is

St. Jean de Losne.

no packing to be done, no bill to be paid, no thought about taking luggage to a station, and whether we are awake or asleep the bed-room itself starts into motion with all our belongings. The only rule to be observed is not to go ashore for a walk between four and six in the morning.

I have promulgated laws about habits and hours.[1] I rise at five and have breakfast at seven with the Captain. This first

---

[1] These laws were well observed during the whole of the expedition. The Patron was not an unpunctual man, and the Captain maintained discipline with military firmness. Our daily round of life went on as regularly as if we had been on board ship.

breakfast always consists of soup only, varied according to the cook's resources. It is the best thing to begin the day upon, as it gives good staying power without embarrassing the digestion. The men, especially the Pilot, follow the common habit of the French working class in the towns and of boatmen on the river, by beginning the day with a heavy dram of undiluted brandy. I have been arguing against this, but who can argue against a custom? Men who get up at three or four o'clock on raw mornings on a comfortless boat appreciate the temporary comfort of a big dram, and on fine summer mornings they repeat the dose from habit.

We have our second breakfast, the *déjeûner*, at eleven and dine at seven. The Captain spends the evening with me and at ten exactly he retires to his own tent. I then sling my hammock, fall asleep as soon as I lie down, and awake at five the next morning precisely.

Our style of living is founded on the principle of decency without luxury. We have a cheap tablecloth and napkins, with the commonest crockery, and silver plate is replaced either by pewter or tinned iron. The Captain has purchased some very handsome silvery-looking forks for three sous a piece. We possess some common wine, and three bottles of good Burgundy which are to be reserved for state occasions. There are also other drinks in the cellar, including a sort of perry that the Patron makes of dried grapes, with pears, and other ingredients. The flavour is pleasant but rather harsh and it provokes one to drink again. The Patron seems to be quite addicted to it, but we have no right to blame him for an indulgence which in the hottest hours could scarcely exceed our own.

Except at meal-times and in the evening, the saloon is my

private room and I can write in it pleasantly even when the boat is in motion. I have never been in anything that glided so smoothly as this boat. The Captain's discretion is entirely to be depended upon. He always leaves me alone except when specially invited to join me. He reads in his own tent, or sits on the forecastle deck observing the scenery with his binocular. He saves me much trouble by taking upon himself all the duty of housekeeping. It is he who buys all provisions. When we stop at a place he immediately lands and sets off to do his marketing, followed by the Patron with a basket on his arm.

Being occupied all day with my writing, I had no time to observe the river except by occasional glances through the window, but I discovered a means of knowing our exact position without even stirring from my seat. In my desk there is a complete ordnance map of the Saône pasted in cuttings in a book, so with this and the mariner's compass I knew at a glance the situation of the boat as we followed the windings of the river. A good large-scale map makes one very knowing. The Pilot is much surprised by the accuracy of my information. He himself cannot make use of a map and is obliged to trust entirely to his recollection of the river itself.

When we arrived at Pontailler the sky was black, and by the time we sat down to dinner we were in the midst of a thunderstorm with rain that would have seemed the heaviest in our experience had we not remembered that it always sounds ten times heavier on canvas. Some water had got through the roof in the last thunderstorm so I had doubled the cloth and this time it resisted perfectly. The canvas walls are of course wetted through in storms but they soon dry again, and no worse effect is produced than the cooling of the interior by evaporation. I have linings to all the tents that might be used if necessary, but they diminish internal space and the Captain thinks it better to do without them. Certainly they make a tent look more comfortable because they hide the wet canvas. This is only an apparent advantage. The real advantage is that if you have a thin worn place in the tent from which the water drops, the lining arrests the drops.[1]

Gray, the Bridge and Weir.

The weirs and locks on the Saône are at the same time telephonic stations from which you may send news relating to the navigation. Near one of these stations I told the Pilot to have our whereabouts telephoned to Gray, where I have friends. The lock-keepers sometimes hold telephonic conversations, and I remember hearing a double conversation of this kind up and down the river at a distance of about thirty miles

---

[1] In winter encampments linings are useful as a protection against snow, which comes through the outer canvas in a fine powder.

on one side and fifty on the other. At the longer distance I recognised a girl's voice, and afterwards a woman's, and the lock-keeper told me that he knew the speakers individually by their voices. The girl said she was afraid, the telephone seemed uncanny to her. Whether uncanny or not, these telephones render immense services to the river navigation as every rise of the water is announced beforehand.

LETTER XII.

NEAR OVANCHES, *June 6th.*

Mr. Pennell joined us yesterday at Gray, and we passed the night there. Not knowing that we slept on board the *Boussemroum* he had retained bedrooms for us at his hotel, but considering that the tug was to start at four in the morning we preferred our usual domicile on board, and recommended our new companion to follow our example.

The Captain told me of an improved kind of camp bed, and we found exactly what he described, the lightest, most comfortable, and most rationally contrived beds for use in tents that I have ever met with. I at once bought two of them for my guests. My own hammock is perfection, and I have no desire for anything else.

Though Mr. Pennell had not expected to sleep under canvas he accepted his fate with a cheerfulness that did him credit—the more credit that tents always look so damp and dreary immediately after heavy rain.

We were all invited to dine at Gray by the kind friends who had been expecting our arrival. It was a strange transition to be suddenly transported from our life on the berrichon to a brilliantly-lighted dining-room with a dinner very prettily served in charming society, and to hear afterwards a duet on violin and piano, our host and hostess being both accomplished musicians. After dinner, amongst other works of art, we were shown a bas-relief executed by a banker in prison. Mr. Pennell and I were both surprised by the rare degree of cleverness, for an amateur, displayed in this attempt. It is not always good to be too clever. The great manual and imitative dexterity possessed by this remarkable banker had been his ruin, as he got into trouble by forging cheques. I remember the man himself very well, having been introduced to him some years ago as to an amateur of a very superior order, at a time when nobody could imagine that his amateurship would go so far as the fraudulent imitation of handwriting. Our host, who is himself in the Bank of France, told me that the forgeries were executed with such astonishing skill that the victims believed the false signatures to be authentic when they saw them, and in one case a victim said his own handwriting was the forgery and the imitation was his autograph. What surprises one most in this history is that a forging banker could ever hope to escape detection. Would he not, in the course of his daily business, be incessantly exposed to discovery?

My friend told me a lugubrious little anecdote. On his first arrival at Gray he had gone to look at an *appartement* to let, where the ground-floor was occupied by a stone-cutter who had filled the courtyard with tombstones. When my friend gave his name the maker of tombstones immediately inscribed it on one of them, in the place reserved for the deceased. "Only the date of my demise was wanting."

Awaking the next morning at my usual hour of five, I found the *Boussemroum* already in motion and going at a superior speed as we had left nearly all our train behind us. At one place we had an emotion. A wire-rope for a ferry-boat was stretched across the river. These ropes can be either dropped into the water, in which case they sink by their own weight, or else stretched high above it. In the present case the rope was not stretched very high and it hung in a festoon. The steamer lowered her funnels and went straight for the lowest part of the festoon. It therefore seemed probable to all of us that the gable of our saloon would be caught. As soon as I perceived the danger I wanted to go forward to be out of the way of the crash and the splinters, but the Pilot stood on the companion ladder and would not let me go. "In a moment," he said, "if we touch, the berrichon will capsize and we shall be all in the water." I care nothing about being flung into water, but have an objection to being crushed and wounded under splintering wood. The steamer went on fearlessly, the wire rope seemed to fly over our heads and the saloon was cleared. The captain of the steamer said afterwards that he had not forgotten my gable but had taken its level. Later, in the ascending voyage, the crew of the steamer made a mistake on their own account, but this requires a word of explanation. On these steamers, quite in the fore-part, there is a small square water-tight well that goes entirely through the vessel. Through this narrow well, or case, a pointed iron stake is worked up and down by means of a crank. This is called a "brick" in French, and as it weighs two tons the mere weight of it ensures its sinking into the mud, where it anchors the vessel better and more quickly than an ordinary anchor. When the boat is in motion the "brick" rises up like a mast. It was in this state, like a mast, when we approached a very low iron bridge near Chemilly, and the man whose duty it was to lower it was suddenly called away to something else which drove the matter out of his mind. Remembering it too late he reached his wheel only to loosen it and rush away out of danger. The "brick" caught against the bridge, and as the upper part of the stake is hollow it broke, and came down with a crash, shattering a wheel and other things upon the deck. There it had to remain, a discouraging little heap of ruins, sadly out of place on a first trip, amidst the pretty bouquets of flowers. Not only were flowers given to the men on the steamer but even bottles of liqueurs were let down from bridges, and round the bottles were bunches of cigars neatly arranged with ribands. Besides this, salutes were fired, and women smiled graciously, and everything had a festal air, but that accident spoiled all. It was a disagreeable duty to telegraph an account of it to the owners.

The first experience of going through a tunnel on the *Boussemroum* was strange and interesting, even imposing. The steamer went more slowly than before and its powerful rhythmic breathings were reverberated along the vault. There was no other sound except the wash of the water against the masonry. There was no reason for any real apprehension, we were as safe in the tunnel as on the river, yet the imagination received one of those solemn impressions that are sometimes produced even when our reason quite understands the means. The train of boats was in fact passing through a vast subterranean hall, dark from its very length, and this hall had a floor of water without stepping-place for the foot of man. In a railway tunnel you could walk if necessary, and the train takes you through so quickly that your estimate of distance is deceived. In a canal tunnel you measure every yard of the distance. The gloom increases to the middle, and then slowly, slowly, the light brightens. At long intervals you get a momentary glimpse of sky by looking up one of the air-shafts, when you see a tiny disc of blue.

I ought, perhaps, to explain that the canals on the Upper Saône are short. They are not lateral canals, like those which run parallel to the less navigable rivers, but they cut off the larger curves and they afford opportunities for gaining a higher level by means of locks. There are sixteen of them altogether, not one of them more than two miles long.

At one of our stoppages to-day a man came and told us that our progress was announced by telegraph to the town of Port-sur-Saône in the following terms :—" A minister, accompanied by three gentlemen, is coming with the new steamer." He said that in consequence of this it was very likely that the Mayor and Common Council would be there to receive us with due ceremony. The explanation is that a donkey, by a pleasantry that does not seem to lose its salt with age, is often called a "minister" in France, not with disparaging reference to Protestant ministers, but to members of the Cabinet. If, therefore, the people at Port-sur-Saône should be taken in the sender of the telegram will shelter himself behind the plea that he only intended to describe our fellow-voyager Zoulou. More probably they will not be taken in.

The steamboat people have a taste for staying in the canals during the night. We are staying in one to-night, near a bend of the river more than six miles long that encloses a considerable peninsula, with three villages. The canal cuts the neck of the peninsula and is about a mile and a half long. It passes under a hill.

LETTER XIII.

CORRE, *June 8th.*

We arrived at Corre at nine o'clock this morning. I wrote last from the canal opposite Ovanches. Early on the morning of the 7th we passed through the tunnel there. I awoke just as the boat was beginning to move and lay quietly in my hammock, as we glided from the bright early sunshine into darkness. I lighted a candle on the table near me and opened a book, but the interest of my own surroundings was stronger, for the moment, than that of literature. The regular and powerful respiration of the engine, the surrounding darkness, the knowledge that this comfortable little room was being taken through the interior of a hill, though it floated so quietly as only to communicate a scarcely perceptible swing to the hammock under me, all this was too novel an experience to be forgotten in the pages of a book. At last the interior of the cabin began suddenly to brighten, then it was full daylight once again, and time to meet the work of the day and to leave off dreaming about the majesty of human enterprises.

I think a human being never feels himself greater as a part of the race or smaller as an individual than in a tunnel. Reclining as much at ease as a prince in a palanquin, I was drawn majestically over currentless waters by the obedient power of fire, through a costly corridor prepared for me in the bowels of the earth. This is the majestic aspect of the matter. The humiliating consideration was that without the help of others I must have walked over the hill exactly as our donkey Zoulou, if he had been put to it. My superiority to him is in my nearer kinship to the makers of the tunnel.

Zoulou's master, the Patron, is rather self-willed, and like many small men has boundless confidence in his own judgment. As we were passing through a lock two or three miles below Port-sur-Saône he went on shore and busied himself about getting fodder for his donkey, paying no heed to our cries. "Plenty of time, plenty of time!" he repeated. The men on the steamer took a malicious pleasure in starting without him, and as they would not stop for him afterwards he had to run on the towing-path about two miles. He ran very well for an old man, and nearly kept up with the steamer, so we got him on board again at the first lock. It is highly diverting to see a man running when you know that he must be in a rage.

Equally amusing was the Patron's first and only lesson in the art of rowing. We have a lumbering flat-bottomed boat that serves us for a dingey and is set in motion with a pair of very heavy and awkward sculls tied to the gunwale with loops of cord. As the Pilot is very strong he can row this thing when he is seated on a loose board set on the gunwales that makes a temporary thwart far too high for any effective pull. The Patron, who is a small man and had never grasped an oar (not to speak of two crossing sculls at once), made a series of most unsuccessful attempts, and ended by declaring his conviction that rowing was a bad way of propelling boats and that the oar was very inferior to a scoop. To demonstrate this, he fetched his own scoop[1] from the *Boussemroum*, and as the water was calm he certainly did succeed in communicating a very slow motion to the heavy boat, on which he chuckled and triumphed, having demonstrated the folly of oarsmen and the futility of their art.

When Mr. Pennell came on board he was struck with the Patron's name, Vernet, as being that of the famous painter, and asked him if his Christian name was not Horace. "No, it is Jean." The strange idea then occurred to Mr. Pennell that the Pilot *must* be called Horace, as Horace Vernet must surely be on board in two persons if not in one; so he went and asked what was his Christian name. "Je m'appelle *Horace*, monsieur." The coincidence is odd in itself, but Mr. Pennell's presentiment about it is much more wonderful.[2]

On reaching Port-sur-Saône we were ready to accord a gracious reception to the municipal authorities, and to present them to the minister, who remained in his private cabin, but no municipal authorities appeared. Evidently the word had been interpreted in its second sense as meaning only an ass; that ancient pleasantry is now too generally known.

Last night we slept on a canal near a village called Bétaucourt, and we came on early, reaching Corre at nine in the morning under a salute of guns. We paid a visit to the steamer and were cordially received by the captain and men who of course invited us to drink. The drink was some green mint cordial which had been lowered from a bridge with a piece of string. The steamer was decorated with a final bouquet on her arrival.

---

[1] A scoop is a wooden ladle used for emptying boats. That belonging to the *Boussemroum* was at the end of a long stick, and so made a sort of awkward paddle.

[2] As Horace is blessed with a fine appetite, his name has been changed by his comrades to *Vorace*.

The accident to the "brick" had thrown a damper over what would else have been a festive occasion.

The crew of the tug, seven in number, had been overworked in the ascent, especially in the locks, but they were fine strong men and took the work heartily, regretting only that they were not ten instead of seven. One of them with a very merry honest face and splendid muscular development had lost patience now and then, but even when most impatient he had been civil. In one of his worst moments, when he had far too much for one man, he exclaimed in a voice of thunder, with a grand vibration of the letter *r*:—

"Il faudrait avoir *quarrrante* mains, et *quarrrante* pieds, et puis *quarrrante* jambes!" The addition of the forty legs as an afterthought to connect the feet with the body, had amused me as much as the omission of the forty arms. I regret to add that on another occasion when particularly embarrassed with the *Boussemroum*, our muscular friend exclaimed in his wrath, "Je voudrais—je voudrais que ce berrichon soit *au diable!*" Afterwards, however, he came on board the *Boussemroum* with all his comrades by special invitation, and was much interested in my contrivances for the maintenance of order.

We have come as fast as we could from Chalon for a convoy travelling in the daytime only, and yet we have spent seven nights on the way, and seven whole days of steaming, besides two half days. And all this to accomplish 150 miles! Was not the Pilot right when he said that the donkey would bring us up as rapidly? No, he was not right, and he has acknowledged his error. The strength of the current in the Upper Saône, now swollen by rain and far swifter than in the low country, acting on a mass like the *Boussemroum*, and aided by a head-wind, would simply have dragged poor Zoulou back into the water and drowned him. We might possibly have made the ascent with a pair of horses.[1]

At the rate of only three miles an hour, and ten hours a day, we should have required five days instead of eight, but the great cause of delay was the locks. At each of these the train of boats had to be disconnected, each boat passing separately, and then the train had to be formed again beyond

The Lock at Corre.

the lock. The fastening of boats with huge ropes takes much more time than the coupling of railway carriages. Sometimes we had to wait at a lock till a descending train had passed through.

Our last lock, at Corre, where we left the steamer behind

---

[1] Subsequent experience proved clearly that we should never have accomplished the ascent with horses, for a reason to be explained later. And as we could not row or sail the *Boussemroum* a tug was absolutely the only thing.

took us out of the Saône altogether, and into the canal that now connects that river with the Meuse and with the canal systems of Belgium and Holland. We are now beyond the navigable Saône, and the *Boussemroum* has reached the highest point of her voyage. We feel that it is an immense deliverance to be disengaged from the steam-tug. The Captain and I have had no liberty for a week. He, at least, could amuse himself by looking at the scenery, but I have only enjoyed it by glimpses, having been so much absorbed in my writing. Still, notwithstanding the confinement to the boat, I have not felt dull for a single minute. Hard work by day, sound sleep by night, are two excellent preventers of *ennui*. It is clear that this system of travelling, in spite of its slowness, has one inappreciable advantage, a retreat is always close at hand if the voyage itself becomes tedious. The saloon has a most convenient bureau, and a small library of fifty volumes in a bookcase. With these, and perfect privacy, no place is ever dull and the worst weather is not depressing.

LETTER XIV.

CORRE, *June 9th*.

It has been a very hard rule for me to follow—that rule of abstinence from all description of what I came to see, namely, the river and the places upon its banks. It was, however, absolutely the only way to avoid confusion. I could not describe places twice over, and yet I wished to tell you something about our ascending voyage.

Corre is the Khartoum of the Saône and Chalon is its

Cairo. As the two Niles meet at Khartoum, so the Saône and the Coney meet together at Corre which is situated on the tongue of land between them. The parallel may be pursued further. Chalon is on the right bank of the Saône, and in the plain, exactly as Cairo is situated; Chalon has domes and an obelisk, and as Cairo has had her Egyptologist, Mariette, so Chalon has possessed her almost equally well-known Egyptologist, Chabas. At Chalon the floods of the Saône are like the rising of the Nile; they inundate the plain.

I traced out this analogy to amuse myself, as it sometimes happens that when there is one resemblance there are half a dozen, but neither Egypt nor Nubia can have anything like the Coney. This delightful stream has its source, like the Saône, in the department of the Vosges at the foot of the *Monts Faucilles*, and after running thirty-eight miles through a wooded country which so far as we could see it was very beautiful, it joins the Saône at a place like a picture, which is the expression of its own peculiar loveliness. The Coney is one of those hill-rivers that seem destined by Nature to be a constant succession of confined but exquisite scenes, such as have delighted poets in all ages and, though so frequently painted, are still favourite haunts of the landscape artist. Utterly unknown to fame, the Coney passes through its long wooded valley, turns its rustic mills, and never in all its course flows near anything like a town. There is a village called Selles on the Coney, a few miles above Corre, where boats are built, and when the stream is swollen by rains these boats are navigated down to the junction with the Saône. This is all the navigation there is upon the Coney, and it

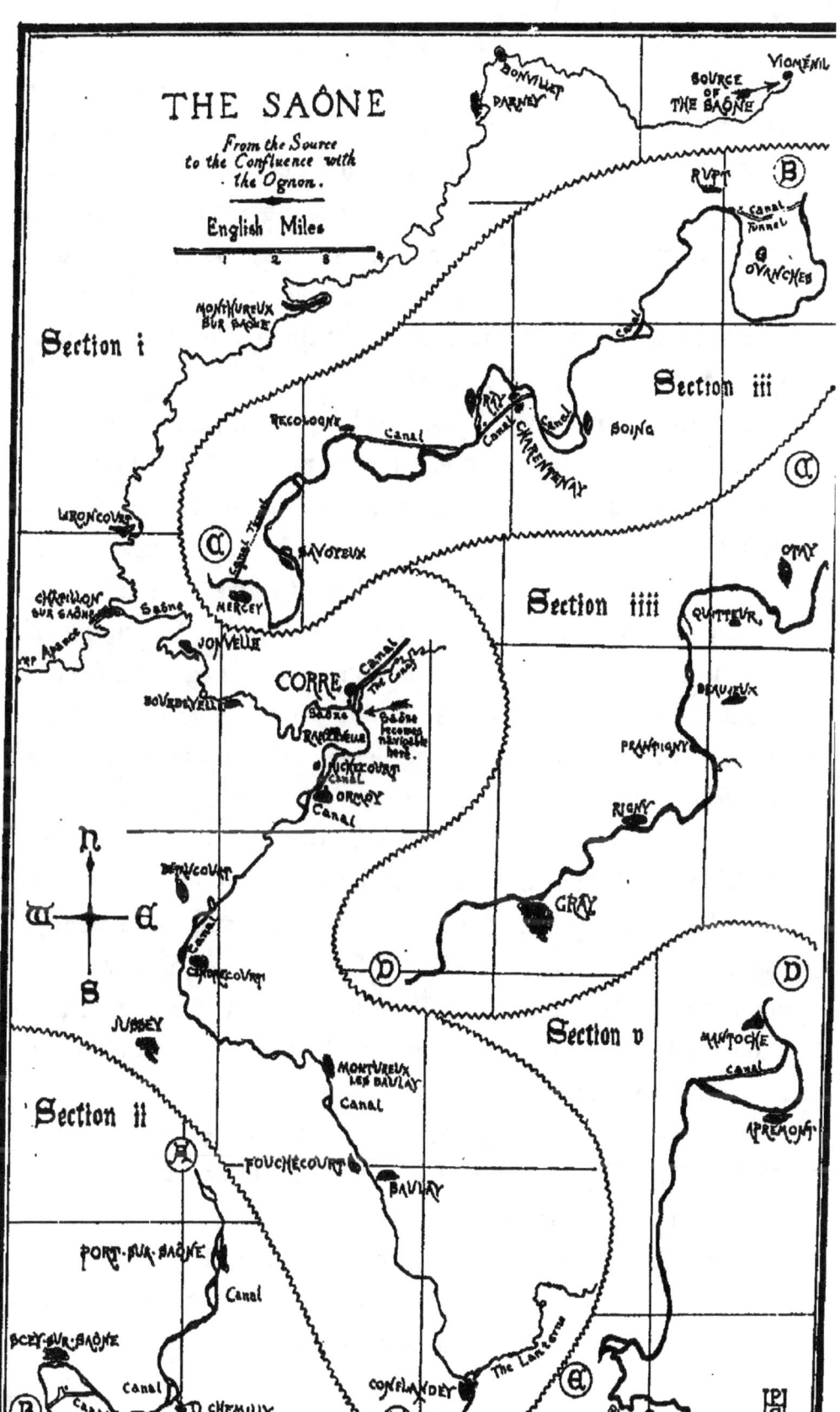

reminds me of a curious fact that our Pilot told me about large boats that are sometimes built near the forests where wood is cheap and yet where there is no river, but now and then there comes a flood and then these boats are floated away for miles over the inundated fields till they reach the banks of a small stream that is a tributary of the Saône—a strange beginning of their voyages.

The Coney narrowly missed celebrity, for the great river might fairly have been called by its name. It discharges at the junction as much water in a minute as the Saône, and its previous course has been almost, if not quite, as long. But if we examine the claims of young rivers to give their names to mature ones we find some remarkable exceptions to the rule, if there is a rule, that the largest and longest of the early confluents ought to preserve its name to the end. The most striking example in my knowledge is the Seine. Where that river meets the Yonne, the Yonne is the stronger of the two, and therefore ought to have given its name to the river that flows under the Pont Neuf. But if we go up the Yonne we find at its junction with the Cure that the Cure is the greater river, consequently the Yonne at Sens ought to be the Cure, and the Seine at Paris ought to be the Cure also. Poor humble, yet beautiful, Cure, known only to artists and anglers, yet having the best of claims to a world-wide celebrity!

The Captain and I visited the Saône above the junction. There it has the character of a shallow rapid canoe river, any other kind of navigation being manifestly impossible. It flows through a plain bounded by steep low hills, and its banks are not wooded like those of the Coney. As I was sketching the young Saône from the road and the Captain sat near me, smoking, we observed two gendarmes in full uniform coming straight at us across the fields. I said to the Captain, "They probably take us for spies and may arrest us." He seemed to think this not improbable; however, although the gendarmes came up to us they simply looked at me, saw that I was sketching, and walked along the road.[1]

The canal that joins the Saône to the Meuse passes between the Saône and the Coney, and meets them exactly at their junction. It is a canal of the greatest commercial importance, as it joins the navigation of the north and south very conveniently for Belgium as well as for Alsatia and Lorraine.

The *Boussemroum* is moored in this canal close to a beautiful private park, with finely-grown trees of different species crowded like an aviary with singing birds. This reminds me very much of some charming places in England. The view along the canal bank leads the eye pleasantly to the old church at Corre, a small Romanesque edifice with a grey tower, certainly one of the most picturesque of old churches, but more suitable for a water-colour painter than for a linear draughtsman. The greys of the walls are cool for the most part, but elsewhere beautifully tinted by lichens, whilst the red and gold of the tiled roofs give an admirable contrast. This old church is perfection at all times, quietly beautiful under a cloudy sky, and splendid against the azure and white of a sunny day.

Our sudden departure from Chalon interrupted the joiner there, and this is the first opportunity for completing his work, so the Pilot sought for a joiner in the village and ended

---

[1] Subsequent events proved that we were watched all along in consequence of a recent law about spies, and a still more recent and stringent order to put the law in force.

The Boussemroum at Corre.

by discovering that there was one on the hill-side engaged in agriculture and with his clothes all earthy. This gave at first the impression of a peasant amateur, but a very short acquaintance proved him to be exceptionally intelligent, and on visiting his house, which is his own property, I had the opportunity of admiring the prettiest and most commodious joiner's workshop I ever saw anywhere, beautifully finished throughout and admirably lighted, with a superb set of tools in excellent order and a

The Church at Corre.

lathe. I then discovered that my new acquaintance could speak English, so I gave him directions about his work in English. This was rather a surprise to Mr. Pennell, who afterwards entered into conversation with the workman, and found that he had lived nine years in the United States. He "guessed" that extensive region to be "a right smart place," an expression which, Mr. Pennell tells me, is very good and pure American.

Mr. Pennell has a great liking for gipsies, which is now a fellow-feeling as we are gipsies ourselves. He was glad to find a group of them with their carts not far from the river Coney. He began to sketch them, on which they very soon broke up their pretty group to hinder him, and he tells me they have a great dislike to being sketched and will always avoid it whenever possible. This may, perhaps, be attributed to the

The Land Gipsies at Corre.

old superstitious feeling about power to injure the human being whose image you possess.

After going to see the gipsies we had an oddly delusive view of the tents and hut on the *Boussemroum*. The canal was completely invisible to us, but the nearer bank of it was just sufficiently high to conceal the boat, so that our habitations appeared to be an encampment on dry land, under the trees of the park. The effect was so absolutely illusory that a photograph taken from our position would have effectively represented a land encampment with nothing to correct the illusion. So much for plain ocular demonstration!

The nightingales sang very well in the daytime in the park close to us, but at night they surpassed themselves, keeping up a wonderful concert in especial honour of the *Boussemroum*. I fell asleep, however, after listening with much pleasure as long as I could, but was awakened some hours later by a serenade in masculine voices. I believe this human music was produced by the sailors of the steam-tug. They sang harmoniously, and I remembered enough of their song in the morning for the Captain to recognise it as *Le Lac de Genève*.

Our Pilot came during the day with a fine bouquet that he had made to put on Mr. Pennell's tent in celebration of his arrival at Corre. I fastened the bouquet on the tent myself and Mr. Pennell kindly shook hands with the Pilot, who seems to have acquired already a special regard for our American guest.

LETTER XV

CORRE, *June 10th.*

This morning I walked down to the junction of the rivers, and on returning saw the Pilot on the canal bank gesticulating violently, and the Patron in the boat nodding his head at the other in a way that he has when he has lost his temper. On a nearer approach it become evident that they were at open war. The Pilot had told the Patron once again how incompetent he is to manage a boat, which is a truth, but a truth that may be repeated too frequently; the Patron had answered in bitterness, and after that each of them had given the other a long through interrupted lecture on his faults and defects in general. For some time it was impossible to stop them, and as they shouted I had leisure to study their attitudes, which were more amusing than their words. All quarrellers have their own peculiar style of quarrelling. The Patron is bitter and voluble, with sarcastic laughs and snorts; the Pilot is tremendously scornful, he expresses the utmost extremity of contempt with a power that would be most valuable to a parliamentary orator. Every now and then, on hearing the retort of his adversary, the Pilot seems to boil over with indignation. Every muscle seems to be stirring, and at such times he looks as if he were about to leap upon his enemy for a death-grapple. Meanwhile the Patron stands pale with rage, sometimes bitterly eloquent, at others silent for lack of words hard enough for his big adversary, and occasionally disappearing behind the bulwark of the *Boussemroum*, yet invariably popping up again as soon as he has shaped or sharpened his rejoinder.

Mr. Pennell is troubled with apprehensions of his own. He says, "Depend upon it, the big one will end by throwing the little one into the water, and as the little one cannot swim he will be drowned!" To this I answer, "Pilot may throw Patron overboard, but if he does that his retriever-instinct will at once compel him to jump in to the rescue. Besides, it will be another life saved to boast of, and that temptation will be irresistible. The fourteen saved lives will be converted into fifteen! Such an incident is most desirable as Pilot would love Patron after saving him and they would dwell together in unity."

I spare you the terms of the quarrel. They were in French of a coarser quality than that which is familiar to you. I think that quarrels are pleasant reading only when the antagonists are refined and excel in the art of saying the most cutting things with urbanity. Even Horace made a mistake when he introduced that coarse quarrelling in the Journey to Brundusium.

My way of dealing with the matter was this. As soon as the fire of the quarrel began to exhaust itself, I took each of the men aside and gave him a private lecture, telling him that if their resentment was not controlled I should put a premature end to the expedition. As I threatened to consult a lawyer the Patron frankly acknowledged that I could turn him out of his own boat which temporarily belongs to me. I discovered that he had spoken disrespectfully to the Captain in my absence, and for this he made an apology which the Captain was good enough to accept. In this way peace was re-established and the men spoke to each other civilly afterwards, but it is only a truce. They are sure to quarrel again as soon as we descend the river, for the Pilot cannot avoid giving orders and the Patron will never endure that.

My own position is embarrassing. When one has organised an expedition everything must, for the time being, be subordinated to its success. Now, it so happens that each of the two men is in the highest degree valuable for the work that lies before us, and Corre is not a port where either of them could be replaced. At Chalon I could have reorganised the expedition if necessary, I cannot do it here. The Pilot, with his great physical strength and his knowledge of the river, will be more than ever necessary when we have no tug to draw the *Boussemroum*, and as we want to live independently on board, a house-servant is also a necessity. Now the Patron, notwithstanding his hot temper, is really an excellent servant, and in everything relating to house-work he obeys me with the most cheerful alacrity. An amusing sign of his turn for domestic service is that he has purchased a blue apron of the kind that French men-servants wear. I might seek a year before I replaced the Patron. I might wait indefinitely at Corre before I got a Pilot comparable to ours.[1]

Our stay at Corre is disproportionate for so small a place, a mere village of six hundred inhabitants, but it has a special interest as the head of the navigable Saône, and Mr. Pennell it delighted with its picturesque character. He has been working incessantly ever since we arrived, and would contentedly remain longer. One could be quite happy in such a place for the whole summer with a colour-box. I have left mine at home as an act of self-denial, and am contenting myself with occasional sketching with a lead pencil on grey paper, leaving Mr. Pennell to work for illustration.

The houses in Corre are almost entirely modern, a few traces of fifteenth-century architecture still remaining, but this modern picturesque is not to be disdained. Almost all the buildings are sketchable and a succession of them is sure to be varied by projecting masses, ample recesses, fine gloomy arches and picturesque doorways. In the doors themselves the boards are often arranged in a sort of herring-bone pattern

---

[1] This opinion of the Pilot's value was fully confirmed afterwards. The Patron, on his part, remained an excellent domestic to the end, but he was nothing more.

Corre, the Main Street.

that has a good effect, and the stone lintels are often tastefully chamfered.

Fifty years ago Corre must have been one of the most remarkable places in France for the quantity of Roman remains that could be found lying about, but these have for the most part been taken possession of by collectors. At one time the villagers of Corre appear to have been almost like children playing in a lapidary museum. Cows might be seen drinking out of a sarcophagus, the *adjoint* used a torso of Apollo for a garden seat, and the washerwomen by the Coney laid their linen on an antique bas-relief. Even now, the owner of the pretty park where the nightingales sing has Roman sculpture for its ornaments. In the course of our walks we find fragments of Roman work in the most unexpected positions. You see a stone close to a house-wall; it attracts your attention by its form, and on a nearer approach you perceive that it has a vase-like swelling, and is adorned with festoons that were carved when men talked Latin at Didattium.[1]

LETTER XVI.

ORMOY, *June 12th*.

Yesterday morning, just after our soup, a little sandy-haired boy came to the *Boussemroum*, and boldly offered himself as an additional servant to drive the donkey. He wore a brownish

[1] It is believed that Corre is the site of the Roman town of Didattium. This is usually placed high on the river Arar (Saône), and the great quantity of Roman remains found at Corre have led to the conclusion that it is on the very site of the ancient town. This is the more probable that towns have often been placed exactly at the confluence of streams.

jacket, nearly in rags, old blue cotton trousers worn very thin, and a cheap straw hat with the broad brim turned up on one side only, in the manner adopted this summer by the most fashionable young ladies. The Pilot was very kind to him, and asked him some questions in a very gentle tone of voice. I, too, questioned him, and found that, if his account was true, he was the orphan son of a quarryman who had been killed in an accident, that his mother was a very poor hardworking woman, and that he himself had been in a place at

Franki and Zoulou.

an inn, but that he had left his situation, and was now seeking another. He offered his services for his food and five francs a month.

The lad had a very honest face, an open countenance wonderfully Scotch in character, such as you meet with about the Clyde, and a straightforward manner that pleased me, so I said that if his story were confirmed he should have a berth on the *Boussemroum*. We first went to the inn where he had been servant, and the people said he was perfectly trustworthy, but had been somewhat disobedient at times. This disobedience turned out to be nothing graver than failure to do everything when he was over-worked, and sleepiness at three or four o'clock in the morning. The lad's mother lived at Jonvelle, so I sent him there to ask for her permission (he being a minor) and for a good-conduct certificate from the

Ormoy in the distance.

mayor. We waited for him at Corre till afternoon, and as he did not appear, I gave orders to start without him, leaving word with the lock-keeper that the boy might join us lower down at Ormoy.

However, when we were in the lock, and the boat was rapidly descending to the lower level, behold the boy and his mother both running along the canal bank, and she began bargaining with me for thirty francs a month instead of five. The bargain was concluded whilst the *Boussemroum* issued from the lock into the river. I promised the thirty francs, as the Pilot said it was nothing unusual for a donkey-boy.

In real life there is often that strange mixture of the humorous with the pathetic, that we find in the works of the best humourists. The scene that now followed was of this double character. As soon as the boat got to the opposite bank the lad and his mother joined us on the towing-path, and she began the tragic tale of her husband's death, which naturally made her burst into tears. Then she gave an account of her present hard struggle with poverty and asked me to advance her seven francs. I gave her ten, as a rounder sum, and then she wept again for gladness at the sight of so much utterly unexpected wealth. She had scarcely dried her eyes on her apron, when the tears flowed a third time in the greatest abundance, on account of the imminent separation from her boy. She was looking forward, in fact, to a very long separation, for the Patron had promised to take the lad on as his own donkey-boy if he did well during the trip. I fancy the poor creature had cried so much since her husband's death that the fountain of tears was ever ready to overflow.

Meanwhile it was only too easy to see that the lad, Antoine Franki, was overjoyed at having got a berth so much to his taste. He said good-bye to his mother, but his real interest was in the donkey, Zoulou, standing already harnessed on the towing-path with the rope fastened to the *Boussemroum*. On the word to start being given, Franki cracked his whip in a most masterly style, and sharply touched Zoulou, who immediately launched out dangerously with both heels. This delighted Franki, who turned to us a joyous face, illuminated with a broad grin that exhibited one of the whitest sets of teeth in France.

It was the old story, the mother tenderly sorrowful and anxious, the son eager to see the world, and make his own way in it.

A moment more and the *Boussemroum* had begun her long descent of the Saône, going down with the stream, whilst the figure of the mother was lost to view as she resumed her weary way back to Jonvelle, saddened by her boy's departure,[1] yet possibly a little happier for the ten francs.

"This," said Mr. Pennell, "is clearly a case of slave-dealing, the difference being that you would never, in the Southern States, have got such a boy for so little money." I ventured to suggest that there might be another difference in the willingness of the slave.

Before Franki had done his first mile it became evident to all of us that he was master of his work. He had the most complete self-confidence, and there was an artistry in his donkey-driving that can only be acquired in youth.

The Pilot looked at me with an air of satisfaction, and uttered the French equivalent of "He'll do." The Captain admired the boy's skill with a beaming smile. As for me, who had just promised his mother that I would be like a father to him, I felt anxious, for every time the whip touched Zoulou he kicked so high and kicked so straight that a hit seemed inevitable, but

---

[1] She had a special reason for more than ordinary grief, which the reader will learn in due time, and which I was ignorant of at the date of this letter.

Franki always stepped aside in time, and looked at us and grinned.

I ought perhaps to explain that Zoulou is by no means a vulgar donkey. He is a handsome, finely-bred animal, quite as intelligent as a clever horse, and both well fed and carefully groomed. His master, though niggardly in other matters, buys the best of hay and corn for Zoulou, and pets him with crusts of bread, besides giving him every opportunity to graze. Zoulou is as observant as a dog. His house has two openings, looking towards bows and stern, and whenever we pass through a lock, or meet other boats, or stop at a village, in a word, whenever there is anything to be seen, Zoulou first opens one door and looks out of it, and when he has exhausted all that is to be seen on that side he does the same on the other. No doubt he has acquired much local knowledge about the canals of Central France,[1] and I am positively certain of this, that he sees the river to be something very different from those canals and is aware that this kind of travelling is an exceptional experience for him.

I wish the *Boussemroum* did her part as well as Zoulou and Franki do theirs, but unfortunately the *Boussemroum*, with so light a load as the encampment, will not answer to the helm when there is a side wind. In a *laden* berrichon the great flat side acts as a keel in the water, in a *light* berrichon it acts as a sail in the air with no keel to resist it. The latter is our present case. There are more than three hundred square feet of oaken

---

[1] The reader may think that this is mere facetiousness, but it is not. Both the pilot and the patron agreed that the horses and asses employed in inland navigation give clear proofs of local observation and strong topographic memory. How could they remember if they did not observe?

wall out of water, and the saloon makes about eighty more above the wall, the Captain's tent about twenty. Besides this we have the permanent donkey-house and the cabin.

To steer well in the river with a wind the *Boussemroum* would require thirty tons of ballast, and I have no room to stow it. The alternative is twin keels, but these would be costly for a single voyage, and I could not get them before reaching Chalon. Leeboards would be applied with great difficulty, and would be objectionable on other grounds. To establish an efficient centre-board with its great water-tight case would cost more than the *Boussemroum* is worth, and, in fact, on account of her great length, two centre-boards would be required. They would also spoil the interior accommodation.

You may think it strange that as an amateur boat-builder I did not foresee these difficulties. Not having any experience of berrichons, I trusted to professional opinion. A great barge-builder said that a berrichon would steer better, when towed, than my sailing-boat. Now, my sailing-boat, which has a centre-board, steers admirably when towed.

There was nothing in the Patron's experience (limited to canals) to make him apprehend this difficulty. Indeed, as soon as we got out of the river into the canal that passes Ormoy, the *Boussemroum* behaved agreeably, and Zoulou drew her with ease. The canal banks protected her from the side winds.

The Pilot, more accustomed to rivers, had foreseen the possibility of bad steering, and had deepened the rudders (there are twin rudders) at Corre, but the boards he added produced no appreciable effect, and were very soon carried away on the stones.

The defective steering will spoil the expedition in this sense, that we shall be very much at the mercy of the wind. In calm weather the *Boussemroum* can be steered, even on the river, but with a side wind this will always be difficult, and sometimes impossible. We shall then have to wait for a change of weather.

Yesterday we had a severe experience. The wind was strong and unfavourable. It did not stop us altogether, but it continually drove the boat on a lee shore, and the Pilot had to keep her off with a pole. She struck the stony bank at least once a minute, on the average, with a shock that made writing and drawing alike impossible. This manner of voyaging combines the extremity of slowness with the extremity of discomfort.

We all admired the magnificent energy of the Pilot, who stood on the forecastle deck, put the end of the pole against his breast, seized the gunwale of the boat with both hands, and bore the shock every time by sheer fortitude. He repeated frequently, "C'est l'orage, c'est l'orage qui fait ça." On the Saône the word "orage" has not its usual French sense; it simply means the wind, any wind, even a light breeze.

Now, you have had quite enough about navigation, and I want to say something about the river. It makes a grand sweeping course between Corre and Ormoy, passing at the foot of a steep height richly-wooded, and the country opposite is hilly, with a well-placed village called Ranzevelle. The river itself is much wider than above Corre, though not comparable to the Lower Saône. The banks are stony, and rich in aquatic vegetation. It is essentially a painter's river here, with well-coloured foregrounds and beautiful blue distances.

Below Ranzevelle the Saône makes another curve and is rapid and no longer navigable. To avoid this part there is a canal which we entered. We moored for the night on this canal close to the village of Ormoy. This is unquestionably one of the most picturesque little places in France, and quite unspoiled.

Ormoy from the Canal.

Finely situated on a small rocky eminence, with the church in the middle of a great open square, it offers endless material for a sketcher. On the rocky side, near the river, you have rude stairs and fine bits of building adapting themselves to the irregular ground—as good material, Mr. Pennell declared, as any he had seen in Italy, and quite Italian in character. But the glory of Ormoy is its fine open Place, with the wonderful variety of the houses that surround it, their grand roofs, their shady arches, and here and there a bit of architectural ornament, especially one gateway with rude, bold, effective carving. We were delighted with the public fountain, a great

Ormoy, the Public Fountain.

circular basin with a lofty stone vase in the middle and in the vase a tree. Then there was such a fine variety of cool and warm colour all about this Place, that it was a torture to draw in black and white only, there were such oppositions of unexpected hues, such depths of sombre browns or purples, such rich reds, such choice and delicate greys! We were so enthusiastic about the beauty of Ormoy that the inhabitants came out of their houses and smiled, though not malevolently, at our strange unaccountable ways.

Close to the canal there is a second public fountain or well near the washing place, but it is forbidden to wash in it and the water is as transparent as air. This being near to the *Boussemroum* was a great boon to us, and we took a supply of it.

A House in Ormoy.

Opposite Ormoy, beyond the Saône, is Richecourt, now a great farm hamlet with the remains of a castle on the side of a steep wooded hill. Richecourt is one of the most picturesque and most beautifully situated castles on the Saône. One or two of the towers still remain and are most finely placed, whilst the other buildings are massive and grand, and compose well.

It is our custom to take a walk every evening after dinner. Yesterday we followed a path through the fields that goes

Richecourt from Ormoy.

Richecourt.

to the banks of the Saône opposite the woods of Richecourt. It was a delightful evening, the twilight passing into moonlight and casting a mysterious glamour over the grey towers, the dark forest, the broad rich meadows, the murmuring, untamed river.

There is a poetical quality in the names of places due to sound and association, often to mere sound only. The sound of many names in this part of France is, to my ear, very

A Country House near Ranzevelle.

melodious. Just above Richecourt, on the height, is the village of Ranzevelle. To my ear, Ranzevelle is in itself almost a little poem. Ormoy is a beautiful name too, I think, and so is Richecourt. A great number of villages not very far from the Upper Saône end with the syllable "court," and many of these names are euphonious and romantic, names to which a man of genius would easily hang a tale.[1]

[1] "Court," in composition, means a "domaine rural," according to Littré. In Normandy it means the ground and plantations round a farm-house, and immediately

LETTER XVII.

BELOW JUSSEY, *June* 13*th*.

After leaving Ormoy on the 12th, we made our way down the river and canal pleasantly to the suspension bridge at Cendrecourt. There being but little wind, and much of the distance lying between canal banks, the donkey served us well. It appears evident now that Zoulou will be useful under favourable circumstances. The uncertainty about getting on gives an additional interest to the voyage. It is quite impossible to foretell what will be the length of the day's journey. I notice with pleasure that the lad Franki is very active and efficient, knowing his work thoroughly and proud of doing it in style. This is especially evident when we come to places where the towing-path changes from one bank to the other, and a rather complicated manœuvre has to be gone through.

As the sun was very hot just above Cendrecourt, I arranged myself in a suit of clean summer clothes, and set off with the captain on foot to see the little town of Jussey, which is nearly two miles from the river. We were caught in a deluge of rain which gave me a miserable appearance, the more unsuitable that I was going to call upon a banker, however, it was not to

---

belonging to it. The name would therefore, in its origin, belong to one farm or château, and afterwards, when other habitations gathered round the first, the name would be retained for the entire hamlet or village. I have made a catalogue of more than sixty villages within a limited distance of the Upper Saône which have the termination *court*. Littré derives it from the low Latin *curtis*, from the Latin *cohors* or *cors*, and from the Greek χόρτος, which has the same radical as the Latin *hortus* and the German *garten*.

negociate a loan. The banker was not at home but I found his partner, and we had a conversation of great interest to us, as we voyagers on the *Boussemroum* have been severed from news ever since we quitted Gray. We now learned the fate of Mr. Gladstone's Irish measures. It was like meeting a ship at sea, and asking for the latest news.

This gentleman also told us about some local events of

A Street at Cendrecourt.

interest. There had been a hail-storm at Jussey a few days before which had cost the little town and neighbourhood no less than 40,000*l.* in damage done to surrounding crops. This is a terribly heavy tax on so small a place. It would be thought a hard impost during a war. Jussey has about 3,000 urban inhabitants.

There is a flat plain between Jussey and the Saône but a

steep hill or *coteau* rises just behind the town. I wish there were a good special English word for *coteau*, which is much more exactly descriptive than the general term "hill." Our word "bank," which comes nearest, gives the notion of something much smaller, like the bank of a river. A *coteau* is a high bank, generally with a table-land above. Seen from below, it very frequently presents the appearance of a real hill.

Jussey, at present, is a rather picturesque little town, remarkable chiefly for its delightfully abundant supply of pure spring

Cendrecourt from the Fields.

water in public and private fountains. The Amance, a tributary of the Saône, passes by Jussey. In the times of the Spanish domination (Franche Comté was a possession of Spain in the sixteenth century) the place was well fortified with a strong castle and ramparts, but these have entirely disappeared.

The banker we were to have seen, and whom I did not know personally, had driven to his garden near the Saône and we had met him on the road without being aware of it. The same thing happened on our return, so we missed each other a second time. On arriving at the *Boussemroum* I learned that an artist who lived part of the year at Corre (M. Dagnan-Bouveret) had sent a messenger on horseback after us to invite us to his studio on the banks of the Saône below Ormoy, but we are rather pressed for time on account of our slow locomotion, and we cannot well go back, even for a few miles.

During our visit to Jussey, Mr. Pennell made sketches in the

A Barn at Cendrecourt.

village of Cendrecourt on the opposite bank of the Saône, and he missed Jussey, but of the two Cendrecourt is the more picturesque, being especially remarkable for its fine roofs. These delighted Mr. Pennell, and he was also greatly pleased with the remarkable unity of character in Cendrecourt. The people there were very civil to him, inviting him to take shelter in their houses during the rain.

On pursuing our way, we had exactly the kind of weather that suits Zoulou and the *Boussemroum*. The water was without a ripple, and even the upper air was perfectly still. To the east, a range of cumuli rose like Alps of a warm golden white, and there was a fine terrestrial distance in that direction.

The joiner at Corre has established a quarter-deck for me on the *Boussemroum*, in front of the donkey's house. This is extremely convenient as we can all three sit upon this deck on camp stools under an awning, and look before us with no other impediment than the narrow peak of the Captain's tent which hides very little of the scenery. Mr. Pennell's tent is much lower and does not impede the view in the least. Nothing can be more agreeable, when the boat is going tolerably well, than to sit in this way and quietly enjoy the scenery. It reminds me of sitting in a canoe, but the much greater height above the water gives a far better command of the shores.

We moored for the night at a beautiful place beyond Jussey where there are fine rocks, coming down to the water, crowned by a wood of the utmost richness with masses of abundant overhanging foliage of a very noble character. Here we passed a ferry and I was pleased by an ingenious contrivance for making the tow-ropes of passing barges go clear over the ferry-boat and its apparatus. Long tapering wands, rather like fishing-rods, are planted in the ground, leaning at a certain angle and in apparent disorder but really with exact calculation. The tow-rope catches the first, and you think it must either break or stop the boat. It does neither, it bends and passes the rope on to another which repeats the motion. In this way, amongst them, they carry the rope clean over the ferry boat and other obstacles, and the driver takes no thought.

We slept at this place close to the towing path, which is contrary to the rule of the river, but we wanted to sketch there. Many boats passed early in the morning, and, if the bargemen had been angry at us, they would have been excusable, but the Pilot went a few yards to meet them, and simply said that we desired to be on that side to make a sketch. The answer he received was always civil, and generally to the effect that the hindrance was of no consequence as the boat could easily pass. The passing, however, cost the bargemen considerable trouble,

Ferry near Jussey.

especially when they were ascending the stream, but they bore it with charming good humour, and we generally had a little talk about our respective destinations, whilst the horses were loosened and the rope was passed over the complicated peaks and gables of the *Boussemroum*.[1] The real good-breeding of

---

[1] If the expedition had to be done over again, one of my first cares would be to establish a curved ridge of wood, starting at the stem and passing to the stern in the shape of a bent bow, clearing all the obstacles presented by the tents and the boat This would enable a rope to glide over them mechanically. All the stationary boats for washerwomen are provided with some contrivance of this kind.

the bargee class on this river was a constant wonder to Mr. Pennell and even to myself, who might be supposed to know them better, but as my other voyages had been usually in a sailing boat they had not brought me so much in contact with the river population. In our present voyage we belong to that population ourselves, the *Boussemroum* having admitted us into the confraternity; the people rather like us for living on board our boat, which awakens their sympathies but causes them no wonder. I was surprised at first that such an odd-looking affair as the *Boussemroum*, with the encampment upon it, did not excite ridicule, but the river people are accustomed to seeing rude huts and tents on barges, or at least cloths which they call *tendues* (only another form of the word *tente*, in Italian *tenda*), so that my arrangements seem to them perfectly rational.

The largest class of boat on the Saône is called a *péniche*, and is not at all like the undecked, two-masted boats which go by that name at Cherbourg and other places on the sea-side. A river *péniche* is a barge of great size, and its tonnage may be anywhere between a hundred and fifty, and three hundred and twenty tons. The prow and the stern rise rather high with a handsome curve, the rudder is about the size of a barn door, and is often hinged that it may be easily reduced in length whilst passing through locks. In many of these boats there is a commodious stable for the horses, and there are good cabins for the "Patron" and his family. These cabins are finished and kept up with a certain amount of luxury. The windows often have little *persienne* shutters (like Venetian blinds) and curtains of white lace or embroidered muslin. The framework of the windows is painted white, with perhaps a red or green line round it, and little flower-pots on the sill. A sign that there are children on board is a little deck before the cabin for them to play upon, inclosed by a railing to prevent them from falling overboard. I made the acquaintance of a mother on one of these boats by lifting her child ashore for her. The child in question was a nice little girl, six or seven years old, very neatly dressed, and perfectly clean. The mother seemed to be of about the same class as a shop-keeper of rather good standing in a provincial French town. She spoke perfectly good French without either patois or vulgarisms, and told me the history of her voyage. They had come from Belgium and were going to Lyons, a distance of a thousand *kilomètres*. As the canals are closed in August for cleaning it was necessary to hurry in order to get back again before the closing, and their boat had come from Belgium to Corre in a fortnight with constant relays of horses night and day. I was shown all over this *péniche*. The cargo, being of iron rails, occupied little space, and was, in fact, mere ballast, so the immense interior served for various domestic purposes like the courtyard of a house, and one part of it was converted into a large dining-room. There was a very well-finished cabin amidships, and another at the stern end. A large *péniche* of this kind exactly fits the gates of the locks. These vessels have often a big mast that can be easily lowered, being hung in a tabernacle and balanced with heavy weights at its foot. When the wind is favourable they display a huge lug-sail, which takes them along speedily with a good breeze. At such times the horses are taken on board, and become passengers like our friend Zoulou behind the steam-tug.

The colour of these boats, which are only tarred, resembles

nothing so much as an old brown violin. In sunshine the transparence of the colour produces the effect of a rich glaze in a picture, and becomes indescribably luminous *within*, the oak showing through the glaze, especially in new boats. The sail is often of a pale green, having probably been steeped in sulphate of copper to preserve it from mildew.

Wood near Jussey.

Visiting the stable on one of these boats, I took upon myself to plead for more care about stuffing the collars, which often gall the horses and produce raws. One man said in answer, "You will never find a raw, sir, on any horse in my care; see, these two are the pair I attend to." On examining them I admitted that their skins were perfectly sound. My companion, the Captain, cannot endure to see anything like maltreatment of animals, and, gentle as his manners usually are, they become quite fierce when he sees any wrong done to the brute creation. One day on a canal bank a man was belabouring an unfortunate horse that he had harnessed before another, and the Captain who was walking there at the time, stopped and exclaimed, with a look of concentrated anger and contempt, "Don't you see that you are an imbecile? That horse is new to the work, and yet you put him first. Remove him from where he is, put him behind, and he will do well enough. There is no necessity to beat him." Such is the force of a superior will that although the boatman was in a furious rage, and had never seen the Captain before, he obeyed without a word, and the horse did his work unresistingly.

LETTER XVIII.

On a Canal near Chemilly,
June 14th.

The Pilot, like the Captain of the steam-tug, has decidedly a fancy for making us sleep in canals. We have moored for the night in this short canal that cuts off a loop of the river. The Pilot moored the fore-part of the boat to a tree, first carefully surrounding the bark with hay to prevent chafing. I admire his carefulness. It was interesting to compare the Patron's slight and inadequate way of doing the same thing when fastening the stern rope to another tree. It made the Pilot shrug his shoulders and put on his contemptuous look, an expression of countenance in which he is excelled by no man.

This is the exact spot where the Patron was left behind as we ascended the river. There is no danger of his being left behind at our present rate of speed! It is, alas, but too easy to overtake poor Zoulou when he is towing the *Boussemroum*. Without that considerable drag upon his motions he is lively enough to lead one a merry chase.

You may remember that my last letter brought us down to a rocky place below Jussey, where I said that the foliage was very fine. The passing of several barges at that place led me into a digression about the floating population.

Soon after leaving the rocky place, the windings of the river, which is very serpentine about here, brought us to a sort of tableland, from which there are most extensive views over blue distances, interrupted by nearer green hills. Here we distinctly realised the fact that we were on elevated ground as we looked *down* into the lower country far away, and it was a peculiar sensation to be floating on a navigable river at a height where, in my previous experience, I had usually found swiftly-descending streams. These distant views were seen in the utmost perfection under a rainy sky in gleams of sunshine between showers. Nothing was to be done for the illustration of such scenery with the means at our disposal. A consummately skilful painter in water-colours might have expressed, at least, the spirit of it. I contented myself with exploring the distances with a binocular, and seeing forest, plain, and distant villages, now in purple gloom under the raincloud, now gleaming with fresh greens in the sunshine, and never for one instant without change.

We passed the village of Montureux-les-Baulay, which differs from most of these villages in being quite close to the riverside, extending itself in length. This place is not so exclusively a peasants' village as Cendrecourt, for example, neither has it the fine character of Cendrecourt. There is a comfortable *maison bourgeoise* with lawn and garden near the church and close to the waterside, as we find such houses on the Thames.

A Curve of the Upper Saône.

A deep lock here brought us to a much lower level, depriving us of distant views, but the near scenery was a compensation. Nothing could exceed the fine reedy vegetation of the river banks, and the water-worn forms of the banks themselves were good. On the right the shore was high and steep, and crowned with a straggling village called Fouchécourt, that reminded us of Dürer's villages, large quaint roofs and high gables crowning the upper ground, and descending amidst firs, poplars, and ash-trees down to the level of the river. This delighted Mr. Pennell, but he was still more pleased with Baulay, a village on the left, at some distance from the shore, in gently sloping fields. This village, with its church tower and high red roofs, is a complete unity in itself without a single discordant element, so that the sketcher has little to arrange, and absolutely nothing to reject. The colour, as we saw

Fouchécourt.

it, was all of the most delightful russets and greys between the green fields and the rainy sky. Mr. Pennell, when he sees a village of this kind, can hardly be taken past it without cruelty, he always wishes to stay there as we stayed at Corre, but we are not advancing quickly towards the south, so I cannot always indulge him. Besides, without colour a village like Baulay loses half its significance. The real beauty of it is in the perfect harmony of all its elements.

At Conflandey we descended another deep lock, and were therefore approaching more nearly to the level of the Saône at Gray. Conflandey is at the junction of the Saône with the Lanterne, one of its most important tributaries, indeed, so important that it is almost equal in volume of water to the Saône itself. The name "Lanterne" is a corruption of lantenne, from the Latin *lantenna*. The dark, swiftly-flowing waters of this river were much purer than those of the Saône when we saw them, the Saône holding much earthy matter in suspension which made it opaque and of a reddish-yellow colour. The village of Conflandey takes its name from the confluence, but I am unable to trace the formation of the word Conflandey exactly. There are analogous names in France, such as Conflans, for example.

Conflandey is situated on the right bank of the Saône opposite a long, curving, beautifully wooded island that reminded me strongly of the finest islands on the Thames. The village is on a rising bank, and is beautifully completed by its church on the highest point. The houses come close to the water's edge and, without exception, are perfect of their kind. Here, as at Baulay, the beauty of the place does not depend on any antique tumble-down buildings, it is the buildings of to-day that are good, being picturesque and habitable at the same time. A village of this quality, so quietly harmonious and unpretending, would be entirely spoilt by a single showy villa. Near the water the houses have little gardens with rugged walls completing the natural rock, and palings on the top of the walls. The day after our arrival the weather was perfectly calm, and the reflection omitted none of these picturesque details.

Some years ago Conflandey ran a risk of being entirely spoilt by the establishment of a great paper-mill, but the mill has fortunately been erected on the left shore of the Saône, where it is hidden by the wooded island. The owner or director of this concern lives in a good house on the island with gardens and grounds, and his communication with the mill is secured by a suspension bridge. As the island is taken possession of in this way by a rich man it is preserved from further injury. The variety of the trees is evidence of careful planting. They include Scotch fir, poplar, alder, horse-chestnut, willow, and

Conflandey, the Village.

sycamore, and the edge of the island is enriched with beautiful aquatic plants. I never saw trees bend more gracefully than on this island, or in more beautiful masses over the water.

The Pilot is always a little fussy (the defect of his qualities), so, as I had expressed some curiosity about the paper-mill, he went to it and came back as if with a message from the owner, saying that he would be happy to show us over it. We went accordingly, and were told to apply to the owner at his house, the Pilot having gone beyond his authority. On this I ordered him to set the *Boussemroum* in motion (if it can be called motion) for Port-sur-Saône.

Between Conflandey and Port-sur-Saône the character of the river scenery is perfect of its kind, and not spoiled by anything,

Conflandey, the Towing Path.

unless it be a long cutting made for the towing-path, which lays the red rock bare on the side of a steep and lofty wooded shore. Poor Zoulou seemed diminished to the size of a rat under these precipices, but he held along bravely, and as the weather, for the moment, was calm, our prospects seemed encouraging. There was a delightful half-hour when the course of the river brought us clear of the hill, and the more open scenery in the direction of

Port-sur-Saône lay before us, but then came a strong gusty wind that drove the *Boussemroum* ashore, and, worse still, impelled her sideways with such speed that Zoulou could hardly keep up with her, and was in constant danger of being dragged into the water and drowned. Meanwhile, the unfortunate but devoted Pilot was constantly receiving thrusts from his pole in the breast, equivalent, at least, to those from a blunt lance in the tournaments of old times, and in this way he succeeded for a while in keeping the stem of the boat a yard or two from the shore. At last, however, we struck with great force, and at the same time the bottom of the boat was caught on a large stone. This, with the great power of the wind on her exposed side, almost succeeded in upsetting her, and clearly convinced me of the possibility of a capsize under properly favourable circumstances.[1] I dare say you have experienced what I have often felt when things were going wrong, a sort of wicked desire that they should go as wrong as possible, so that the powers of evil, instead of troubling us with mere *taquineries*, might give us something serious to complain of. I do honestly confess that there was a moment when I wanted the *Boussemroum* to capsize. The thing had plagued us by abortive attempts at capsizing, and there would have been something colossal in the upsetting of a canoe of eighty tons burden. Mr. Pennell sat on the quarter-deck making the most disparaging reflections on our yacht. The Patron, at the stern, popped up his head at every bump, and flew into a fresh passion, as if such collisions were quite new to his experience. As for the Pilot he had not much time to talk,

---

[1] A berrichon only *seems* stable because it is very heavy and big, and the weight of a man in one part or other of it makes very little difference. A fly probably believes that the crankest of canoes has stability. So it has, relatively to the fly.

on account of the groans occasioned by the fearful thrusts of the blunt lance, but whenever an opportunity occurred he repeated the same formula of words, "C'est l'orage qui fait ça, c'est l'orage!"[1]

As we got nearer Port-sur-Saône we were more accustomed to the incessant shocks against the stones and managed to admire the beautiful grey rocks and green sward on the steep shore, all in bright sunshine or broad shadow.

Port-sur-Saône is a little town of two thousand inhabitants, beautifully situated at the foot of a steep wooded hill. There is an island in the river here larger than that at Conflandey, but not so beautifully wooded, and a long old bridge goes over to the

Port-sur-Saône.

mainland. Mr. Pennell made a remark here about the rarity of old bridges on the Saône. The truth is that the frequent wars of which the Franche Comté has been the theatre have led to the destruction of bridges, and the scientific work of the modern engineers has replaced others, besides creating many bridges where there were only ferry-boats in old times.

[1] The word "orage," on the banks of the Saône, has not its usual French meaning, as I noticed in Letter XVI. In ordinary French it means a storm, generally a thunderstorm, but on the Saône it means the south wind, and by extension any wind, even a light breeze. Our Pilot called the faintest breezes "l'orage," which produces the oddest effect till one is accustomed to it. The English reader may realise this by supposing that in some part of England faint breezes were always called thunderstorms by the inhabitants.

There is a fine Renaissance church at Port-sur-Saône, of simple but serious and dignified architecture, that rather surprises one in so small a place. It was much more like a minor church in a great city. The body of it is stately and plain, the east end rich with a moderate display of gilding on dark panels. An interior of this kind must produce a strong effect on country people who are not accustomed to see dignified architecture.

Port-sur-Saône— the Little Bridge.

Although there are few visible remains of antiquity in this little town at the present day, it is one of the oldest in France, and the scene of the martyrdom of St. Vallier.

We made the acquaintance of a tall pilot at this place who was soon very friendly, in fact, we had become acquainted on the ascending voyage. These pilots are physically picked men by natural selection, as their work requires great strength. Our new friend was perhaps not quite so powerful a man as our own Pilot, but he was a fine specimen of well-preserved activity in mature life. He had mighty hands and a lively, vigilant eye; he was muscular, without an ounce of superfluous flesh; altogether one of the finest men I have met with upon the Saône.

In striking contrast to this noble-looking pilot was a podgy cantankerous little man, who came to the boat attracted by curiosity, and presently began to scold young Franki as he sat peeling potatoes in front of the cabin during the absence of the others. I was writing at the time in the saloon, and came out to see what this scolding creature was, but being immediately convinced that the fellow was drunk, I retired after merely telling Franki to take no notice. So Franki went on quietly peeling his potatoes and smiling at the other's noise. This incident would not be worth mentioning were it not that the drunken man said, "There's money that's honestly earned, and there's money that's earned in other ways. I would not earn money as you do by serving foreigners who make plans." This is the only expression of the spy mania that I have yet observed in the country. It may possibly create some inconvenience if the man goes on talking and induces people to believe him.

We quitted Port-sur-Saône in the golden glow of a splendid evening. The weather being now perfectly calm the *Boussemroum* kept off the shore and took us down to Chemilly, through beautiful reaches of the winding river, which is here broad enough to be majestic. The shores here are richly wooded, there being a great forest on the right bank and a large communal wood on the left. To the south was an open hilly distance, so that under this charming effect the whole made a succession of the richest landscapes with fine, broad masses of shade and the most harmonious glowing colour. Mr. Pennell and I both enjoyed this deeply as we sat at ease on the quarter-deck, but we agreed that it was beyond the possibilities of any linear drawing, and Mr. Pennell thought that the tranquil, majestic beauty of such a scene was even beyond the art of painting

Port-sur-Saône— the Channel between the Islands.

itself. It cannot be *realized* in paint, but Claude, Wilson, and Turner have all conveyed the impression of richness and tranquillity that charmed us. A broad winding river, richly wooded shores rising to gentle eminences, distant hills of a tender grey approaching, but not too nearly, to a pale azure, a sky all full of heaven's own calm and light, and everywhere Nature's sweetest summer rest—these are the elements of a scene too perfect for description, but so impressive that even the rude boatmen were touched by it and stood quite silent in their places, the only sound being the occasional swish of the tow-rope after being caught an instant in the glassy surface, or Franki's cheerful cry of encouragement to Zoulou. At length we heard the sound of falling waters, the river became a lake, terminated by a great weir, and after falling in a cascade, it flowed away in a noble

The Boussemroum in the Canal at Chemilly.

curve by islets and shallows to the old castle of Chemilly. Here, of course, as at all the curves that are not navigable, a canal opened its gates to the *Boussemroum*, and shortly after, we were moored to the shore beneath a brightening moon.

Nothing can exceed the tranquillity of an evening spent in such a place as this. The shore of the canal is like a lawn;

it has been freshly mown, and the hay is in little heaps. The thin, delicate young trees stand in their peaceful order, whilst beyond them the untamed river flows in its old channel as it has flowed for a thousand years, and the murmur of it comes to us without ceasing, here in our protected rest.

To my taste there is nothing in our present voyage more charming than the hours when the *Boussemroum* is moored for the night. Even in the worst weather we enjoy the evenings in the saloon, when the Captain sits in state in the one arm-chair we possess, but on fine evenings we enjoy a sauntering walk, without any definite object. This evening was especially delightful with the clear bright moonlight and the absolute calm. The *Boussemroum* lay quite alone in the canal, motionless on the motionless water, as quiet a home as the most solitary cottage in the midst of its silent fields.

LETTER XIX.

In a Canal Basin, near Scey-sur-Saône,
June 16th.

Early in the morning we went to see the village and château of Chemilly. At this place the shore of the river is steep, high, and well-wooded. Then it slopes down suddenly to the river Durgeon, which falls into the Saône at this place, and the village is situated by the confluence, on a steep road, the castle being partly on the height with some towers down by the river.

The little bridge over the Durgeon has quite a superior air with its statue of a good bishop on the bridge, not a mere doll, but a piece of respectable eighteenth-century work. It is wonderful how immediately a piece of sculpture of the slightest artistic merit ennobles and refines the things about it. Here is this little two-arched bridge, for

The Bridge at Chemilly.

example, made distinguished amongst bridges by the possession of its stature, and the whole village gains dignity from it.

The river Durgeon, Drugeon, or Dregeon, passes by Vesoul, which is here less than seven miles from the Saône as the crow flies. Vesoul is the capital of the department and a place of some interest, but in the present voyage we confine ourselves to the shores of the Saône itself which afford us ample occupation.

The castle of Chemilly is inhabited. The square and massive

The River Durgeon at Chemilly.

donjon tower stands high on its rock in the midst of what is now a beautiful garden, and the tower itself is the chief part of the modern dwelling. It has been modernised, and is now surmounted by a sort of dome, perfectly incongruous yet, strange to say, by no means ineffective at a distance, where it crowns the composition with some nobility. Such of the other towers as still remain are but little injured, the most interesting of all being a small *tourelle* low down on the river shore which is in a wonderfully perfect state of preservation. It is of pale grey hewn stones, most carefully finished and fitted, and round the moulding that supports the projecting part of the wall there is a band of delicate sculpture that one discovers only on coming near. It was quite a surprise to find such a finished piece of work as this *tourelle* on the banks of the Saône, where the old military architecture is generally rude, and especially to find it so close to the water's edge, where it must have been exposed to every flood.

Much of this beautiful castle was destroyed at or about the Revolution. The charm of what remains is enhanced by the garden with its quaint mixture of order and irregularity. Just before the donjon there is a terrace, from which you look down a sheer precipice upon the roofs of the towers below, and whence you have one of the finest river views in France. The wild Saône, here quite unspoiled by engineers, and navigable only in a small boat, comes with a magnificent curve, washing reedy islets in its course. Far in the distance you have villages with their towers and, fold behind fold, the endless forest-covered hills.

On the height behind the donjon there is a convent, now unoccupied, except that the chapel of it is used as the village church, and the villagers come up to service here, through the beautiful grounds of the castle.

The singular charm of this village of Chemilly is appreciated by the people of Vesoul, who come here in excursion parties, and feast in leafy bowers at the meeting of the waters.

The weather had been fair during the morning, but on leaving the canal we found ourselves in a deluge of rain. Zoulou and Franki held their way bravely with empty sacks on their backs. The Pilot got wet through, whilst I was

From the Terrace, Chemilly.

sitting well-sheltered in the saloon, hard at work upon a chapter of *Imagination in Landscape Painting*. The readers of our books know little of the strange circumstances in which some parts of them are written. I have never worked more comfortably than on board the *Boussemroum*, even when the rain was clattering most noisily upon the canvas.

After a mile or two of natural river, we discovered a water-gate on the opposite shore. Whenever you see a water-gate you must enter it, as its existence is a proof that the river is not navigable far beyond. Zoulou had to be conveyed across in a ferry-boat, which the Pilot called for in a voice of thunder: but there was only a woman at the ferry, and as the rain was still pouring heavily, she preferred to be somewhat deaf. At length, however, Zoulou was taken across, and we shortly found ourselves on a magnificent canal. This canal is the finest hitherto seen in the descending voyage. It is broad and straight, between banks green as English lawns down to the water's edge, and on the top of the bank there is a stately avenue of poplars, four ranks of them on each side and all of magnificent growth. Beyond this on the left side rises a steep forest-covered hill. The impression produced by a canal of this kind is not at all that of a merely utilitarian work, such, for example, as that between Liverpool and Leeds. Here one's impression is that of being admitted into some royal demesne on artificial waters intended for state and pleasure. Mr. Pennell expressed our feelings exactly when he said that the rude *Boussemroum*, quite in her place on the natural river, was unworthy to float on these canals where the only suitable craft would be a boat of the most finished beauty and elegance. I said it ought to be a gilded barge, with a glass saloon, or at the least, a gondola.

We had excellent evidence, in this canal, of the utility of an ordnance map. I never travel without these maps, and have extracted from them a complete atlas of the Saône. Our Pilot, like all his brethren, is full of confidence in his own knowledge, which is derived from ocular observation and memory, and never refreshed by a reference to any document in the intervals of his voyages. Midway through this canal is a large basin, and the Pilot was leaving this behind, when I suddenly came out of my cabin and ordered him to turn

Canal between Scey and Chemilly.

back and moor the *Boussemroum* in the basin itself, and on its eastern shore. The Pilot defended himself by affirming that he was going to Scey. I said he was going away from that place (which was quite invisible from the water) and cut short all discussion by a peremptory command. When the

The Boussemroum in the Basin at Scey.

boat was moored, I said: "You see we are close to a road. It goes straight to Scey, which is one kilomètre from here." The Pilot went upon the road, and saw the little town straight before him. This impressed him with a fresh respect for the ordnance map. I would willingly make a tracing of the whole river for him, but he could not read the names.[1]

Zoulou was set as usual to graze after the *Boussemroum* was moored for the night, but being in a more than usually frolicsome temper he escaped to the woods, and Franki was despatched after him. After dinner the lad sent me, by the Patron (not venturing to enter the saloon himself) a bouquet of wild strawberries that he had found time to gather for me during his chase of Zoulou. He had heard me say to the Captain that the weak point of our feeding was the absence of dessert, and that we got neither strawberries nor cherries in the villages. I was pleased with his attention, and charged the Patron to thank him, when, glancing at the open door, I spied the donor of the strawberries in person, watching the effect of his present with that broad grin which, with him, expresses all the shades of satisfaction.

This basin is the most beautiful place in which the *Boussemroum* has hitherto been moored for the night. It measures about 200 metres by 150, and is surrounded by towering trees. Its surface is adorned with the yellow water-lily. We had it all to ourselves, except that two men were repairing a small boat on the bank. After dinner, the evening being fine with splendid moonlight, we walked on the road that goes to Besançon and

---

[1] Even a good reader may be unable to use a map, from the lack of the topographic sense. There are many comparatively educated people for whom a map has no distinct meaning. During the Franco-German War an officer in the Garibaldian army told me that many of his brother officers were quite unable to make any practical use of maps.

winds up through the wood. Mr. Pennell observed in what perfection this road was kept, the impression being rather that it was a drive in some English nobleman's park than a public way through a forest.

The next morning I made the discovery that the skin of Franki's feet had been rubbed off in many places by his hard boots, which he wore without socks, so I took him to Scey and made him a present of shoes and socks in return for his strawberries. The poor lad has a most beggarly appearance, yet in spite of this everybody at Scey treated him with almost parental kindness. The shoemaker's wife behaved like a mother to him, and helped me by wise counsel in the selection of socks. The lad asked for a trifle out of his wages, and this he immediately invested in fishing-tackle, so he will have an amusement for his leisure hours.[1]

At Scey I found the Captain seated in a goodly dwelling and talking to the lady of the house, who was a very handsome, fine looking person, as if he had known her for twenty years. The Captain's manners, always gentle except when he is reprimanding a man for mistreating some wretched animal, become imbued

---

[1] The shoes remind me of a little difficulty I experienced before Franki joined the expedition. The Patron is not precisely my servant, but only a boatman who has voluntarily taken upon himself the office of cook. The Pilot is not my servant either, but simply a river pilot engaged to manage the *Boussemroum*. I therefore felt some delicacy about ordering them to clean shoes. I had a large supply on board (Mr. Pennell called them my "regiment") and by managing carefully I contrived to make them last till we got to Corre. Meanwhile the Captain appeared every morning with boots of unsurpassable blackness and gloss. I asked if he had persuaded either of the men to give them this beautiful appearance. "No," he replied with a merry twinkle in his eyes; "I am not unable to clean boots myself, and as I have plenty of time on my hands it gives me a little occupation." When Franki joined the expedition I found he was ignorant of this art, so I placed him under the Captain as a

A House in Scey.

with I know not what grace and deference when he is speaking to a woman, and it does not take him more than a quarter of an hour to be treated as an old acquaintance. I began to tease the Captain a little on this subject, when he extolled the strong sense of the lady he had just left. French people have a wonderful facility for passing in conversation from the lightest trifles to matters of the gravest import, and for talking about the serious things quite seriously after laughing over the trifles a minute before. I should not have been in the least surprised if the Captain and his new friend had held a dialogue on the immortality of the soul; however, when I discovered them they were only comparing the Apostles with modern priests, to the disadvantage of the latter.

The position of Scey is one of the most beautiful in France. Here the Saône, as at Chemilly, makes a great curve, during which it is not navigable. Close to Scey are some well-wooded islands, not too large, and there is a slanting weir above the islands, down which the water rushes tumultuously. Above this weir and close to the water's edge is a picturesque house with a turret, and a quantity of rich foreground material, such as a garden wall with quaint stone ornaments, and, nearer still, a sort of Constablesque confusion of reeds, willows, palings, and boats.

pupil. No painter except Knaus could have done justice to the perfect subject that one of these lessons presented. They were given in the interior of the Captain's tent, in itself not a common-place interior. The master gave his instructions with a becoming dignity and gravity, whilst Franki, most anxious to learn, was kneeling and watching him with rapt attention. The consequence was that the lad became an excellent shoe-black, and all my "regiment" shone wonderfully. I was much amused one day when standing on a quay in a town to feel something about my feet, and, on looking down, to discover the lad Franki, who had perceived that my boots were a little dusty, and unbidden had fetched his apparatus from the *Boussemroum.*

Beyond this house are two or three fine distances, rich in various kinds of dark and light trees, and then a remote distance with a lofty mount. All this is as you look up the river. In the other direction is a fine well-wooded park with a stately gate in the main street of the little town itself. This park stretches away to the hills, and on the first rise of ground at their feet one may discern the stabling of a country seat, which belongs to the Duke of Beauffremont. We did not observe anything noteworthy in the little town itself, except a fantastic building with a turret, all evidently modern, but decorated with fragments of old carved stone and strange water-worn natural stones put together indiscriminately. At some distance the thing looks as if it would be interesting, but on a nearer approach one discovers the cheat with vexation.

LETTER XX.

On a Canal near Ovanches,
June 17th.

On leaving Scey we were soon on the river again, but only for a very short time. Brief as it was, in all our voyage we had not a more exquisite hour. The time was late afternoon, with golden sunshine, the scenery a reach or two of calm river, reflecting shores all beautiful with rock and tree and the freshest verdure. It is one of the advantages of this rainy summer that the shores of the Saône are as green as if it flowed through the west of Ireland.

An impressive contrast awaited us when we had to turn aside from this golden sunshine, these cheerful pictures of cattle grazing in happy pastures under beautiful groups of trees, or merry peasants passing in the ferry-boat—an impressive contrast awaited us when we came to the gloomy portals of a tunnel. We came upon it suddenly as we turned aside from the pleasant river and saw close before us the grim

Tunnel below Scey.

entrance, with its severe monumental architecture, its sad-looking firs and pines standing on each side, silent on the green sward, all dark in the shadow of the hill. There was nothing to help us through the dark vault but the very slowest of all imaginable streams, produced artificially by a partial opening of the water-gates beyond. By an almost imperceptible motion this stream took us into the darkness, and then, for our encouragement, it tranquilly sent us back again. After what seemed an interminable delay, the stream slowly drew us a second time under the vault, and then, as if to make us forget our lugubrious surroundings, the Patron cheerfully announced dinner. The saloon was lighted, the blind drawn, and we tried to make-believe that we were dining exactly as usual. It is impossible, however, to forget one's surroundings, and for my part I find tunnels depressing to the imagination. It was clear to me that the bargemen felt the same oppressive influence. One of them, on the boat that led the train, began to fight against it by singing in a powerful and very musical voice. His song was a monotonous ballad that seemed to have no end, but it certainly helped to pass over our forty minutes of funereal gloom. This ballad being at last concluded, the singer gave us the magnificent *Chant du Départ*, with admirable power and feeling. Most men would hesitate about following so fine a voice, but the Patron was restrained by no such feeling of prudence. The last note of the *Chant du Départ* had hardly died away when the Patron jumped upon the little platform before his cabin and announced in a loud voice that he was about to favour us with a ballad entitled *Corsican Vengeance*. It was a sanguinary history, sung to an air of the most lugubrious character, and with a voice that for tone and tune resembled the raven much more nearly than the nightingale. This completed our wretchedness, and we felt it as a deliverance when Franki, in joyful accents, announced that we should very soon be out. Daylight became visible once more, and our one musical dinner was over. Music is a luxury, no doubt, but one glimmer of daylight, as you emerge from the bowels of the earth, is more cheering than all the powers of song.

We afterwards passed the boat that had led the train in the

tunnel and I paid the singer a merited compliment, on which he modestly replied that he could sing better than a horse, but that the horse could tow a boat better than he could. From the extreme promptness with which this answer was given I have reason to believe that it is kept in readiness for such occasions. I commend this plan to authors who receive sudden compliments about their books, than which nothing is more embarrassing. "Your last work was *so* delightful, you write so *very* charmingly." *Answer kept ready :* "I write better than a solan goose, but he employs his quills for loftier flights than mine."

After this tunnel the canal sweeps round a long majestic curve between fine stone quays, and above these is a steep slope on each side of well-kept grass, planted with fir-trees. Emerging from this cutting, which is more like English "grounds" than anything else, the canal goes in a straight line to the lock, and the country is open on both sides. This canal is a short cut across a large peninsula, where the Saône makes a curve of six miles. In this peninsula are two or three villages and one of them is Ovanches.

During our ascending voyage we had walked to Ovanches in the evening and had been enchanted. The mellow light after sunset, the mysterious twilight slowly increasing, gave an indescribable charm to our exploration. Everything in the place seemed part of one beautifully coherent rural poem. It was a Sunday evening, and the people were seated in groups about their doors. We noticed especially one group of women, composed like a picture, their sun-browned handsome faces enlivened by their talk. I asked them some trivial question, and they received me with such easy politeness that we thought the place must be a little centre of civilisation. And all the buildings around us were so picturesque! The houses were delightfully various, a few of them had turrets and balconies, or *loggie*, and projecting roofs. The oppositions of advancing and retiring masses, of light and dark spaces, of warm and cooler colour, were all that an artist could desire. Besides this picturesque material, there were two edifices of greater severity, the public

Ovanches—the Cross.

washing-place and the church. The washing-place had evidently been designed by an educated architect; it was a little classical edifice, carefully and regularly composed, with its columns mirrored in its own oblong basin, dark masses alternating with the golden glow of the reflected evening sky. The church, a grey and simple edifice, stood near, occupying with perfect dignity the finest site in the village. Everything was as it ought to be in such a place, and there was not a discordant note.

We decided that, on the return voyage, we would both work at least for a whole day at Ovanches, so after a night's rest on the canal Mr. Pennell rose betimes in the morning and went there to his work. I was too much occupied with writing to quit my study on the *Boussemroum*.

About eight o'clock Mr. Pennell re-appeared with an expression of the blankest disappointment on his face. "What *has*

A House at Ovanches.

happened?" I inquired. "Ovanches is nothing," he answers; "there is positively nothing at Ovanches!"

I had done well not to return to it, and so to preserve for life the Ovanches of enchantment in my memory. Still, although the effect was gone, the tangible material must have remained, the quaint houses with their *loggie*, their external stairs, their little turrets, their clambering vines. The classical washing-place and the church must be there yet, and the village must still be as beautifully situated as ever on the gently curving land that descends from the hill to the river.

The reasons for Mr. Pennell's disappointment were, first, the difference between an excessively poetical effect and a most prosaic one; and, secondly, the invaluable freshness of eye that he brought from London to Ovanches, as he had not seen a village of that quality before. Subsequent hard work at Corre, Ormoy, and Cendrecourt, had habituated him to the peculiar quality of these villages.

I have mentioned this incident at length as it is striking evidence of the importance of freshness in impressions and of the power of effect upon the mind. The immediate consequence of it, for me, was that I declined to return to Rupt this morning, having walked there last evening in the twilight. You shall have my first and only impression of Rupt in my next letter. Meanwhile I may observe that the natives do not pronounce the name like the second syllable of *bankrupt*, but like the French word *rue*, yet more curtly. Vibrate the *r* well, pronounce the *u* clearly, but cut it off short and sharp, even as a woodman chops off a twig. On no account may you introduce a dying English cadence after your *u* for the sake of a softer effect.

LETTER XXI.

OPPOSITE RAY,
June 18th.

As usual, we are moored in a canal. The length of this one is about a mile and three-quarters, and it differs from the others in being bordered with a much greater variety of trees. It has Scotch firs, besides other kinds of fir, ash, poplar, &c. The

Rupt, the Church.

banks are rather high, in two terraces one for the towing-path the other for the trees.

This gave an excellent opportunity for observing the difference of effect between monotony and variety in trees. At Scey the magnificent canal avenue was all of one species—poplar—at Ray it is of many kinds. The answer, as to effect, is easy. The monotonous avenue far excels the other in power and solemnity of effect, but the varied one is pleasanter to stay in. The trees in a private park ought to be as varied as possible near the house, and monotonous in one or two more remote places, to be visited in more serious moods.

In my last letter I promised some account of Rupt. This is a village of 440 inhabitants on the right bank of the Saône (but not close to the water), at a place where the river becomes navigable again after its course about the peninsula of Ovanches. There is a castle on a precipitous height, of which the principal remnant is a great, tall, round tower, of admirable masonry in a fine state of preservation.[1] Close to this, nestling, as it were, under the shadow of it, is the modern dwelling, a commodious but ordinary house. The top of the hill is entirely occupied by a considerable park and other domains, surrounded by a wall, and the owner has farms in the plain. The owner is a widow lady with four sons and four daughters, so the estate is destined to a minute division.

During our evening walk in this village, we had been much struck by the strange effect of seeing the place for the first time in twilight, not a golden twilight as when we visited the enchanted Ovanches, but a grey twilight that was only a mitigated darkness. This caused us to see all things in masses,

[1] There is a tradition in the village that the tower once had a roof as tall as itself.

and the chief open place of the village seemed really grand, with its church high on the hill on one side, and the castle

Rupt—the Round Tower.

tower lording it on the other. There were a few *tourelles*, especially those of a whitened old house with an enormous well-trained hedge in front of it, a grave-looking, orderly, old-fashioned place, exactly suited for aristocratic old maids. To our great surprise we discovered two fountains, one with a bronze figure of Abundance, the other with a good bronze lion, and we immediately concluded that they must be gifts from the great lady at the castle, but next day the Captain ascertained that the village municipality had ordered and paid for the bronzes. Few villages are so artistic in their tastes!

In a minor degree, Rupt in daylight disappointed Mr. Pennell as Ovanches had done, especially with regard to one view, that of the great Place. Here, in the evening, the houses were half seen, and only the fine general arrangement was appreciated, with the Place rapidly narrowing to a steep street leading up to the church, reminding one of Gustave Doré's mediæval street scenes. When, however, Mr. Pennell revisited Rupt in the morning, he found that view less impressive, as it had lost its mystery, but it was all the better adapted for pen-drawing.

The weather seems dreadfully cold at present. I say it *seems* cold because the thermometer hardly gets below fifty in my cabin, but we began our voyage in overpowering heat, and the transition is hard to bear. I am wearing a winter overcoat and other warm clothing that I brought in case of a change of temperature. The Captain wears his *tricot*, which is a knitted over-shirt fitting like a coat of mail, and the Pilot has one too. It is always a good rule in boat-travelling to have warm things, whatever the season of the year. They are easily laid aside in the heat, and even in the French climate there is not a day in the year when you are sure that it will not be cold. Mr. Pennell compares our present weather to that of an English May, he might almost have said an English March without the winds. It rains almost as in the Highlands of Scotland. Everything on the *Boussemroum* is damp, the tents have no time to dry. As we have no fireplaces in our habitations we are fain to warm ourselves at the galley fire, and I have begun to administer hot grog in the evenings, which is much appreciated.

From Rupt we came on to Ray, passing Soing, which is comparatively without interest. There is a canal here cutting off a loop of the river, and after this canal the Saône is beautiful again, with green shores, rich woods, and pretty villages. Charentenay, to the left, is the ideal of a modern village, not romantic or picturesque, but clean-looking, with its little church and pleasant houses in the midst of trees and greenery.

Here we entered the long, straight canal opposite Ray evidently a loss to our voyage in this sense, that we missed one of the most beautiful of the great curves on the Saône, though the canal itself is remarkable. I had thought of bringing my canoe with me simply for amusement, and now regret not to have done so for a more serious reason. It would have been easy, with a canoe, to explore these great curves of the Saône.

Ray is the most romantic of all the villages passed in the course of our voyage. An old castle of considerable extent, and still inhabited by the Duke of Marmier, crowns a steep height with its towers, and below is the old church and the village in which there is hardly a house that is not picturesque, whilst the whole composes admirably with the beautiful river, and the hilly distance. The Saône here is rapid and flows in irregular channels past several islands. We had to cross it from the canal which is on a much higher level. The lock-keeper has a son only nine years old, certainly the most active boy of that age I ever saw out of a circus. He ferries you over between the islands in a heavy boat across a strong current. Bare-headed, bare-legged, with

The Saône, near Ray.

nothing on him but a light blue blouse and trousers, he came to the *Boussemroum* and offered his services in the kitchen, lying full-length on a plank, and peering over into the galley. Finding that Franki could shell the peas without assistance, the lad turned head over heels as a convenient way of removing himself, and then began gyrating like a wheel on the canal bank. The next thing he did was to hop along the very edge of the lock, one of the deepest locks I ever beheld, which looks a frightful gulf when it is empty, and then he crossed the narrow plank on the lock gate. I took a great interest in this boy on account of his extraordinary liveliness, and inquired if he had learnt to swim. No, he had never been taught. This made me speak seriously to his father.

Lock on the Ray Canal.

"Here you have a boy," I said, "who is hopping about and turning somersaults on the side of a canal with a deep lock, and you neglect to teach him to swim. Can you swim yourself?" "Yes, sir, I swim very well," the father answered unwilling to sacrifice his own aquatic reputation. Before I left, he promised positively that he would teach the lad this summer.[1]

There is an extensive pasture of short lawn-like grass that occupies the plain before the village, and would be a fine cricket-ground if the French appreciated that game. It would also be a delightful exercise ground for galloping horses. There are several of these fine plains on the banks of the Saône, some of them wonderfully extensive, as we shall see,

Ray.

in the course of the voyage. At Ray, the plain has a picturesque value by its contrast with the castled steep.

Ray is a little place that still entirely preserves the aristocratic *cachet*. The château and the church are everything at Ray. In the church are found the dignified seats of the reigning family (I mean in this little dukedom), with elaborately carved coats-

[1] On the Lower Saône all the boys swim at an early age, and some of the girls learn too. There is an annual death-rate from drowning, but more from imprudence than inability, and there would be fewer rescues if the knowledge of swimming were less general.

of-arms, and there is more mediæval sculpture, including a wonderful scene of the Entombment, with a crowd of figures three feet high, all standing on the church floor. What is chiefly interesting in these old country churches is the almost invariably picturesque character of the chancel. It is seldom *correct*, seldom in architectural harmony with the rest, but quite as rarely dull or bare. At Ray the woodwork of the chancel is all of renaissance carving, not without delicacy and taste. Then you have the romanesque and early ogival arches, whilst externally the incongruity of the chancel is repeated by a tower of the last century, not at all offensive in the distance.

The Captain, who as you know is the provider of the expedition, tells me that he can hardly procure anything at Ray. Whatever there is goes to the château. The commissariat would be a serious difficulty in these parts if we did not change quickly from place to place. The *Boussemroum*, uniting the produce of many villages, is better supplied than any village separately. The Captain purchases what he can, and what is unprocurable at one place is absurdly cheap at another. All along the Upper Saône we could not purchase a strawberry; at Scey we got excellent strawberries at the rate of nine great platefuls for three-pence. Here, at Ray, we are promised some beef for to-morrow, but the condemned ox is even now wandering in his native fields, unconscious of his doom.

I notice, in this village, that the tradesmen have pictorial signs explaining their occupation to the illiterate. Over the baker's shop is a painted representation of loaves of bread, the joiner's workshop is indicated by portraits of his tools, the smith's by painted horse-shoes. A single pictorial genius may have originated these and other signs of the same kind, scattered throughout the village. The graphic arts, as we see, may sometimes excel literature in practical utility. I observe that there is no more proportion between the painted objects, as to scale, than there is in heraldry; in fact, these paintings are a sort of heraldry.

The impression produced by Ray is that of a social position now belonging to the closed pages of French history. The great house rules over everything from its lordly height, the church is the refuge of the arts, and the people humbly lead a narrow

The River Bank near Ray.

life under the shadow of church and castle. It is happily and curiously in harmony with this entirely unspoilt relic of the past that the engineering works for the Saône navigation have been executed at a respectful distance, and have left it safe with the river flowing past it in the old neglected way. Some modern river improvement, some quay made only too perfectly, would have been the destruction of Ray. The canal is well hidden by its own trees.

LETTER XXII.

BETWEEN BEAUJEUX AND RIGNY,
June 19th.

We quitted Ray yesterday afternoon. We are now in a nameless place nearly equi-distant from Beaujeux and Rigny, and the reason for our being here is simply because we have no choice. Do you know what being *collé* (glued) means in French nautical language? It means what the unlucky *Boussemroum* is at the present moment.

To be *collé* when you are in a boat is to be pushed sideways by wind or water so as to be fixed by pressure against some obstacle and kept there in such a way that all the forces at your disposal are insufficient to release you. A canoeist is *collé* when the stream carries him sideways against boulders in a current, and he cannot obtain deliverance on account of its steady, unrelenting pressure. With an ark the size of the *Boussemroum*, more than eighty feet long, it is rather a serious matter to be glued. We are so most completely just at present. The Pilot, though he got us off at another place, has just come to me and announced that we are hopelessly fixed till there is a change of wind. Add to this that the weather is that of a wild March day and you may imagine the pleasures of our situation.

There are, however, certain compensations. We have provisions on board that may last till the wind changes, and both Mr. Pennell and I can occupy ourselves with our work. As for the Captain and Franki, they have taken to their fishing, so we have nothing to do but consider the *Boussemroum* a house on land for the present, and renounce all ideas of locomotion.

Such a state of things is highly favourable to writing. I know that the boat cannot stir, so at least it will not bump against the stones, that is one satisfaction; moreover, the Pilot will not be coming for sailing orders. The *menu* of our dinner is settled, we are to eat what we have on board, and may be thankful that the larder is not altogether empty.

The Captain takes these incidents most philosophically. Even a complete stoppage in the worst of weather is unable to disturb his serenity. Mr. Pennell is not quite so patient; he is young and energetic, and an American, and has not yet accepted the consolatory doctrine of middle age that the enforced halts of life are Nature's own havens of tranquillity. Franki is patient for another reason. To have no work to do, and free permission to fish for gudgeons, is perfect bliss for him.

We are fixed in a very odd position. The *Boussemroum* lies just across the mouth of a currentless rivulet, and is fixed by stem and stern to the banks on each side of a little bridge. The wind is strong enough to keep her moored as effectually as a pair of cables.

It may possibly have occurred to you to wonder where Franki sleeps. By the merest chance I had brought with me a small boat tent that was used last summer on my sailing boat, so this has been set up under the quarter-deck in the space called "la Cour Pennell," and Franki sleeps in it on plenty of dry straw. In wet weather his tent is doubled by an external covering of canvas, the lining of the saloon which has not been required. Franki is perfectly comfortable, and very glad to have a little place to himself instead of sleeping aft in the cabin with the men. In the wildest weather there are no draughts in his tent.

Whenever there is a new-comer in a small community he is

K

likely to cause a division for and against himself. In the poop cabin there is a party for Franki and a party against him. The Pilot is Franki's strong friend and supporter, the Patron is evidently inimical. It is one of the Patron's peculiarities never to be able to remember where he has put things. Before Franki's arrival there was nothing for him to do on these occasions but grumble; now the lad is always accused of having lost the article, which is generally found soon afterwards in a situation clearly revealing the Patron's own negligence and forgetfulness. As it is simply impossible to stop the Patron's tongue, and I cannot do without him till we get to Chalon, I have told Franki to pay no attention to these attacks, and as Franki has healthy nerves and a merry disposition he only laughs at them. Nothing is more amusing than to witness the glee on Franki's face when the Patron has accused him of losing something and it is triumphantly found, to the old man's complete discomfiture.

After leaving the canal at Ray boats only enter the Saône to leave it again at once by another canal of considerable length, that takes them to Recologne, a small grey village of striking beauty with some thatched roofs still remaining. The alternation of river and canal, canal and river, has the charm of change and variety, but, grand as the canals are, it is to me always a relief to get into the natural river again, especially when there is an old village on its banks of the quality of Recologne. The misery of this voyage consists in leaving such places without staying a week at each to sketch in water-colour.

The next time we left the river it was to enter the canal near Savoyeux, one of the most magnificent in the voyage, with avenues like those already sufficiently described at Scey. There is a keeper on this canal, who lives in a house provided for him and is called a "guard." There is no lock near him, but he is not far from the entrance to the second tunnel. An incident occurred in connection with this official. He asked me into his house, and told me that he had received a telegram. "This," I thought, "must be some bad news from home." To my relief the telegram turned out to be only an official one, ordering the guard to make inquiries as to our nationality. I answered these in writing, and then we proceeded on our voyage, but the nature of the questions shows that the authorities have their eye upon us, and it is not impossible that we may be arrested at Gray. The guard's manner to me was perfectly civil, and his questions were in themselves quite reasonable, yet I thought he was rather grave, like a man who perceives a situation to be more serious than it appears. On reflection I connected this incident with the visit of the tipsy man at Port-sur-Saône, who reproached Franki because he "worked for foreigners who made plans." Perhaps, too, the appearance of the gendarmes at Corre, when I was sketching the Saône, may not have been purely accidental.

This time we walked over the tunnel, which gained me time to sketch the canal on the other side, pending the arrival of the *Boussemroum*. Here it passes through a dense wood, the trees nearest the canal forming an avenue of the stateliest character, less formal than that to the north of the tunnel. This is one of the grandest things we have seen on the voyage. When, after long delay, the *Boussemroum* did at last emerge from the darkness, I stopped her that we might sleep on the canal. The great dense wood was filled with singing-birds, or at least with the sound of their voices.

The canal opens upon a fine country, a little south of the village of Mercey, which was the object of our evening walk.

This village consists of a single, long, straight street, of great width, with farm-houses and their farm-buildings on each side, an odd contrast to the streets in great cities. At the end stands the church, dominating over the whole, and the Captain made a remark which is worth repeating. He said that the French habit of congregating rural habitations in villages tends greatly to maintain the power of the clergy, because the priest is far more influential in the village, where the population is under his eye, than he would be over the same population if it were scattered on isolated farms. We noticed here the remarkable civility of the people, who all said, "Bon soir, Messieurs," in a hearty fashion as they lifted their hats and looked us straight in the face. There was a frankness in their manner that pleased us greatly, and I noticed that the Captain put more than his usual heartiness into his replies.

On our walk back from Mercey to the canal we saw the finest and most pictorial effect that has hitherto occurred in the voyage. The trees in the great wood are extremely dense, in grand opaque masses, but those on each side the canal, seen obliquely from the opposite side of the Saône, appear to become gradually more open, till the most advanced of them stand out separately. There is, consequently, a gradual passage from the dense and close to the open, which is always pleasing and has long been known to artists. In the effect of the 18th of June this was imitated in the sky, but in reverse, the clouds being dark and dense opposite the dense trees and more open as they approached the forest, till behind the open trees the sky was lightly clouded and coloured like mother-of-pearl. There was consequently every appearance of an *intentional* and most felicitous arrangement of dark opposing masses and a gradual opening of both at

On the Canal near Savoyeux.

a luminous centre, but more than this, the whole was reflected in the river, which made the wonderful unity of the scene far more strikingly manifest. It was one of those very rare occasions, far rarer than is generally believed, when Nature herself turns artist and makes a picture. I have only to add that the more open trees were of indescribable beauty and elegance, and that the colouring of the whole subject was as rich as the finest Titian or Giorgione.

The region below Mercey has a peculiar beauty which made us greatly desire to linger there, and sadly regret the necessity for moving southwards. Here the Saône winds in great curves between hilly shores, and the land is diversified by woods, each of considerable extent and separated from its neighbours by fine open spaces of brightly coloured fields. It was a cheerful landscape, and its cheerfulness was heightened by sunshine, delightful after fog and cold.

At the ferry between Quitteur and Otay, where the towing-path changes from one bank of the river to the other, and Zoulou had to be taken across, we found a stout old ferryman, of rubicund aspect, who was evidently a character. My acquaintance with him lasted about ten minutes in all, and I did not get nearer to him than shouting distance, yet he contrived to tell me that he had great experience as a pilot both on the Saône and the Rhône, and to offer me his services in case I had *quelquechose de volumineux*. In boating all our estimates depend upon previous experience. For that old pilot the *Boussemroum* was merely *ce petit berrichon là*, for me it was "voluminous" enough.

There is a village called Beaujeux about a mile away from the left bank of the Saône. This attracted me by an old tower and a church that promised to be beautiful, so we walked over to it.

Here was another proof of the utility of the ordnance map. It had been suggested that we should go to this village from a higher point, a very roundabout way, but the short cut across the fields was marked on the map and we found it, a mere track about a foot wide. The village was a disappointment to Mr. Pennell, because prosperity and repairs had nearly killed the picturesque. The church, too, had been thoroughly and expensively restored, and though the restoration was very clever and learned, it inevitably made the building look new. This church is an excellent specimen of romanesque architecture with transition towards gothic. In the interior the general sobriety of the style is relieved by the rich and various sculpture of the capitals, and by the abundance of stained glass. The ceilings are of oak, that of the nave being slightly stencilled, and those of the aisles undecorated. The stairs leading to the organ loft are peculiar, every step being on a corbel projecting from the wall like the machicoulis in military architecture. The effect is that of unnecessary heaviness. The stone spire of this church is one of the best I know. It is simple, and rather sturdy than elegant, yet very finely proportioned.

As we ascended the hill to the tower we met with an old woman who told us that this tower was the last and smallest of seven that had belonged to the old castle of Beaujeux. It is now enclosed in the garden and vineyard of a modern house. This garden pleased us by the irregularity of the ground and by the great variety of the trees—fine walnuts, Scotch firs, epiceas, ash, and other species. The views in every direction were most extensive, including a distant view of Gray that rose pale from the plain. The principal church of Gray being on an eminence is visible from a great distance and crowns the place superbly.

There is a ferry at Prantigny below Beaujeux where the wire-rope is stretched across the river, which alarmed us during the ascending voyage. This rope gave us a second alarm in descending, as the ferryman was extremely deliberate about raising it, which he did by suspending himself on a long lever inserted repeatedly in a winch. Meanwhile the *Boussemroum*

Ferry at Prantigny.

was carried forwards rather rapidly by the current and at one minute an accident was not improbable. I have a peculiar objection to seeing the safety of all my things dependent on the quickness of a man unknown to me.

It was below Prantigny that the side-wind fixed us to the

shore, where we are now inhabiting a real *immeuble*, like a house, for the *Boussemroum* can no more be stirred than a dwelling of bricks and mortar. After our gipsy life a fixed residence ought to be accepted as evidence of an advance towards a higher state of civilization.

LETTER XXIII.

GRAY, *June 22nd.*

My last letter left us fastened to the shore by a side-wind and in a state of philosophical resignation. We spent the evening in the saloon as usual, amidst a storm of wind and rain that cheered the Captain and me with a pleasant sense of being comfortably sheltered. But not even the storm could cheer our younger companion, Mr. Pennell. He was at the same time too polite to desert us and too much discouraged to be anything but sad and silent. The unprogressiveness of the *Boussemroum* is a trouble to him, and I wish we had a steam-engine in her for his sake, though certainly not for mine. Of the two evils I prefer stoppages to steam-engines.

To console Mr. Pennell I promised to make every effort to be progressive in the morning, and kept my word in the rain against a head-wind. The *Boussemroum* can be towed with the wind in her teeth, though at a slow speed. Franki flung a sack over his shoulders, and went bravely on with Zoulou, similarly caparisoned.

Early in this dismal morning, before we started, we met with the first instance of incivility from bargemen in the course of the voyage. We had been stopped on the side of the towing-path, and were therefore rather in the way of a great *péniche* that descended the stream. The driver of the horses treated us exactly as if we did not exist, and when our Pilot begged for a moment's delay to get the rope over our saloon and masts we heard contemptuous expressions from the passing barge about the nature of our " machine." We learned afterwards that the same bargeman who had been uncivil to us broke a ferry-rope at a place lower down. No doubt he went straight on as when he passed us, taking a bitter pleasure in not accommodating himself to the convenience of others.

We had *déjeuner* inside the deep lock at Rigny, where the lock-keeper left us in peace. This arrangement was due to the Pilot. He said we should be much quieter in the lock than on the river, and the keeper consented, first letting us gently subside to the lowest level, so that we could see nothing out of the window but the huge, grim walls and gates. It was quiet enough certainly, but the reverse of cheerful. However, I thanked the men for their good intentions and pretended to be quite pleased, though I never breakfasted in such a dismal place before. The solemn tolling of a church bell at a little distance made us feel as if we had been lowered into the grave.

Between the lock and Gray the Patron had one of his noisy fits of ill-humour, because the Pilot had given him an order; so to put an end to these quarrels I told the Pilot that I placed myself under his orders as common sailor, and that he would find me both silent and obedient. This removed a difficulty, as the Patron could not row, and it might now become frequently necessary to put the Pilot ashore in the boat whilst the *Boussemroum* was in motion. He soon asked me to do this, and I obeyed with silent alacrity, but not without some effort, as our boat is the most unwieldy thing I ever attempted to row, and I had to overtake the *Boussemroum* with it afterwards, which Zoulou was towing vigorously. However, I got alongside, and clambered up into the berrichon. The Pilot was pleased with this, as it makes him more independent of the Patron and his temper.

I have not said much about the wonderful quarrels that are constantly arising between these men, but as they always spring up in the same way, a very short description may suffice. The Pilot commands on the river, giving authoritative orders, on which the Patron invariably flies into a furious passion, and becomes voluble beyond all the powers of stenography to follow him. I could not remember or invent the tenth part of what he says on these occasions, but I can recollect every word of the Pilot's answer. With a gesture of supremely scornful dignity, he cries, " Attend to your soup, *cuisinier*, attend to your soup ! That's all you are fit for. You are of no other use on a boat."

The strangest thing in the conduct of these two men towards each other is, that five minutes after their fiercest quarrels they are civil and even amiable, rendering each other little services with a graceful readiness, or asking for them politely. As the Pilot is unable to read, the Patron kindly reads the newspaper to him, or any letter. The Patron is very ready with his needle, and I believe he does the Pilot's mending ; if not, he would be quite willing to do it. In ordinary times the Pilot calls the other " Papa " with an affectionate tone of voice.

In the new generation of French people there will be nobody unable to read. Already there is a wonderful difference between the men of the Pilot's time and their grown-up children. He showed me a letter from his daughter that any young lady might have written. It was in faultless French, and charmingly graceful and tender in its filial affection. The great rough man —rough only on the outside—is proud of his children, and always speaks gently of his wife. He told me a story about her which is worth preserving.

The Pilot had taken his wife and daughter on a pleasure trip down the Saône and Rhône to Arles, on one of the common barges, and as they came back, against the current of the Rhône, they had to be towed by the wonderful grappling tug that has a great wheel working on the bed of the river with prodigious steel teeth.[1] At that time there was a dangerous passage at the Pont St. Esprit, so the Pilot said to his wife and daughter, " Now, whatever happens, you have only one thing to do, which is to keep perfectly silent. Promise me that you will not open your lips." They promised, and the Pilot went about his work elsewhere. However, a minute later, one of the sailors cried out, " Il est mort ! " on which the Pilot's wife set up a piercing shriek, and exclaimed, " Mon mari est mort, il est mort ! " He immediately re-appeared and said, " You promised to keep silence, and you have not been silent more than a minute." The explanation is that the word " dead " is a technical boating term on the Rhône, meaning simply that the momentum of a boat has expended itself.

The approach to Gray from the north is one of the best town views on the Saône. Gray is finely situated on a hill rising suddenly from flat meadows, and the principal church, which

---

[1] This wheel is a marvellously audacious invention. Of course the bed of the Rhône is very irregular, and the wheel has to rise and fall with all the differences of level, and yet be kept in motion. It is the roughest work that steam has ever done for the transport of merchandise.

has a characteristic tower with a domed roof, is the finishing ornament of the whole place. The ascent to this church is so steep that the only direct road to it is by a series of stairs on the hill-side. Quite on the top of the hill is one of the finest promenades in France. The town is, to my taste, a delightful little place, being clean and picturesque, at the same time with a sufficiency of old remnants to give the priceless air of antiquity, whilst the modern dwellings have an inviting aspect of prosperity and order. A French monarch, I forget which, committed a

Gray from the North East.

pun in praise of this town when he said, "Je trouve Gray à mon gré," and the place has long been surnamed Gray la Coquette. It has important historical associations, and at the close of the thirteenth century was the seat of a university. It was the favourite residence of a royal lady, Jeanne de Bourgogne, when separated from her husband and during her widowhood. Gray was much valued for military reasons by the Emperor Charles the Fifth. In connection with the power of Charles the Fifth on the left bank of the Saône it is interesting to note that

Gray from the North.

a reminiscence of it has been preserved down to the present day, from mere tradition, by the bargemen. They call the left side of the river "Empire," and the right side "Royaume." But of all the historical reminiscences connected with Gray there is not one so fine as the courageous answer of the mayor, Mongin, when Louis XIV. had entered the town in consequence of a treacherous capitulation. The mayor had to perform the

Old Shop in Gray.

painful duty of giving up the keys, but he found some consolation in saying boldly to the magnificent king, "Sire, votre conquête serait plus glorieuse si elle vous eût été disputé."

It requires an effort to bear in mind how very recent is the final establishment of French authority in the Franche-Comté. Even so late as the year 1688 the French abandoned Gray again, and demolished its fortifications. Sometimes, to tease Frenchmen a little in a friendly way, I tell them that the Saône is both the natural and the historical frontier of France, but I observe that, like all other peoples, they are warm advocates for natural frontiers when they imply an extension of territory, whilst they obstinately object to them when they imply the slightest diminution.

One consequence of the past Spanish domination is that the

Courtyard at Gray.

villages and small towns in this region have rather a foreign aspect even at the present day. Mr. Pennell noticed this from the first, and said he hardly felt himself in France. He sketched one or two courtyards in Gray which have a very Spanish character. Such villages as Ormoy and Ovanches remind one sometimes of Spain and sometimes of Italy.

I have very kind friends at Gray who had received us hospitably on our ascending voyage, so I conceived the audacious notion of inviting them to a state dinner on board the *Boussemroum!* The Captain's house-keeping abilities and Mr. Pennell's taste were brought into requisition. It was thought at first that we ought to give the dinner simply with the resources of the *Boussemroum*, that is, with our own service and our own cook. To order anything from a restaurant seemed a sad confession of inadequacy. It was decided, finally, that the Patron should do the cooking, except the roast and a *pâté*, and that we should get knives and forks from the *restaurateur*, as our own forks were but of tinned iron. Half the art of giving a festal appearance to a place consists simply in having plenty of light and flowers, so I employed a tinner to make ten sconces for the walls of the saloon, which, as the tin was quite new, had very brilliant reflectors, and the Captain went to a gardener, who gave him a vast quantity of flowers for a very little money. The saloon was put in order, with the table in the middle and my military chest of drawers for a side-board, and the two tents were neatly arranged as *salons de réception*. To spare our guests the inconvenience of walking along the edge of the *Boussemroum* two bridges connected the vessel with the shore. It had been intended at one time to illuminate its exterior with Chinese lanterns, but as this would have attracted public attention the idea was abandoned.

Our guests were but three in number, my friend and his wife, and the director of the Bank of France. When they arrived, the tents were not lighted, but left in twilight and without flowers, so that the transition to the brilliantly lighted saloon should produce its full effect. This effect may, perhaps, have been excelled by the Royal Yacht Club, on state occasions, but assuredly neither the *Boussemroum* nor any other berrichon had ever been the theatre of such a brilliant scene before. Mr. Pennell had adorned every sconce with roses, and placed flowers, with infinite art, in all the most conspicuous positions. The oddity of our surroundings made the lights seem brighter and the dinner better, and the hours passed quickly and merrily. In addition to his serious labours in decoration, Mr. Pennell, at my request, had kindly toiled during the afternoon in the production of *menus*, each with an original design on the back of the card. Mine represented Franki with Zoulou kicking viciously, the others were recollections of the Saône. Of the three bottles of good Burgundy which were put on board at starting, two were consumed on this great occasion. The Patron received high compliments for his cookery which were but in part deserved, as the roast was erroneously attributed to him.[1]

The church at Gray is one of those which charm the traveller at a distance, but rather disappoint him on a nearer approach. There is a poor new porch before you get to the old Gothic doors. The interior is more picturesque than beautiful. The renaissance ornamentation in various marbles round the walls near the altar is on the same principle as at Autun but less

[1] During our talk the director of the Bank of France told me about a recent alarm at the bank, which was in some degree connected with ourselves. During our absence on the Upper Saône he was seated one afternoon in his private room absorbed in his accounts, when, at five o'clock precisely, he heard a horrible noise, and could not, on the instant, make out the nature of it. He had, however, time to think "This is an infernal machine that has been placed in the bank by some scoundrels, and it is now in action. In a few seconds the explosion will take place." The noise appeared to proceed from a small brown paper parcel, which he opened to discover an alarum clock. I regret to say that the alarum belonged to me, and that it was I who had set it to the hour of five. On ascending the Saône I had left this dreadful thing at Gray, for some trifling repair, and it had been sent to the bank to await my return.

elegant. The lancet lights above are also a heavier repetition of those at Autun. The architecture of the church generally is an inferior Gothic, more likely to please a painter than an architect.

A Little Bridge at Gray.

It may be observed that there is but little architecture on the Saône above Chalon. At and below Chalon there are a few interesting buildings.

LETTER XXIV.

Below Apremont,
June 23rd, Morning.

The voyage from Gray to Mantoche was one of the most agreeable in our experience. The day was calm and cloudy at the beginning, but the sunshine afterwards struggled through. In the absence of "l'orage" Zoulou was well able to tow the boat. We sat on the deck enjoying the beautiful scenery, a succession of quiet pictures. There were many interesting things on the shores (or what artists consider such,) as for example, a little picturesque riverside restaurant with arbours for the people of Gray to come to as those of Vesoul go to Chemilly. Here and there were a few houses, but Mr. Pennell remarked that the country was very thinly inhabited in comparison with America. The difference is due chiefly to the French habit of concentrating the rural population in villages, so that when you do not see a village the country has all the appearance of a solitude. The scenery increased in richness and beauty as we approached Mantoche. There was a large, dense wood on the left shore, and also a remarkably rich reedy foreground with an aquatic vegetation of such luxuriance that Zoulou was absolutely hidden by it, and the only sign of his existence was the tow-rope which advanced in a great curve, bending the reeds before it. As usual in these woods, there were many singing-birds, this time including the cuckoo.

We passed a man in the middle of the river who was scooping sand into a boat at anchor. Evidently his solitude was a burden to him, for he at once entered into conversation with our Pilot and their talk lasted till they could hear each other no longer. It was a curiously friendly bit of talk about the hardships of life and the wisdom of enduring them with patience. The Pilot called this man "Papa," affectionately, though he had never seen him before.

Although we were by this time quite accustomed to the extreme civility of the bargemen we were still surprised by it a little above Mantoche. We caused some delay to an ascending boat which had to detach its tow-rope and pass it under the *Boussemroum*. Whilst this was being done, the men on the

Near Gray.

barge talked with us in the friendliest manner. A day or two before, our own tow-rope had been passed under a great German boat, and there had been a hitch and a long trouble to set it right, but not a word of impatience on either side. These little delays usually end with a hearty expression of thanks and a "Bon jour" or "Bon voyage."

Mantoche is one of the most picturesque places on the river. It has two châteaux, one low on the shore, another on a hillside, and the Saône exactly resembles a pond, entirely surrounded by dense woods. All the buildings seen from the river are picturesque, with several little towers having the bell-shaped roof common in the Franche-Comté, and the colour of the whole place is rich in ochres, reds and yellows. We landed to explore the interior of the village, and the first thing we came upon was a fine bartizan *tourelle* of grey stone, in excellent preservation. This was at the corner of the château, and supported on a corbel with good mouldings. The church is not beautiful, it is too low, but its architecture is harmonious, being

Mantoche.

a pure and simple old romanesque. There is a large low arch before the choir, placed on one side. The sanctuary was impressively gloomy and mysterious, as seen from a little distance, with its dark rich ornamentation against which the great silver candlesticks stood out in picturesque relief. I noticed a gilded *console* (half-table) of eighteenth-century carving, set against the wall to the right, probably a gift from the château. These incongruous things are often met with in village churches in France, but the unpretending and picturesque aspect of the whole interior makes us indulgent, so that they hardly strike us as being out of place. Walking southwards we found a renaissance house so quiet in character that it might easily be over-looked, yet it must have been, when newly built, a rarely perfect example of delicate, quiet taste in architecture. Not an ornament is overdone, yet not an inch of the whole front has been carelessly or neglectfully treated. I regret to say that the large windows with their delicately-moulded framework of stone, are now blocked up with bricks, and the most vulgar modern windows are inserted wherever required, with the most absolute disregard for the original scheme of the architect.

Nothing is more depressing to a lover of art than this perfectly brutal and blind disregard for the better taste of a less barbarous age than ours. Advance of refinement, indeed! Here is refinement ravaged by vulgarity! This is exactly one of those really refined pieces of architecture that the vulgar of all classes, educated or not, pass by as unworthy of attention because there is nothing loud or obtrusive in the design.

I made a drawing of the bartizan before mentioned and whilst at work on this was accosted by an infirm man, who evidently took an intelligent interest in art. He invited me to his house, and showed me some studies in water-colour by no means destitute of native colour-faculty, but inadequate in drawing. There was an old volume on his table, bound in calf with faded gilding, and red-edged. He had been reading this, and he told me that for many years his chief resource against *ennui* had been the enjoyment of literature and the practice of art. At the age of twenty-five he was a notary, when a stroke of apoplexy, utterly unexpected, left partial paralysis behind it, and deprived him of all hope of an active life. He therefore sold his *étude*[1] and lived on his private means. I was much impressed by the beautiful patience with which he bore his infirmity and the loss it had occasioned him. He congratulated himself that the right arm was free, and that the paralysis of the left leg had so far diminished that he could move about, though slowly. He thoroughly appreciated the beauty of the village where he lived and the convenience of access by rail to several more important places. Let no one say that artistic and intellectual pursuits are without a serious value as a mitigation of the ills of life! Here was a man of refined tastes who found it endurable under one of the most severe and most hopeless afflictions, when a vulgar nature, in such a maimed existence, would have tormented itself in endless *ennui*. I quitted this new friend with a profound conviction that there are men in health less happy, less contented, less truly fortunate than he is, and our talk left an impression upon me that lasted the whole day. It was neither gladness nor melancholy, but rather a silent satisfaction. I had been in one of the dark places of human life and had found light even there.

Soon after leaving Mantoche we entered another of the canals that scarcely differed from the magnificent one near Scey, except that here the straight avenue may have been longer. Zoulou did wonders in this place; he brought us along so quickly that we actually passed a boat drawn by horses,

---

[1] An *étude* is a notary's office. These offices are limited in number by French law, and are sold to successors as commissions used to be transmitted by sale in the English army.

and the driver dropped his rope for the *Boussemroum* to float over it, an event most worthy of record!

The same driver gave us an account of the peculiarities of his horses. One of them, he said, was so voracious that he did not eat his corn, he *drank* it, which I thought one of the strongest and most original expressions I had ever heard.

A stately *péniche* travelled for some time on our left in this canal, so I had a talk with the people on board about our voyage and theirs. They paid me some compliment on the ingenuity of my arrangements for living on the *Boussemroum,* which I returned by telling the lady of the *péniche* that they were but of a rude and provisional character, whereas it was evident from the pretty lace window-curtains of her cabin that it must be delightfully neat and well-kept inside. She appeared gratified with this piece of flattery, if agreeable truth is flattery.

Contrarily to our usual custom we emerged from the canal before mooring the *Boussemroum* for the night. She was then moored to the left bank, and a sudden exclamation from Mr. Pennell drew my attention to a charmingly perfect distant view of Apremont, a village situated on that curve of the Saône which the canal had made us avoid. The current here is strong and in consequence of the rains the water is heavily charged with mud and vegetable refuse.

During the whole night the weather was boisterous with wind and rain, but that makes little difference to us when the boat is moored. It is in the roughest nights that we best appreciate the convenience of the *Boussemroum.* With a small open boat in this place we should have had to go on foot to Apremont, as the curve of the river is not navigable, and we might have failed to find a lodging there. My first advice to all boat voyagers is to have sleeping accommodation on board. Without it, there is no independence.

This morning the rain continues, with a north wind and an increased current in the Saône. The landscape is French but the effect is Scottish. We have rather a depressing day before us, a voyage through a great forest, under the gloomiest of skies.

The first thing we learned this morning was that a boat in the canal had been seized by the police. The skipper had brought a pilot with him from Corre, but had declined to pay his wages. The pilot calmly waited till they arrived at the next lock and then told the lock-keeper, who immediately refused to let the boat pass and telephoned for the police. This barge belonged to foreigners, who probably were not aware that every lock is a telephone station, and every lock-keeper an agent for the preservation of order. The police work of the river is done very quietly but most effectually.

LETTER XXV.

PONTAILLER,
June 23rd, Evening

The *Boussemroum* had been so manageable from Gray to Apremont that we had almost forgotten her defect and had come to think that she was like any other river boat. If we needed a reminder we got a very effective one this morning. We had a favourable wind, that is to say, for a thing that floats entirely on the surface of the water, one of the most uncomfortable of all winds. It may sound like an exaggeration, but it is the simple truth that a contrary wind is better for the *Boussemroum*. We began by swinging across the river soon after being unmoored, and after that we progressed mostly sideways, with the constant and well-founded apprehension that Zoulou would be dragged into the water and drowned. The Pilot and Patron were both in high excitement and quarrelling almost without a pause. I remember one situation that gave me five minutes of real anxiety. We came to a passage between an island and the right bank of the Saône, when a strong gust of wind made the entire hull of the *Boussemroum* lie across the river like a bridge, but a bridge that was moving with the current. The *Boussemroum* is very long, and it did not appear certain that, in this position, the stern would not catch the island, and the prow the shore exactly at the same time. If this had happened, the boat would have immediately become a weir, and I know by canoe experiences what follows. In such accidents the water rises, the boat heels over and fills, and those on board have no resource but swimming. Fortunately in this case there was room to pass, though very little to spare.

As soon after this incident as the *Boussemroum* could be put straight again for a few minutes, we told the Patron to jump ashore, and made him walk with a rope in his hand that was fastened to the stern of the vessel. By this means she could be kept tolerably on her course. For several miles we passed through an almost uninterrupted forest. This is one of the most extensive forests in France, and we only crossed it in a comparatively narrow part. Its character is at first monotonous and the trees are uninteresting, but as you descend the river the beauty of the forest increases greatly, and you see many fine trees, especially well grown oaks. This led Mr. Pennell to make a remark that opens one of the most important questions in criticism. He said that this forest had not a French character. I asked why not, and then Mr. Pennell went on to say that the trees were too grand and that a French character required very thin, small, elegant trees. I argued against the narrowing of

In the Woodland.

the idea of what is French to a part only of what is contained in France, and said that if in literature and art we gave the English public only one part of French things, and always the same part, the consequence must be that our public would not learn to know the real France with its great variety, but only a monotonous, imaginary France. The argument may be extended to other subjects, and particularly to the characters of men. People form to themselves an ideal for some class, and then, if a novelist represents a person belonging to that class who does not in all things answer to the preconceived ideal, he is blamed for want of truth, whereas he may be truthfully representing the variety that is in nature.

There is considerable variety in this great forest itself. It increased very much in sylvan beauty and interest as we came southwards. At first it was only vast, and had so little definite local character that it would have been difficult to know the scenes again, but afterwards they became recognisable.

The Pilot told me that during the terribly cold winter of 1879—1880 the river here was entirely frozen over, and that great numbers of wild boars migrated from the right bank to the left, probably in search of food. I can hardly imagine a more desolate scene, even in Russia, than the frozen river in this forest with a troop of wild boars upon the ice.

When on the point of emerging from the woodland we came upon the finest of the Saône islands, remarkable not only for its great size, but for the extraordinary beauty of its trees, their noble height, their stately grace, their admirable grouping. The finest of them were trembling poplars.

In the part of the forest which approaches the island the sylvan beauty is much increased by the better massing of clumps of trees, no longer in confusion as where the wood was denser.

An important affluent, the Ognon, falls into the Saône just below the island, and then the river emerges from the woods completely and enters upon a treeless plain. If I had to choose between a dense wood and an open plain as a residence, I should prefer the plain. This may seem strange in a lover of trees, but there is nothing in which excessive quantity is less desirable.

On the present occasion, after being shut up in the woods all day, it was a great relief to see the horizon once again.

Franki and Zoulou had some difficulty between the forest and Pontailler because the Saône was high enough to overflow the lowest banks, producing many little pools. At the first of these Franki stopped, but the Pilot ordered him to go forwards, so he dashed in, and after that made his way through

Pontailler, from the Second Bridge.

the others without hesitation. They were not very deep, which was lucky, as Franki cannot swim.

The boat is moored for the night at Pontailler, and we have just explored the place. Considering that it is an ancient city, and that there was a royal palace there so far back as the time of Charles the Bald, its strikes us chiefly as being extremely modern in appearance. The reason for this is historical. The entire town was destroyed by General Mercey, whose name resembles mercy more than his actions. The place had offered

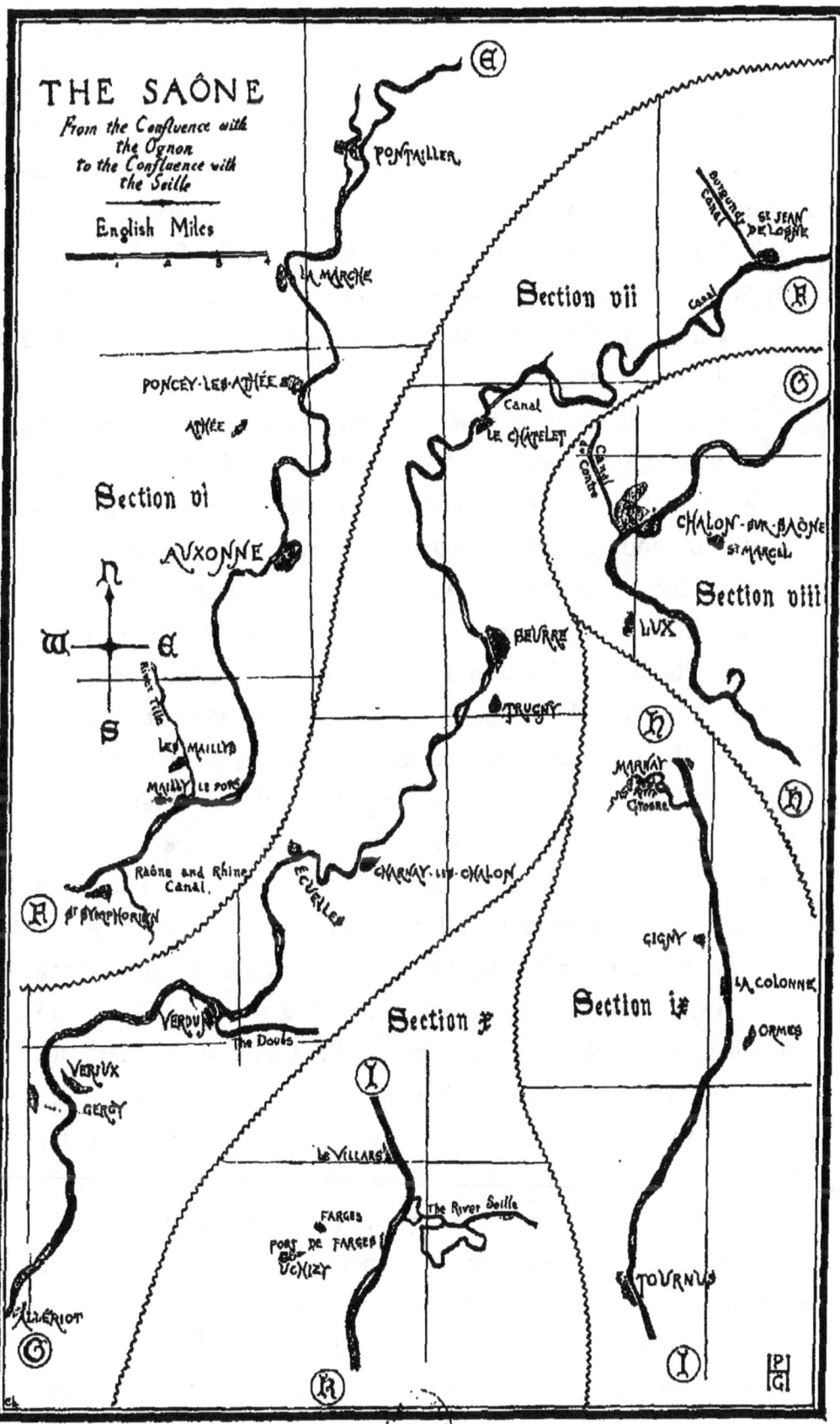

a gallant resistance which put him out of temper, so he gave it up to fire and sword on the 28th of August, 1636. The year following a sort of public inventory was made from which it appears that only five houses had escaped from the conflagration, whilst no more than twenty-two inhabitants had been left alive after the massacre.

Part of the town is now situated between the present bed of the Saône, and another bed of the same river which makes a long and very pretty lake shaded with some of the most beautiful and graceful groups of trees that I ever beheld, and bordered by gardens with pleasant-looking residences in them. The lawns here are as pretty as those on the banks of the Thames, and the gardens seem to be particularly well kept. The church is on the space of land between the two waters. It is a modern renaissance edifice, very plain and simple outside, but tastefully decorated in the interior after the present Parisian fashion. There is a bridge over the "false river" which leads to the quarter of the town near the railway. Altogether Pontailler is an agreeable little place, but quite uninteresting except for the singular beauty of the false river. To the west is the Mont Ardou, a hill of no picturesque interest, and to the north a flat green plain up to the limits of the forest that we traversed yesterday. The present bridge over the Saône is a modern iron structure on brick piers. The old bridge was blown up by the inhabitants during the Franco-German War, but this did not preserve the town from occupation by the enemy. Mr. Pennell much regretted this useless destruction as there are now so few old bridges upon the Saône. During our walk to-day we passed along a road upon an embankment where men were busy erecting an important iron bridge over a small marshy place. It seemed out of all proportion to the need, but the explanation is that it is placed there to relieve the upper grounds in the floods. At such times the flat country above Pontailler must be an extensive lake.

Pontailler, on the Old Saône.

LETTER XXVI.

PONTAILLER,
June 24th, 10 A.M.

You will perhaps be rather surprised to learn that we are at this minute in a state of arrest. We are prisoners, though allowed to remain on board the *Boussemroum.*

When we had just finished our morning soup I happened to look out of the door of the saloon and beheld four gendarmes coming towards the boat in a deliberate manner. At first I thought their visit was one of simple curiosity, but I was very soon undeceived. When they were close to the boat one of them said to me, "You have an individual on board who makes plans." "No," I answered, trying to establish a necessary but difficult distinction, "we have an artist on board who makes drawings, but that is not the same thing."

"Yes, he makes plans," said the gendarme. "I myself saw him doing so this morning; let me see what he did this morning." I then asked Mr. Pennell to hand over his drawing, which he did immediately, and the gendarme *holding it the wrong side up*, with an air of the gravest disapprobation, repeated his assertion about plans, on which an argument arose. The Captain and I, with small success, endeavoured to make our visitor understand the difference between a plan and a perspective drawing. It was a waste of time to attempt this, because amongst the uneducated French *tirer des plans* is a generic term which includes both geometrical and landscape work of all kinds. For them the work of a land-surveyor and that of Corot or Daubigny is the same. Afterwards we thought the man might understand the drawing a little better if he held it the right side up, an unlucky idea, for when its position was rectified the change only led to a new difficulty. Mr. Pennell's way of drawing is this: he uses Bristol boards, and first sketches upon them in pencil, making out his whole subject in that way; he then proceeds to draw over the pencil in black ink, and often in the ink drawing he introduces changes to improve the composition. Now, it so happened that in the drawing of Pontailler which the gendarme held in his hands there was a pencil sketch of a house-roof that had not been effaced, though it was destined to be so, as there were no ink marks upon it. The gendarme had not noticed this so long as he held the drawing the wrong side up, but when its position had unfortunately been rectified the mystery of the pencil marks immediately began to disquiet him, and he insisted upon it that they were intended to represent the Mont Ardou, which, he declared, was a place of the greatest importance in time of war. Our repeated assertion that it was merely a house-roof was of no avail, though we showed him other drawings with pencil-marks left here and there. It is, however, a difficult task to begin the artistic education of a man who has power to arrest you, as he may not quite like to be taught. This man got rather angry, though the three others kept their temper well, and the angry one declared that in his view Mr. Pennell's culpability was established, and that the case must be referred to the authorities. We then underwent an examination about our "papers," by which a French gendarme means passports or other documents establishing the identity of the bearer. I explained that as passports were no longer required at the frontier it was not usual for Englishmen or Americans to be provided with them, and that we possessed nothing of the kind.[1] He then asked Captain Komprobst if he had papers. Now it so happens that the Captain never travels without all his most important papers, from an idea that they are safest in his own keeping, so he had all the documents concerning his military position and produced them.[2] The gendarme, before examining these, would have it that the Captain had

---

[1] Our conduct in travelling without passports has been represented as singularly careless, but, in fact, I had often sketched on the Saône before during boating excursions, and had never been asked to show a passport. Our critics may perhaps be able to answer the following question: *How were we to anticipate the stringency of instructions that were issued to the gendarmes after the "Boussemroum" had started on her voyage?*

[2] The French newspapers took no notice of this important fact, but said that we were all three without papers.

chosen the Prussian nationality, but that was easily disproved, then he said it was not clear how the Captain was free from military service before the usual time of retirement, but the wound explained this. Finally it was admitted that the Captain was a French officer, but under suspicion of communicating information to foreigners who were engaged in making plans. In this way it turned out that my military friend, instead of being a protection to us, rather added to the danger of our situation. I nearly lost my temper when the Captain was accused of being an unpatriotic Frenchman, he who has the sentiment of patriotism in a far higher and purer form than most Frenchmen, and in a degree which is rare at the present day in all countries. I have not the slightest doubt that Captain Kornprobst would march quite cheerfully to certain death if by doing so there would be even a chance of winning back Alsatia and Lorraine.

One of my arguments was a decided failure. I said that real spies would never travel with such a visible and peculiar apparatus as the *Boussemroum* and its contents. But the gendarme replied, with more *finesse* than I expected, that an appearance of extreme openness and frankness might be made use of to conceal illegal designs, and that it was even possible to sketch in an innocent manner in order to obtain opportunities for sketching otherwise.

The same gendarme then read his instructions to us, which empowered him to arrest persons found making plans or *sketches* of roads, rivers, canals, and public works such as bridges, in short, of all means of communication. Our drawings included all these interdicted subjects, so it was useless to deny that the gendarme had right on his side, in the literal sense, though he had begun by misinterpreting our work. I then said that I should place myself under the protection of the higher French authorities through the mediation of a Prefect, and mentioned three Prefects who were likely to assist me, and to whom I intended to address telegrams. After this we noticed that the gendarme assumed a less authoritative tone. The others had exercised, from the beginning, a sort of moderating influence. They were perfectly civil to us, and listened with patient attention to everything that the Captain and I had to say in our defence.

In order that the whole matter might be fairly judged, I offered to give up all my own drawings in addition to all those of Mr. Pennell. The gendarmes were not aware that I had made any drawings whatever. They counted the two collections, and promised to return them if permitted to do so by the authorities. Meanwhile, we and the *Boussemroum* were to be detained.

The Brigadier is gone to Dijon by the morning train, taking all our drawings with him. He mentioned both the *Parquet* and the General when he left us. I hope the matter will not be referred to an ordinary legal tribunal, as we may be kept in prison at Dijon till the case is tried. I should much prefer a reference to the military authority, which will settle the matter at once.

Mr. Pennell is a little dejected, for a particular reason. He is convinced that he will never see his drawings again, which would be painful to him, independently of their pecuniary value. My opinion is that they will be restored, but perhaps not immediately.

We are guarded by two of the gendarmes with revolvers in

their belts. I am, however, allowed to go to the Post Office and send off telegrams and letters. I have even sent a packet of corrected proofs, which might have been drawings. The Captain and Franki are both fishing close to the *Boussemroum*. Mr. Pennell is drawing in his tent, not venturing to work openly, whilst abstinence from the practice of his art would be, for him, an almost unbearable privation.

Old House at Pontailler.

The Captain and I have had a leisurely conversation with our guards since our arrest or detention. The tone they now adopt is conciliatory and rather apologetic. They admit that we may be innocent of any evil design, but affirm that they dare not let us proceed further without an investigation, and do not feel competent to decide the matter on their own responsibility. They received special instructions to be exceedingly strict about a week ago. I have reason to believe that they got orders to look after us, by telegraph, from Gray.

We all thought at first (as other people will think) that the gendarmes had made a ridiculous mistake because they do not distinguish accurately between plans and sketches, but, after hearing their instructions, I do not see how they could avoid arresting us. If we escape being put in prison, it will only be because the authority to whom the matter is referred takes a liberal and reasonable view, and sees the absolute innocence of our intentions. A narrow-minded, ill-tempered judge, with a dislike to art and artists, might cause us most serious inconvenience.[1]

We are anxious, all three of us. I am anxious, not because we are in danger of severe punishment, but because an expedition, on the success of which I had set my heart, may be brought to a close prematurely. We may be distinctly forbidden to go on with our drawing. The Captain is anxious, because it would be unpleasant for a military man to find himself entangled in a trial of "spies." Mr. Pennell is anxious for the fate of his drawings, which form a quite unique series of

---

[1] Amongst the numerous references to our case in the newspapers, the point of real importance was generally missed. The newspaper correspondents seem to have believed, and some of them affirmed plainly, that we had been drawing fortified places, and they were kind enough to let us understand that we ought to have known better. One correspondent said that we had been arrested for drawing a fort at Pontailler, and that I had admitted we were in the wrong. There is no fort at Pontailler. Others said we had drawn fortifications at Pontarlier. Considering that Pontarlier is fifty miles from the Saône as the crow flies, we must have had excellent eyesight to see the forts there, supposing them to exist.

No; the point of interest and novelty in our little adventure was the discovery, quite new to us, that artists are liable to arrest in France for drawing *ordinary landscape subjects* even when, like ourselves, they *carefully avoid military works*. Our surprise was, to learn that we were in fault for having drawn a quiet river and its sluggish canals, and for having sketched some unfortified villages on its banks, with here and there a bridge, or a bit of rustic road.

illustrations of the Upper Saône. No artist, in the future, will ever be able to execute such a series of illustrations of this river without all the practical conveniences afforded by an organised expedition like that of the *Boussemroum*.

1.30 P.M.

Before closing my letter, I may tell you that our guards have disappeared, and the Pilot has heard in the town that a telegram has arrived at the gendarmerie. Possibly this may be in our favour, but the Brigadier who took the drawings to Dijon is not expected at Pontailler till evening.

LETTER XXVII.

PONTAILLER, *June 25th.*

After writing my letter to you yesterday, I remained idling in or near the *Boussemroum* all day. The Captain fished almost the whole day, and Mr. Pennell went on sketching privily in his tent.

At six in the evening, being in that part of the boat which we call the "Cour Pennell," a square space in front of the artist's habitation, I saw two gendarmes approaching, and one of them carried a large parcel under his arm. "What news?" I asked, when they came near, and they answered, "Bonnes nouvelles."

I confess that this was an immense relief to both of us, for the reasons I mentioned yesterday. One of the gendarmes was the same who had spoken rather sharply to us in the morning. His manner was now very different, and he offered an apology; but I answered that he and his brethren had only done their duty, which is really my view of the matter. Besides, they might have annoyed us much more seriously.

The drawings were now counted, and faithfully returned to us. They had been submitted to the General [1] commanding the district of Dijon, who had examined them and declared that there was nothing in them to disquiet the military authorities. He gave directions that we were to be allowed to pursue our journey peacefully, but he sent us at the same time a friendly message to the effect that it would be well not to sketch at Auxonne (which is a fortified place) nor in its immediate neighbourhood. I promised that this advice should be acted upon, not simply because Auxonne has little artistic interest, but because I was glad to have an opportunity of showing deference to an officer who had dealt so fairly with us.

The gendarmes appeared anxious to atone in some way for the annoyance they had caused us, and volunteered to write or telegraph to the gendarmerie at St. Jean de Losne (our next town after Auxonne) to say that we were not to be molested. I accepted this proposal, and we parted in a friendly manner, the gendarmes wishing us a pleasant voyage.

[1] General Tricoche, an artillery officer of very high reputation in the French army.

I am waiting here to-day, because recommended to do so by a Prefect who has applied to the Minister of War. Mr. Pennell has resumed his sketching at Pontailler, and it amused me this morning to see one of the gendarmes passing within a few yards of him. They salute us, especially the Captain, with much politeness, which makes it difficult to restrain a smile. I have now discovered that Mr. Pennell pitched his sketching-stool close to the gendarmerie itself!

We have learned something about the extreme strictness of the military authorities here. It appears that we are in the second line of defence, and although Pontailler has no fort it is within the range of the great guns on Mount Roland. The road surveyors are not allowed to make new plans of any part of the roads without special permission, and a landowner cannot freely make a new path upon his property. All the means of communication are considered to be military. This may seem an excess of precaution, but it may be well to ask ourselves whether, if a French army occupied Sussex and Kent, the English military authorities would not be equally strict in Surrey.[1]

A rather strange incident occurred this morning on the quay.

---

[1] Railroads and canals are in some cases believed to be expressly made by the State for military purposes, though used for ordinary traffic in time of peace. For example, the non-navigable Saône above Corre is crossed by a railway not yet entirely finished, which is one of several strategic railways either completed or in progress. It is possible that the great engineering works that have been executed during the last decade on the Saône itself, making it navigable from Gray to Corre, and thus connecting it with the canal and river systems of the north-east and north, may have had some strategic as well as commercial motive also. However this may be, the military authorities look upon all navigable inland waters as a part of the national defence.

Now, it so happened that one of my drawings which were shown to the General at Dijon included a canal with two bridges and a tunnel, one of the bridges being that

All the bargemen and labourers were talking about the news that the Government had decided to expel the Princes, and they were unanimous in disapproving the measure. Our Pilot had been with them, and also felt strongly on the subject. Generally, when men are indignant, they exaggerate the cause of their indignation, and these men believed that all princes whatever were expelled. I explained the real limits of the measure to the Pilot, and shortly afterwards the bargemen sent him to ask if I would talk to them. It is always a delicate matter for a foreigner to speak on a political subject, but there could be no harm in removing a misconception, so I went and explained the case. The men listened most attentively, and were much relieved to hear that the measure affected the Pretenders only. I said that the necessity might be regretted but that, as a matter of fact, it had always been the custom of all Governments to expel Pretenders. The feeling showed by the bargemen and labourers did them credit. It did not arise from political partisanship, as I believe they were all Republicans and quite loyal to the existing Government, it arose from the sympathy with what they believed to be an unmerited misfortune. "Are they not," they asked when speaking of the princely families, "are they not French citizens like ourselves?"[1]

of a railway, which is probably a strategic railway. The canal itself, and especially the tunnel, might be regarded as works having a possible military importance.

In a case of this kind it is clear that the artist is completely at the mercy of his military judge.

[1] The expulsion of the Comte de Paris has since been justified by the manifesto in which he undisguisedly assumed the position of Pretender. That of the Duc d'Aumale, regretted by every lover of the Fine Arts, and of all high culture whatever, was not expected in June, 1886, and appears to have been intentionally provoked by the form of his letter to the President.

LETTER XXVIII.

ST. JEAN DE LOSNE,
June 26th.

A steam-tug came down to Pontailler yesterday about noon, so I resolved to avail myself of it, and to have telegrams and letters forwarded to this place.

The speed of tugs with trains of boats behind them is, as you know by our experience on the Upper Saône, remarkable only for slowness, yet a tug is preferable to our poor friend and inadequate servant Zoulou, who is liable to be stopped at any time by a side wind, and who cannot, at the best, take us over more than ten miles in the day. The distance from Pontailler to St. Jean de Losne is about twenty-three miles by the Saône, and this took us from one o'clock in the afternoon till ten in the evening without other stoppages than a very few locks, yet after going behind Zoulou the steamer gave us the illusion of a relative swiftness, an illusion greatly aided by the washing of the water against the clumsy boats. They do not cut it and glide through it like a yacht, they butt against it noisily, and leave a whirling commotion in their wake.

The scenery between Pontailler and St. Jean de Losne is at first wooded, and the views are not extensive, but they gradually become more open, approximating in character to the Lower Saône. The horizon is hilly, without having much character at first, though as we descend the river the hills increase in interest. The dominant height is Mount Roland, with its church and a few houses on the crest of it, situated just like a Gaulish oppidum. There is a strong, modern fort on this commanding position, which can bombard the whole country round with its far-carrying heavy ordnance, but modern military works are

Coming down behind steamer.

so little conspicuous that this fort was not visible from the river. The mount is, I believe, called after the famous paladin who fought at Roncevaux, and this union of modern strength with ancient romance and some natural grandeur gives it not a little dignity.

The character of the buildings in the villages and by the river is often grand with their lofty peaked roofs. Mr. Pennell managed to sketch a great shed that would have attracted Rembrandt. In the churches we noticed a peculiar taste for sharp spires. Each village has its spire, and in one of them, La Marche, there is a new church with the luxury of two spires, both rather thin and needle-like. This taste may be explicable by the example of Auxonne, which possesses a fine taper spire that must have set the fashion.

The river here winds about so much that without the help of a map any one approaching Auxonne from the north would believe that he had left it far behind and was going directly away from it. Afterwards the river seems to return to the city, which is visible in the distance chiefly by the tall spire just alluded to.

Poncey-les-Athée is a village on the right bank of the Saône. The name might strike an Englishman at first as meaning that the inhabitants were atheists, but *les*, in this connection, means *near* (from *latus*), and indicates that this Poncey is near the village of Athée, which, in fact, is about a mile to the south. Poncey attracted our attention by a great building, ugly enough to the bodily eye, but beautiful to the mind's eye when one knows the origin and the use of it. A rich man in the neighbourhood erected it at his own private cost as an asylum for the poor.

In this part of the river Mr. Pennell remarked that the shore of the Saône was an "arrangement" in green and red between the two blues of sky and reflection. Beginning at the top, this arrangement may be described as follows, in bands: Blue sky, dark green trees, bright green grass, reddish bank where the earth is eaten away, then the reflections producing all these bands of colour over again in reverse order and in deeper tones. We agreed that this was very pleasant to the eye in nature, and that the repetition of it for miles was not at all fatiguing, but how impossible to make a picture with these bands of colour, unless the painter had recourse to other materials to interrupt and relieve them!

I mention this arrangement as particularly characteristic of the Saône. I have never seen a river on which it was so frequent and maintained for such considerable distances. I may add that on the Lower Saône the band of dark trees is frequently absent, and is replaced by the blue of distant hills. The grass of the shore is extremely fresh during our present voyage on account of the recent rain, and the contrast of the red earth for colour and the dark trees for tonic value is such as to enhance the brightness of the green shore to the utmost, particularly under sunshine.

The fortifications of Auxonne are not very visible at first from a boat on the river. The aquatic traveller sees little except soft-looking green mounds, but on looking attentively he may discern a narrow line of grey stone below the green. On approaching the bridge the strong wall is very visible behind the avenue that has been planted on the left bank of the Saône.

Being anxious to observe the General's friendly hint about Auxonne in appearance as well as fact, I decided that none of the party should land there, and for some time before and after our arrival Mr. Pennell ceased to make the rapid memoranda which occupy and amuse him during our ordinary boat travelling.

As we passed under the bridge Mr. Pennell and the Captain observed that a gendarme was watching us, and that he remained in sight till the *Boussemroum*, after a short stoppage, had resumed her voyage. I hope his vigilance was rewarded by the assurance that we made no sketches at Auxonne.

As we did not even land I cannot describe the church to you except as seen from a distance. It was a matter of regret to me not to visit this edifice, which has some architectural peculiarities. There is a vast porch under the western towers that must produce a fine effect of shadow. The church has five towers in all, only one of them being completed.

The misfortune of a place of this kind is that the ages efface their predecessors. Nothing is so dull, so destructive of the past, as the work of modern military and civil engineers. Auxonne has suffered from both. Who that sees the monotonous walls under their green mounds can think of Auxonne as it must have been when the nobility of Burgundy gave their brilliant tournament in the year 1444? It is difficult when you see the red-legged French soldiers lounging on the long iron bridge to remember that Auxonne was once the capital of a little independent sovereignty belonging neither to the duchy of Burgundy nor the kingdom of France. It is a curiosity of history that there are two small ex-capital cities on the Saône, Trévoux and Auxonne. Such weak little States can hardly last, and this one ended naturally by being incorporated with the duchy first and afterwards with the kingdom.

One of the most recent historical associations of Auxonne is, that Napoleon had his sledges made here for the audacious passage of the Alps. There is more real sublimity about the rough work of the carpenters, who made these things in a hurry, than in the finished craft of a Parisian coach-builder. The grandeur of such a scheme as the passage of the Alps makes the rudest instruments sublime. Auxonne is still so military that the soldiers are four-tenths of the whole population, and are to be seen everywhere. We met groups of well-mounted officers riding along the canal banks (they stared with wonder at the tents on the *Boussemroum*), and there were soldiers in the fields about, and everywhere, even in the very waters of the Saône itself.

In the lock below Auxonne I took occasion to scold young Franki seriously, this being the first time that I have spoken a harsh word to him. The lad gives me real anxiety in such places. He cannot swim a stroke and he is recklessly active, running along the edges of boats like an old *marinier*, and climbing in and out everywhere, up the vertical iron ladders in the locks, and in general wherever there is the attraction of danger. Now, the danger in locks is really serious, for if you fall into the water between a boat like the *Boussemroum* and the wall, or between any two of these big boats, you are likely to be crushed to death.[1] The bargemen are constantly placing themselves in situations where a false step would have this result, but their wonderful skill makes the false step itself very unlikely to happen. With Franki the case is different, he is not a young *marinier*, bred on the river, but only a farm servant.

Since the establishment of our little quarter-deck, as we call it, in front of the donkey's house, from which we have an

---

[1] The best chance of safety in such an accident would be the following, but it would require both presence of mind and good diving powers. One might dive at once beneath the boat and swim under it to the stern, where there is sure to be a little room about the rudder, sometimes all the room there is in a lock crowded to the utmost.

unimpeded view of the river, we have acquired the habit of sitting on this deck when we are towed, especially if the scenery is interesting. Few hours of our voyage have been more delightful than those spent on the quarter-deck between Auxonne and St. Jean de Losne. After a splendid day came an evening of enchantment with effects that could hardly be painted, and of which no conception whatever can be conveyed with the simple

Our Quarterdeck.

art of pen-drawing. After passing through the lock at Auxonne the voyager finds himself in a broader river with the character of the Lower Saône. This character may be described generally in a few words. The Upper Saône is more or less closely hemmed in, either by near hills or by woods, but on the Lower Saône (with the exception of the extreme south, of which more will be said later), although there are hills and woods still, the hills are generally distant, and the woods only occasional—a great wood here and there—whilst the especial character of the scenery is *extent of plain*, giving such a sense of space that it reminds one of the desert or the sea. This latter comparison has so often occurred to me that I was struck by the coincidence, when Mr. Pennell exclaimed, "This is a new sensation on a river; it is like being on the sea!" After a brilliant sunset came the finest effects of all. In the after-glow the sky was of greenish mother-of-pearl, with delicate films of rosy cloud slowly darkening, and a line of fiery crimson over the intense azure of the distance. The effect lost nothing of its poetry by our knowledge that those distant hills were not mere sterile rock and bog but the richest vine-lands where the juice of the grape has attained its mellowest perfection, the world-renowned *Côte d'Or* seen across the great plain of Burgundy. The perfect calm of the river was disturbed only by the passage of our train of boats, which took vast and majestic curves that gave it at times a picturesque beauty, the strong steamer holding steadily on her way, transformed by distance and by the magical evening light into the poetic essence of steamships instead of the hard mechanical reality. Many of the boats were covered with great cloths, in colour a pale faded green, that gave the train the appearance of a vast floating camp, and our own tents in the foreground added to the illusion. As the twilight deepened, the river seemed broader still, the shores more mysterious and more remote, and at one place on the right bank[1] we saw a wonderful effect of

---

[1] I learned from the map that this place was *Mailly-le-Port* by the mouth of the river Tille near the village of *Les Maillys*, which is situate about a mile farther inland. The river Tille has this remarkable peculiarity, that it is formed of three streams, *each of which is called the Tille*. The three meet in a small lake from which

extreme obscurity in contrast with beautiful light. Mr. Pennell was enchanted with the fine arrangements of some dark farmhouses and cottages, composing themselves at times with such strange perfection that it seemed intentional. These dark houses with high thatched roofs stood on a band of dark plain between a sky still glowing with pearly light and its counterpart in the calm water, the only other element in the simple composition being the dim indefinite hills of the Côte d'Or, still retaining their azure, but darkened to an incredible depth. At this time

Sunset on the Broad Saône.

Mr. Pennell's enthusiasm knew no bounds, and he continued taking rapid notes in his sketch-book till he could see no longer. The scene was so rarely and so completely beautiful that he declared it was the finest and most perfect without any exception that he had ever witnessed in his whole life—such was the overpowering effect of the impression at the moment. He must have thought me unimpressionable in my taciturnity, as I did not sketch and remained almost entirely silent; but I am his senior by twenty-five years, and time causes us to take the

the united river flows. In the way of river nomenclature I do not know any similar instance.

greatest pleasures calmly. To me the delight in all this beauty was tempered by infinite sadness, for it brought suddenly to my recollection scenes of the same rare quality witnessed in other lands and in what is now an irrecoverable past.

In this part of the Saône are two large islands, one above Mailly-le-Port opposite the village of St. Seine-en-Bâche, and the other below Mailly. Neither of these islands is wooded, and they increase the melancholy of the scenery by their dreary aspect in the midst of the waters. A rushy shore, a stretch of land surrounded by water, and that is all. Beyond the lower island, on the left shore, are some grey buildings with what looks like a mediæval pont-levis, the whole presenting very much the appearance of the entrance to some ancient town. This is the beginning of one of the most important canals in Continental Europe—it connects the Rhône with the Rhine!

There is such a glamour in history, and poetry, and art, that the mere names of these most famous rivers, in their curious similarity, awaken a thousand associations. Gazing on this simple entrance to the canal I came to see it no longer, but, in place of it, a rapidly changing vision of romantic cities, castled heights, and swiftly-flowing waters. Rhodanus makes his way from his great blue lake to a sea of sunshine, Rhenus flows from another great lake to lose his divided identity in the flat sands of a foggy northern coast; yet this humble result of human toil, so insignificant in appearance that we might pass it without notice, has made them as one river, and a boat may go from Ehrenbreitstein to Avignon.

I have just spoken of the glamour of history. Is there anything in history more romantic than the Crusades, or any crusade grander in the courage and hope that inspired it, and in the fortitude with which a great disappointment was endured, than that expedition of Saint Louis to the Nile, described by the good Sire de Joinville? Well, during our voyage from Auxonne to St. Jean de Losne, it was impossible not to think of the hopeful setting forth of that expedition. De Joinville tells us that the baggage belonging to the Count de Sarrebruck and himself was sent in carts as far as Auxonne, "there to be put on the river of Saône in order that it might go as far as Arles by the Saône and by the Rhone." In the same chapter he says, "I and my companions ate at Fontaine l'Archevêque before Donjeux, and there the Abbot of St. Urbain gave a great number of beautiful jewels to me and my nine knights. From that place we went to Auxonne, then with our baggage that we had caused to be put in boats we went from Auxonne to Lyons descending the Saône; and, by the side of the boats, our great war-horses were led."

This passage is intensely interesting for several reasons. It proves that in those days the Saône was navigable from Auxonne downwards, and also that there was a towing-path, without which the horses could not have been led continuously along the shore. Yet the river itself must have been at that time comparatively in a natural state, as the engineering works are recent. There are now eleven locks between Auxonne and Lyons which have made the navigation incomparably easier.[1]

When you are on the river in such an evening effect as that which enchanted us near Mailly-le-Port—effects of that rare

---

[1] The Saône appears to have been navigable up to Gray in the thirteenth century, as the increase of the town at that date is attributed to the commerce by the river. It was navigable from Lyons to Chalon in Roman and in ancient Gaulish times, but there the natural difficulties are not great, and the worst evils were probably nothing more than a few places with a strong current and some shallows in hot weather.

beauty being in the highest degree stimulating to the imagination—it becomes possible almost to *see* the train of boats with the Crusaders and their "grands destriers" led along the bank. 'Tis a glimpse of a vanished past, and only a glimpse. Where are the brave, simple-minded, enthusiastic knights, and the strong steeds, and the boats and river "mariners" of those days? It is like asking where is the water that carried them, as they believed, towards the deliverance of Palestine. Yet surely we know that they passed here, between these shores, where now the steam-tug draws the barges and the *Boussemroum*.

At length in the deepening twilight we made out the towers of St. Jean de Losne, and soon arrived and anchored there, if the dropping of a heavy stake can be called anchoring.

How delightful it is to be exempt from the trouble of seeking for an inn when one arrives at a place at night! We stop at St. Jean de Losne at ten, in the starlight, and there is nothing to be done. The *Boussemroum* ceases to move, that is all. I give orders to the Pilot to moor her to the south-eastern quay in the morning, near the entrance to the Burgundy canal, and I know that she will be there when I awake.

LETTER XXIX.

St. Jean de Losne,
June 27th.

As soon as the post-office opened in the morning I presented myself and found a short telegram from a Prefect, not very explicit, but enough to satisfy me that the Minister of War has given a favourable answer. It is to be regretted that I have not the terms of the Minister's despatch, as I have nothing to show to a gendarme.[1]

We have had evidence this morning that the gendarmes at Pontailler have been as good as their word. Mr. Pennell, as usual, went straight to the gendarmerie to draw, and was not disturbed. Later in the day he was drawing the church and I was standing near him when a gendarme appeared in sight. He was in full uniform, not excepting the cocked hat,[2] and bore down upon us as a ship of war might come upon two defenceless merchantmen. Our first impression was that we were to be captured as prizes, but instead of arresting us the armed man

---

[1] I learned afterwards that there had been a double mistake. The Prefect had intended that the Minister's despatch should be forwarded to me, and a copy of it sent to the Prefect of the Doubs, where he believed me to have been arrested by the common confusion between Pontailler and Pontarlier. This caused me afterwards much trouble in correspondence, and to this day I have not been able to procure the Minister's despatch, although the Prefect had explicit permission from the War Office to communicate it to me.

[2] All I regret about the gendarmes who arrested us at Pontailler is that they did not wear their cocked hats. They carried revolvers, it is true, which might have been more efficacious weapons, but a gendarme without his cocked hat is hardly a complete gendarme. Mr. Pennell wanted to add this imposing ornament in a sketch of our arrest, but I insisted that the drawing ought to be historical.

saluted us and smiled upon us, oh! so sweetly. Two quotations rushed into my mind together, one was from Macaulay's *Ivry*:—

"Right graciously he smiled on us,"

the other was from a French ditty:—

"Et avec un sourire
De ravissante douceur."

The church of St. Jean de Losne which Mr. Pennell sketched, is to my taste the most picturesque—I do not say the finest—on

The Church at St. Jean de Losne.

the Saône. The colour of its warm old brick-work was a great comfort to the eyes after the colder stone-work on the upper river, and it was a pleasure after the severe modern renaissance architecture at Pontailler and Port-sur-Saône to come upon the fanciful and elegant renaissance of a more inventive age, even though out of place, as it was patched upon a sort of gothic.

The west end of the church at St. Jean de Losne is indeed sad patchwork and yet pathetically interesting. The gothic has been removed about the entrance to make way for a renaissance doorway so exquisitely beautiful as to be utterly out of harmony with the general rudeness of the edifice, a work of accomplished art that ought to have been taken when new and put safely away in the hall of some museum. Too delicate even to be exposed to the common vicissitudes of the weather, far too delicate to be entrusted to the vandalism of ignorant and careless men, it has met its inevitable fate, and is now ravaged and ruined. Columns are broken away and leave their capitals hanging in the air; the perfectly carved canopies over the niches remain between the little brick and plaster shops that fill up the recesses; mouldings once sharp and well defined are now clipped and broken away. Above the cornice the vandals have built a blank wall and placed in the midst thereof a barbarous old statue, and above this wall is a huge window without mullion or transom, consisting of nothing but common panes of glass, and having no more style or taste than the windows of an engine-room or a weaving shed. The work of the renaissance artist has been attacked from below as well as from above. It is partly buried by the raising of the level of the street, and instead of ascending to his beautiful doorway you go down to it. Nobody has cared for all his skill and taste. The blind forces of Nature would have treated his work with as much care and intelligence. It might almost as well have been entrusted to the grinding of an Alpine glacier or the wash of the Atlantic wave.

Still, shattered as they are now, and out of place as they

must ever have been on a rude gothic edifice like this, these remains of a too exquisite beauty have the preciousness of a finer civilization. There is no really refined work in the little town, except this. I can fancy some youth, born and bred there, and getting his notions of refinement in architectural art from these broken fragments only. The church itself is interesting in quite another way. It would be a capital subject for water-colour drawings, and the picturesque draughtsman would not object to the little shops that nestle between the buttresses. One of these is actually a small café, with all the appliances of a café in miniature, even to seats outside and orange-trees in green tubs. Another of these tiny establishments is a fruit-shop, with its pretty display of fruit close to the church door.

The interior of the church is picturesque, but there is nothing in it so delicate as the renaissance work about the doorway. The reason for this appears to be that the renaissance artists who worked inside used marble, and thought that the richness of the material released them from the labour of invention. There is a great Italian marble baldacchino above the altar, with a hemicycle of marble columns behind it, and a flourish carved in marble above. There is also a heavy and expensive red marble pulpit—a monolith. It seems to be almost a rule that the more marble there is in a building the less mind; the pretty material seems to be taken as a substitute for mind.[1] Another great evil of rich marbles is that they bar the way to a judicious restora-

---

[1] A striking instance of this is the choir at Chartres, where the carvings were removed in the time of pseudo-classical vandalism to make way for plain slabs of coloured marbles, not better than the common work in chimney-pieces, only bigger and more expensive.

The Main Street at St. Jean de Losne.

tion. At Gray and Autun the intelligent modern architects have not dared to remove the marbles, for fear of a popular clamour.

I observed in this church an arrangement of stalls radiating round a column, which was effective and new to me. There is a fine view of a side chapel through intersecting arches, and in the chapel is a large gilded figure of a bishop. High in the air hangs a big votive model of a ship, with a tricolour of disproportionate size behind; but there are suspended relics of greater historical interest.

The little town has a glorious surname, *Belle Défense*, because in 1636 the inhabitants successfully defended the place against the imperial army under General Gallas. The helmet and sword of the officer who commanded the defenders are still preserved in the church, and the event is celebrated by a public festival which was at first intended to take place every hundred years. The interval of a century was, however, thought to be too long and that of fifty years was adopted instead, which fixes the celebration in the year 1886. The people were planning the details of their festival during our stay. It has the good effect of making them remember a bright page of local history. That year 1636, marked with unutterable horrors for Pontailler, is splendid with successful heroism for St. Jean de Losne.

There is an event in the earlier history of the place which is a comedy and a tragedy in one. In the year 1273 the lords of Franche-Comté sent five hundred men to surprise St. Jean de Losne, and to effect this the more easily they were disguised as women. However, the inhabitants found them out and slaughtered all the five hundred.

The warlike annals of this little place come down quite to our own times, as the Garibaldians resisted a German advance in a combat here in 1870, after which the Germans retired to Dijon. There are still fortifications about St. Jean de Losne on the land side, bastions and a ditch, but the place is not a *ville fermée* like Auxonne. However, there was quite enough to give a pretext for the imprisonment of Mr. Pennell if we had not been in favour with the military authority.

He noticed that the people at St. Jean de Losne were extremely civil to him, and appeared to understand art. They admired his rapid skill, and especially his power of drawing with the left hand.[1] When it rained they invited him into their houses, an attention which he contrasted with the rudeness of the people in a northern city. I, too, had my own experience of civility here. I went to a café and found myself unable to pay for what I had taken, so I explained my case to the lady. I owed five sous and possessed but four. Having paid all but the last sou, I was leaving when by accident I discovered just one sou in another pocket which enabled me to clear myself of debt. Then the lady said, "This is a disappointment for me, monsieur, for so long as you were my debtor I was sure to see you again, whereas now I am no longer sure." A trifle, but pretty in the thought and extremely neat in the expression.

Another trifling incident pleased me. I was drawing the Saône with a steam-tug in the foreground and the tug was ready to start with its train of boats. The captain, however, saw me at work, and came ashore to say that he would postpone his departure a little if my sketch were not yet finished. It is true that he was the same captain who took us up to Corre, but

[1] Mr. Pennell always drew with the left hand during our voyage, and I believe he finds it more convenient than the right, but he is able to use both.

Steam-Tug at St.-Jean de Losne.

sketchers are not accustomed to so much consideration from anybody.

Whilst I was drawing, a great boat came suddenly round the corner out of the Burgundy canal, and we had to get the rope over the *Boussemroum*. The Pilot was fast asleep in the cabin, and the Patron far too much absorbed in his cookery to heed anything. Luckily Captain Kornprobst was on board, so he and I passed the rope, which is difficult when boatmen are not accommodating.[1] The men in the big boat were engaged in a furious quarrel at the time, so they had not leisure to be considerate. We heard them quarrelling till we lost sight of them through the bridge.

Franki asked permission to absent himself for half-a-day. He wished to go to the village of St. Symphorien (where the Rhine canal begins) to inquire after his brother, of whom nothing had been heard for two years. This lad had quitted his situation without leaving an address, and had not written to his mother or to any one. A girl who had been in these parts said that news of him might be had at St. Symphorien, but Franki came back disappointed. His brother had indeed been there, but he had gone to another situation which he had quitted, and then all trace of him was lost. I am often struck by the wonderful non-communicativeness of the poor. In this present instance I asked Franki if he would not write to his mother. "No" he said, "it

---

[1] A horse walking at the rate of four kilomètres an hour (which is the pace when a boat is light) does about sixty-six mètres in the minute, or about one mètre per second. The length of the *Boussemroum* is twenty-seven mètres, consequently, if the driver is in a bad temper and will not slacken his pace, you have twenty-seven seconds to pass the rope over all obstacles, and it is a most awkward thing to get hold of, especially as it may sometimes have a combination of two motions, forward and diagonal.

is not necessary. She will understand that there is no news about my brother."

Franki had been very kindly treated by the people at St. Symphorien, especially by the curé, who gave him his dinner, with cherries, to console him for his disappointment.

LETTER XXX.

St. Jean de Losne,
June 28th, Morning.

Last evening we walked to see the Burgundy canal. This great canal, which joins the Saône to the Yonne and therefore to the Seine, is a convenience for the internal navigation of France, as it connects the Atlantic with the Mediterranean, and yet, if such an expression is permissible, it is a most inconvenient convenience. The number of locks is given by Malte-Brun as 251,[1] and there is a tunnel at Pouilly so long that the steam-tugs take an hour and a half to pass through it, and nearly suffocate you with the fumes of their coke. For the bargemen who do each day's work as a matter of business, it matters little whether time is spent in a lock or in travelling, but amateur boatmen see in every lock a wearisome trial of patience. I therefore looked

---

[1] The bargemen confirmed this number, but on reference to the log of the *Princess*, an English yacht that passed the canal in 1880, I do not find quite so many. Malte-Brun, the geographer, and the bargemen are probably right. I certainly will not decide the matter by going to count the locks in the canal itself.

The transit by the Burgundy canal from the Saône to the Yonne occupied the steam-yacht five days.

upon the *Canal de Bourgogne* with a quiet but most firm resolution never to attempt the navigation of it. As a picture, it was curious and rather beautiful from a bridge. It is perfectly straight, and would present a curious example of perspective lines converging at an apparent vanishing point, were there not a lock in the remote distance that just prevents the view from being infinite. The long avenue of poplars had its own sublimity, especially as they were dark in the evening with an afterglow in the sky behind them, and the whole was reflected in the still water. This canal, however, is but of an ordinary width, and therefore not comparable to the noble canals on the Upper Saône. It seemed to me so melancholy in its monotonous length, that the natural ending of it must be a cemetery whereto the funeral processions might go in black boats moving silently on the stagnant pool.

During our walk round the outskirts of St. Jean de Losne, we saw many picturesque farm-buildings that delighted Mr. Pennell and gave us a succession of charming rural domestic pictures, as the people had not yet gone to bed. It was Samuel Palmer's favourite hour, and the scene before us presented the rich darks that he loved, and the mysterious penumbræ with centres of glowing light in the interiors.

There being nothing to detain us at St. Jean de Losne I have seized the opportunity presented by a descending train of boats which is stopping here for an hour or two. I have agreed with the captain of the tug to have the *Boussemroum* towed directly to Verdun.

This is quite contrary to my principles as a traveller, but is a concession to unfortunate circumstances. If the *Boussemroum* had possessed lateral resistance enough to tow well I should have hired a pair of horses, the great evil of steam-tugs being that they only stop at the locks. I value the power of stopping at will more than anything else in travelling, more than either comfort or speed. It is a mental torture to be dragged past an interesting place without being permitted either to explore or sketch it. However, a berrichon is a berrichon and we have to accommodate ourselves to the peculiarities of our vessel. It has come to this, that we look upon the steam-tug as our only chance of ultimately reaching Chalon. Even the tugs are very slow. The distance from St. Jean de Losne to Verdun is under thirty miles, yet it will take us the whole day, and this without the privilege of stopping.

LETTER XXXI.

VERDUN,
June 28th, Late Evening.

Our place in the train of boats was by the side of a great Belgian *péniche* which gave me the opportunity for examining one of these interesting vessels at leisure. The long open space in the middle is covered with hatches which (though quite loose and easily removed at any part for loading) are so well contrived and fitted, with grooves for drainage, that no rain-water enters. After the rude barges that one is accustomed to meet on the Saône, which have probably not been altered in shape or finish since the middle ages, a Belgian *péniche* strikes one by the perfection of all its details. This perfection is carried out in everything, both in the thorough workmanship of the builders, and in the orderly, conservative care of the boatmen, who are often owners. The *péniche* we travelled with might have been converted into a most respectable house-boat without any change in its external appearance.

On Board a Péniche.

Just behind the central cabin there lay on one of the hatches a little model of a sloop with its sails set. "That vessel," I said to the boatman's wife, "makes me know that you have a little boy on board, though I have not seen him yet." Instead of brightening at the reference to her child as mothers generally do, this mother looked sad and pained, and she answered: "Yes, I have a little boy, but he is ill." I hoped the illness might not be serious, and the subject dropped till the afternoon, when the mother came on deck with a child in her arms that did not look very well. "Is this the little ship-owner?" I inquired. "No, sir," she answered with the same expression of profound sorrow on her countenance, "he is older, he is five years old." I concluded that the boy must be seriously ill and made no further allusion to him, as his mother did not seem able to bear the subject. The same evening, whilst we were at dinner, she came near the berrichon and had a talk with the Patron who was in the galley. The tone of her voice was very sad, and after some time she gave the reason. "We are in great affliction, we lost our son a fortnight since." "What age?" inquired the Patron. "He was *five years old*." So this had been the owner of the little model sloop, and his mother, not being able to utter the dreaded word *mort*, had said *malade* to me instead. How differently different people bear these sore afflictions! In the same situation I could have said quite easily, "My child is dead," but I could never have borne to see the little toy-ship every time I came out of the cabin; *that* would have been beyond my fortitude.

There is a little grave in some churchyard in a village by the Saône or the Meuse where that *péniche* will stop, you may be sure, on every one of its future voyages.

At a place called Le Châtelet there is a lock, and here we found quite a collection of boats, so picturesque that Mr. Pennell was put ashore to sketch them and got caught in a heavy shower. Amongst these boats was a charming house-boat of moderate dimensions, with a black hull and a white house built upon it. As house-boats interest us just now we had the curiosity to peep inside as we passed, and saw a very tidy little dwelling of several well-furnished and orderly rooms. This is the floating residence of the admiral of the dredging boats, and in this way he inspects the work done in different parts of the river, on which he has his own home everywhere.

At Le Châtelet there were picturesque houses on the shore with roofs of thatch and moss, and some quaint balconies. To console Mr. Pennell for being taken away from these by the inexorable tug, I promised him other thatched houses on the

A House-boat.

Lower Saône, but I doubt if he will find anything quite so good. It is such a torture to him to be dragged past interesting places that I am obliged, at times, to lure him on with promises that may not be *quite* fulfilled.

At Seurre, which is a town of some importance, the houses have quite a different character, indeed Seurre does not resemble any village or town that we have hitherto seen. They remind one of Holland and even of England. They are of red brick, and some of them are both tall and ugly. There is a gaunt brick building with two wings near the bridge. This is not out of keeping here, and gives a sort of grim dignity to the place.

O

This town has a punning motto to its arms, "Loyale et Seurre." Its history goes back to Roman antiquity, but there it becomes cloudy. In the middle ages it was besieged several times, and twice in the seventeenth century. As the town had taken the side of Condé against Louis XIV. the king made himself master of it and then destroyed its fortifications.

Charnay-les-Chalon, below Seurre, is one of the most beautiful villages on the Saône, partly by the pretty grouping of its buildings, but especially by the unrivalled richness of its trees, which form quite classical compositions. The ground, too, is in itself beautiful with its sloping lawn-like fields, and the river has almost a lacustrine character here as there is a weir, with a lock

below. The Pilot told us a dreadful story about this beautiful place. He said that a former mayor having an enmity against the schoolmaster (*instituteur*) had set fire successively to all the houses in the village except one, as at that time they were thatched and burned easily. He then accused the schoolmaster of this incendiarism and got him transported. Later, on his death-bed, the mayor confessed his crimes, and the schoolmaster, who was still alive, was declared innocent. He was released, of course, but he declined to return to the country where he had suffered such a terrible wrong. The subject has been successfully dramatised.

Between Charnay and Verdun we had one of those evening voyages which, when the effects are favourable, delude us with wondrous enchantments. As usual, on these occasions, we all three sat on the quarter-deck, enjoying the rare beauty of the hour. The effect this evening was not brilliant, but it was full

of charm—a soft decline of day in a grey and delicately tinted land, where everything was poetical and vague. The village of Écuelles, on the right bank, composed admirably with its old romanesque church, its rustic houses, and its steep little road coming down to the water, Mr. Pennell said it was like one of the prettiest of Italian villages. As usual in such cases he was

Écuelles.

miserable because the merciless tug dragged us past it, so to console him I suggested the idea of rowing back here the next day with the Pilot, but with no real intention of encouraging a re-visit to-morrow that might renew the disappointment of Ovanches. An impression is not given by a place but *by a place and an effect together*, and the material earth and houses are like dry bones when the soul that gave them unity is gone.

In this part of the Saône the shores are wooded and steep, with great curves, and the stream is comparatively narrow. Afterwards it widens and the shores become flatter.

Nothing could be finer than the *turnings* of the great train of boats at the curves of the river, in the twilight, going majestically on the broad silvery stream between the dark and apparently distant shores that became more and more mysterious as the night deepened, with only a thin line of azure hills beyond them in one direction and nothing in the other. We passed a chain of flat islands that looked unutterably desolate and dreary. There was a warm light in the sky, and by the time we reached the basin above the lock at Verdun the stars were reflected in the calm water. Here the train of boats came to a standstill, and it was not long before sleep reigned from stem to stern of the *Boussemroum*.

LETTER XXXII.

VERDUN, *June 29th.*

The first event in the morning after our arrival at Verdun was a great quarrel between the Belgian bargeman on the *péniche* and the crew of the steam-tug. It was due, in the first place, to the foreigner's misunderstanding of the customs prevalent on the Saône, and in the second to the mere fact that he was a foreigner.

When a boat forms part of a train it is evident that the bargeman may, if he chooses, remain inactively on board, but a custom of mutual help prevails on the Saône by which the men on all the boats are expected to offer their services at certain times, as when locks are passed and there is hard labour in separating and re-forming the train. On all such occasions I am represented by the Pilot, whose mighty strength and merry goodwill make him one of the most popular men on the river; but that unlucky Belgian had remained all day on board his own boat, and he had not even done his duty well on that, so two men from the steamer were sent to belay the towing cables better. He was impolitic enough to protest against their presence as an intrusion, and to assert that he was master on his own boat, which was a technical error as when a boat forms part of a train the entire train is commanded by the captain of the tug, who can send men wherever he thinks they may be needed. The two powerful fellows who had come to belay the cable were not men to accept a slight, and they gave the Belgian the benefit of a thorough Saône scolding, threatening to throw him into the river, which at one moment they seemed quite likely to do. The scene was grandly Homeric as an expression of strong men's wrath and scorn, and it interested me as a study of primitive manners. The men came on board the *péniche* repeatedly for their work, and I noticed that when they were in personal contact with the Belgian the quarrel flagged, but when they stood on another boat it regained its vigour, and the voices their loudness. Of course they called the unlucky man a Prussian, to which he answered with more courage than prudence, " I am not a Prussian, I am a Belgian, but the Prussians are better than you think. You do not know the Prussians," a word in favour of the enemy that had the effect of petroleum in a conflagration. At last his wife was so ill-advised as to interfere. A woman of good nerve, she calmly told the Frenchmen that they were very rude and brutal, but she unexpectedly met her match. One of them turned to her with quite an altered manner, showing that he had his temper well under command, and he uttered these words deliberately: " This is not a place for a woman. What has a woman to do on board a boat? Your proper place is in a house on land, and you ought to be there, minding your own work and bringing up your children." Rough as they were, these men were hearty good fellows, but they had an unaffected contempt for a man who shirked his work, and that natural hostility to foreigners which exists among the common people everywhere.

I was sorry not to have an opportunity for explaining to the Belgian where his mistake lay, as our boats immediately separated.[1] He was one of those unfortunate mortals who lack heartiness and openness of manner, a fatal deficiency on the

---

[1] He had spoken English to me with a strong London accent, leaving no doubt about the place where he had picked it up.

Saône, where a frank readiness to offer and accept services is the prevalent characteristic of the people.

After passing the lock I had the *Boussemroum* warped across to the mouth of the Doubs, and moored her in its green, bright waters in the morning of a splendid day.

The effect of a lake upon the mind depends upon what you *see*, that of a river on what you *know*. I could not see the waters of the Doubs at Verdun without thinking of all its beautiful course from the frontier of Switzerland to Besançon, and from Besançon to Verdun. It is one of the loveliest streams in France, but not classed as navigable, except from Vougeaucourt, a village

Verdun, the Ferry from the Island.

on the extreme east of the department of the Doubs to Dôle, in Jura. During this distance of about fifty-four miles, it is made use of by the canal from the Rhône to the Rhine, and canalised on exactly the same principles as the Upper Saône; in other words, its bed is used whenever possible, with short links of lateral canal from time to time. The navigable part of the river passes through the beautiful valley above Besançon. I have never attempted to ascend it from Verdun to Dôle as the voyage would be impracticable for my boats.[1]

---

[1] A light rowing boat, manned by four strong young men, can just accomplish this ascent. It was done in 1882, but not easily, by a four-oared gig from Lyons,

This is the second of the three most important confluences on the Saône which are, with the Coney at Corre, the Doubs at Verdun, and the Rhône at Lyons. In each of these cases the volume of water is doubled.

At the junction of the Doubs and the Saône there is a beautiful island adorned with most graceful masses of foliage. The views of the island from the town, and of the town from the island, are so interesting that, although there is not much else

Verdun from the Island in the Doubs.

at Verdun, a lover of the picturesque might yet be content to live there. And he would have the contrast of the two rivers— the Saône, sluggish and often opaque, the Doubs, swifter, clearer, brighter, but less navigable.

Notwithstanding the beauty of the day and of the place, it was a sad day for us as our friend the Captain was to leave the

Le Quadrille. The rowers found "the navigation extremely difficult, for the river has many windings, and there are numerous islands amongst which it is not always easy to select a channel. There are also mill weirs, only to be overcome by carrying your boat. The current is often very violent, in some places comparable to that of the Rhône."

In the canalised Doubs the navigation, of course, is easy, but there are many locks— twenty-eight between Dôle and Besançon only.

Verdun, the Foot-bridge.

expedition here. He would have gone with us southwards, and had actually made sacrifices to stay with us so long, but he had to make a removal that required his personal superintendence.

I said that for the last day he must have a better *déjeuner* than the *Boussemroum* could give, so we sought out Mother D—, who is famous amongst all boating men on the Saône. We found her at last, a fat woman, shelling peas in the shade.

"Are you Madame D—?" I inquired, as Madame seemed more respectful than Mother.

"Anyhow," she replied, "I am a good part of her."

"Then there is enough of you here present for our purposes. We want *déjeuner*."

"Yes, I know," she answered imperturbably. "The Inspector told me so."

"That surprises me, I was not aware that the Inspector could be so well informed about our intentions."

"*Mais*," she said, "all these gentlemen have *déjeuner* together. You are with the schoolmasters."

The truth was that Mother D— was expecting twenty *instituteurs* to *déjeuner* that day and had quietly concluded that the Captain, Mr. Pennell, and myself were three French schoolmasters. It was the first time that we had been taken for members of the same learned profession. It gave us quite a new feeling of brotherhood and elevated us in our own estimation after being arrested as foreign spies.

I then begged Mother D— to let us have a *pauchouse*, for which she is celebrated. Perhaps the inhabitants of London do not telegraph to Mother D— for *pauchouses* ready prepared, but certain Parisians do, and all along the Saône the fame of them is like that of whitebait at Greenwich. A *pauchouse* is composed of different kinds of fish and served in an abundant soup-like sauce on buttered *croutons*. It is an intermediate invention between the *matelotte* of the Lower Saône and the *bouille-abaisse* of Provence. Red wine is not used in it as in the

A Corner in Verdun.

matelotte, nor saffron as in the *bouille-abaisse*. White Burgundy is used, and the dish has a pale, golden colour, with an extremely delicate flavour. It is one of those excellent inventions, that have been found out by the common people. Neither *pauchouse*, nor *matelotte*, nor *bouille-abaisse*, was discovered by Parisian cooks or gourmets. The common fishermen on the Saône and the Rhône found these things out long ago. With their different kinds of fish, a bottle of white or red wine, some fresh butter from the nearest farm, some crusts of bread, and an acute culinary genius, those poor unknown men made their immortal discoveries.[1]

The Captain left by the afternoon train. We all accompanied him to the station. The Patron and the Pilot carried his small trunk, the boy his valise. He had a kind word for everybody on leaving, and everybody was a little affected at the separation. Franki could not endure it, but left the station by himself before the train came, and we noticed that he was wiping his eyes with the back of his hand.

"Monsieur Amandon,"[2] said the Pilot to me, "you will weep also."

"Pilot," I answered, "an Englishman never weeps, but when I get back to the *Boussemroum*, and see the Captain's tent empty, it is not impossible that my eyes may be just a little moist."

[1] All the boatmen on the Saône take an intelligent interest in the culinary art, and many of them excel in it. They know by tradition a considerable number of really excellent dishes, and they live quite as comfortably as any yachtsman need wish to live. Having been familiar with the opposite extreme of culinary ignorance and incompetence amongst the Scottish Highlanders, and also amongst some French peasants, I must say that the Saône boatmen have the best of it. In a wandering life a knowledge of cookery is independence. Without it you must either eat at the inns or live miserably when at a distance from them.

[2] My real name, in any pronunciation, was beyond the powers of both Pilot and Patron. At first they called me Ermenton, and afterwards, for some unknown reason, they invented Amandon, and used the two indifferently, as they found by experience that I answered to both. I think Amandon is rather a pretty name, prettier than my real one.

We have a feeling as if the whole expedition had collapsed with the Captain's departure. No human being could be more perfectly adapted to the share he took both in the business and the pleasure of the voyage. His watchful management left me without a care, free to give all my thoughts to my own work, and in my hours of rest and recreation he was always the same cheerful friend and companion. I hope and believe he enjoyed the voyage; as for the little hardships and inconveniences of our life on the *Boussemroum*, he only laughed at them.

"Monsieur Amandon," said the Patron to me when we got back to the boat after the Captain had left us, "it did me good to hear him and you always talking so pleasantly and merrily at table. How happy you were together, and how well you agreed, and how you always knew how to say the word that would make him laugh!"

The possibility of a disagreement between the Captain and me is so utterly unthinkable that I must have seemed unable to understand what the Patron was saying, so he went on:—

"What a pity it is that it should be so different with us here in our cabin!"

This is delicious!—the Patron laments the discord which is all his own making. I seized the opportunity and argued in favour of the Pilot throwing in a word of blame to make the rest acceptable. I even flattered the Patron by pointing out that there was a difference of education, and that it was for him, as the better educated man, to be tolerant of the faults of the other. Then he frankly admitted that the Pilot was a good fellow; but we shall see how he takes an order from him to-morrow.

Mr. Pennell and I visited the church. It has round-arched windows with stained glass, and a vast nave, quite realising the old idea of *la nef* (the ship[1]). It is all of wood with tie-beams, one vertical post resting on each beam, the whole of the arch being boarded. It is exactly like a ship turned upside down with the apse for a prow. On the altar were many candles glittering, yet not enough to dissipate the gloom in the great dark apse, on one side of which a black-robed priest sat silent in his stall, turning over a leaf of a large volume at almost regular intervals, this turning of the leaves being the only motion or sound in the whole edifice. There was an old-world quietness and solemnity in all this, full of repose for the mind after the noise

The Bridge at Verdun.

of modern life, or even after the mere echo of it in the newspapers.

On setting out for our evening walk we met two priests, who took off their hats with the greatest politeness, a salute that we returned ceremoniously. We met them a second time on our return, and then we took care to be the first to salute. After being treated as liars and spies we appreciate a mark of respect.

The evening was exquisitely still and beautiful, and we went to the suspension bridge over the Saône, from which we gazed a long time on the smooth, broad river, silvered here and there by faint breezes, and going far away into a misty distance, not a

---

[1] The French crusaders always called a ship a *nef*. Our own word *nave* is nearer the Latin *navis*, but only etymologists remember that it means a ship.

boat on the whole expanse of it except one creeping close to the shore with a woman sitting in it and a man poling, silent dark figures as in a picture.

LETTER XXXIII.

CHALON, *June 30th.*

Yesterday, June 29th, we had a fresh instance of the spy disquietude amongst the authorities. I had gone with Mr. Pennell to the island and left him there sketching. On my return to the *Boussemroum*, I found a gendarme in full uniform and two men in civil costume standing close to the boat and evidently waiting for me. One of the civilians presented himsel as the Justice of the Peace, and said that the other civilian was the greffier.[1] He asked to see my papers, and required an explanation of the fact that we were making plans, and of the general purposes of our voyage.

It is wonderful how rapidly we get accustomed to new situations. I have no doubt that if a man could be guillotined twice, the second time it would seem to him a trifling matter. I am already accustomed to being arrested as a spy, which gives me a great advantage. "My position," I said, "Mr. Justice of the Peace, is somewhat complicated, but I hope you will soon understand it. I have been arrested already at Pontailler as a spy, and at once applied by telegraph, through a Prefect, to the Minister of War, who accorded me his protection, yet I have nothing to produce in proof of it." This, in fact, was the peculiar embarrass-

---
[1] Something like a Town Clerk.

ment of my position. If I said I was not protected I told a falsehood, and if I said I was I seemed to be telling one, which, as the world goes, is considered a hundred times worse.

I was then questioned rather closely and my answers were taken down by the greffier. The gendarme meanwhile contented himself with looking on, not discourteously, but ready to arrest me when the Justice of the Peace should give the order. At length it occurred to me that perhaps if I showed the very brief telegram I had received from the Prefect of the Lower Alps it would at least prove that I had been in communication with the authorities, so I proposed to fetch it from the saloon. The Justice at once eagerly assented to this, and I perceived that he wished to penetrate into the interior of the *Boussemroum*. A moment's reflection convinced me that it would be imprudent to allow this. The telegram was in my table-bureau. I could not open that piece of furniture without displaying a quantity of manuscripts and memoranda, with maps and a mariner's compass, quite enough to arouse the suspicion of a Frenchman in these times, especially as the writings were in an unknown tongue.[1] I therefore went on board as fast as I could, and found to my dismay (there being not a moment to lose) that the Patron had laid the cloth for *déjeuner*, and all the things upon it. I had to remove these and find the telegram before the Justice could get in, and I knew he was following me. But here an unforeseen hindrance told effectually in my favour. His worship was a corpulent man, and the only access to the galley was by passing the hut on the narrow gunwale. My visitor found this

---

[1] Since then I see that a traveller has been arrested as a spy in Brittany and imprisoned by order of the Procurator, the evidences of his guilt being that he had *maps and a mariner's compass!*

passage very difficult, and soon the greffier and the gendarme, anxious for his safety, implored him to desist. I deeply regret to have missed this little scene, which must have been worthy of Charles Lever.

The telegram was as follows:—

"*Transmets télégramme Ministre Préfet Doubs.*"

It did not prove very much, but was accepted as evidence that I was not unknown to the authorities. After this I had a short but agreeable conversation with the Justice of the Peace, and he kindly recommended me, on arriving at a town, to go at once to the mayor and tell him who I was. "By taking this simple precaution," he said, "you will in future avoid all annoyance." I thanked him for his advice, which we shall certainly follow at Chalon, and we parted with the utmost politeness on both sides. The magistrate offered an apology for having disturbed us, but I answered that I was by this time clearly aware of the vigilance required by the new law.

Mr. Pennell had come back from his sketching in the midst of the colloquy. "I cannot understand," he said, "how you have the patience to go on reasoning with those men and answering all their questions." The truth is that interviews like those at Pontailler and Verdun are games of patience, and if you lose your temper you go to prison.[1]

[1] A newspaper correspondent at Verdun sent the following paragraph about us to the Chalon newspapers, from which it was copied by those of Mâcon and Lyons:—

"*Verdun sur le Doubs.*—Trois individus, un Anglais, un Américain, et un ancien officier français résidant en Alsace, ont été surpris levant le plan du barrage de la Saône, celui de la ville et des rives du Doubs et de la Saône. Interrogés par les autorités locales, ils ont déclaré être chargés d'une mission topographique (we said nothing of the kind) n'avoir pas de papiers, et être autorisés par le Ministère de la

After the civil authorities came the ecclesiastical. The two priests who had so politely saluted us the evening before approached the *Boussemroum* in a manner that implied curiosity mingled with discretion. I therefore went to meet them, and invited them to come on board and inspect our habitations. They were greatly interested in all the details of our establishment, and rather surprised by the comfort of that saloon which the magistrate had missed. Mr. Pennell kindly brought his drawings out of their hiding place. Our new friends—themselves untouched by the spy mania—were mightily amused by the history of our adventure at Pontailler, and the visit of the authorities at Verdun. Such is the opening effect of sympathy and kindness, that these two gentle ecclesiastics learned more about us and our labours in half an hour than the

Guerre. Le brigadier de la gendarmerie de Verdun est parti immédiatement pour Chalon demander des instructions à ses chefs et au parquet. Tout porte à croire que ce sont des espions."

I need hardly observe that we did not draw the weir at Verdun, which no artist would think of drawing.

A few days later, a Mâcon paper spoke of us quite positively as spies. A boat passed that place, drawn by a horse, and of a shape not common on the Saône. The name of this boat was painted upon it in foreign characters, and three men on board spoke a foreign language, which (of course) was German. "Cet incident," continued the Mâcon newspaper, "est à rapprocher de l'arrestation de trois espions à Verdun sur le Doubs, occupés à lever les rives de la Saône."

On the appearance of the first paragraph a military friend of mine was seriously asked if it were true. "Certainly," he replied, "but the case is even worse than it has been represented. Mr. Hamerton tried to force the stockade at Verdun in order to ascend the Doubs to ascertain whether, in case of war, the German artillery could not be brought down the *Saut du Doubs*." This is a celebrated waterfall over a vertical precipice on the Swiss frontier, in the wildest part of the river; however, such is the ready credulity of people during the prevalence of a spy mania, that the victim of this prodigious pleasantry believed and spread it abroad. I need hardly add that there is no stockade at Verdun, and that the *Boussemroum* is not a steam-ram to break through obstacles.

P

gendarmes could ever have extracted from us with all their questions.

After their departure I told the Pilot to take the *Boussemroum* to Chalon, and start immediately. As we had no other motive power than Zoulou, the Pilot said it would be necessary to take another man to hold a rope's end and manage the boat. By the time we were in motion I observed that this man had become two, but the Pilot informed me that the second was the son of the first, and would be content with a present. I had decided to let the Pilot have his own way in everything that day, as I was curious to see how he proposed to manage the *Boussemroum* on the Lower Saône.

The men began by towing the boat themselves. An attempt was made to land Zoulou, but he objected so strongly (as his plank went down into the water) that he had to be left in his stable. Afterwards he landed on the firm bank of the river.

The wind would have been delightful for a sailing-boat. The distance to Chalon, sixteen miles, would have been a run of two or three hours under canvas, but with the *Boussemroum* such a wind is an enemy. At first we went along sideways, independently of the men on shore, afterwards we were pushed against the right bank, which, fortunately, was soft in these parts with an abundance of rushes, so the boat did not stick fast as in the adventure above Gray, but rubbed along with enormous friction, the devoted Pilot standing at his post and receiving the thrusts of his pole in the chest, lance-like, after the good old manner. I need not add that our progress was as slow as it was painful. The men on shore worked most devotedly, and so did Franki and Zoulou.

Meanwhile I sat in my arm-chair in the saloon and meditated. My crew had been increased already at Corre by the addition of Franki, and here were two men more, making five in all, and we were accomplishing an average speed of about two miles an hour, without any of the pleasures of boating; on the contrary, it was misery to me to see the water rippled by such a fine sailing-breeze and know that I had a sailing-boat lying idle at Chalon. Here were we scraping along the bank, travelling literally with the greatest possible friction, when anything that could carry

canvas would have been going freely and merrily in mid-stream. The result of my reflections was, that the berrichon should stop at Chalon, and the crew be paid off, whilst the remainder of the voyage should be done on my own boat, the *Arar*.[1]

This being settled I offered Mr. Pennell a place on the *Arar*, but he honestly told me that, although he had taken part in a yachting expedition, he was not a practical sailor. Neither Franki nor the Pilot knows anything about sailing, so I determined to postpone

[1] The men could be discharged at Chalon without any breach of contract on my part. The contract was that I hired the berrichon and men for one month at least, and as much more as I chose to keep them, *subject to the condition of bringing them back to the port of Chalon*. Our arrival at this town left me, therefore, quite at liberty to terminate the engagement, but I could not have done so at Lyons, even if I had kept the *Boussemroum* a month longer.

the voyage of the *Arar* till I could have my own trained crew, which is composed of my eldest son and a nephew. It was finally decided that Mr. Pennell would visit the Lower Saône by himself, making use of the public steamer.

In consequence of this decision the rest of our voyage from Verdun to Chalon at once took a new character for us, and had rather a melancholy interest. With all their faults we had become attached to the *Boussemroum* and its crew, so that the last day on board seemed like the last in an old home. By an illusion common to all great changes in one's manner of life,

A Haystack.

our residence on the *Boussemroum*, from its novelty, had appeared much longer than the days marked on the almanack. To me it seemed three months since I had slept on shore.

The scenery between Verdun and Chalon is of a kind that is always pronounced uninteresting, but to me it is interesting from the extreme purity of its character, a purity that nothing mars. I always enjoy a strongly peculiar kind of scenery, whatever it is, provided there is nothing discordant. Here you have a broad, tranquil, almost currentless river, reach after reach of it, between soft green pastures, and with so few trees that the winds blow freely on its waters. Amidst these pastures, sometimes near the water, sometimes at a little distance, are quiet, prosperous looking villages, no longer with the fine character of those on the Upper Saône, but cheerful with all the evidences of well-being, all the houses and churches having a look of newness and of

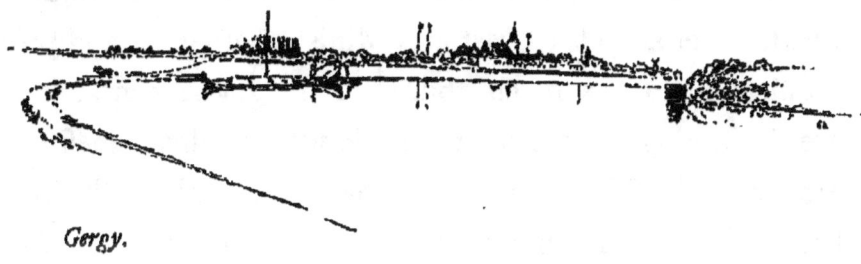

Gergy.

good repair. The appearance of such a village, from a distance is usually that of a thin line of white houses stretching on the green plain like an encampment, and crowned by the inevitable church steeple. One of them, Verjux, is connected with a romantic page of contemporary history. Some years ago a poor girl left that village as a laundress, and finally found herself in Paris, where she married a shopkeeper who afterwards died, and she now keeps the shop.

A Village in the Plain.

"Well," you will think, "my correspondent must be lamentably at a loss for materials to tell me such a commonplace story as that, and call it romantic! Such things happen every day." Yes, but there are small shopkeepers and great ones, just as there are little bankers and the Rothschilds. The young laundress of Verjux is to-day the queen of all the shopkeepers in the world, and maintains her royalty after a fashion of her own. She is famous for three things—her wonderful business abilities, her prodigious wealth, and her untiring kindness of heart. Her shop is as vast as a Ministry of State, and probably requires at least as much ability for its government, her coffers are like a king's treasury, and her kindness rains benefits on all around her.[1] She revisits, occasionally, the banks of the Saône on her way to her Mediterranean villa. I wonder if the Parisian lady can recall to memory the hopes and anxieties of the poor young laundress of Verjux!

Like Verjux, on the left bank of the river is the village of Allériot, that I mention because it is near a small hill, where formerly stood the Château Gaillard. The Seine was not the only river with a castle so proudly named, though I am not aware that history has anything to tell of the vanished Château Gaillard on the Saône. It has not been associated with such great events as the proud stronghold of King Richard that looks down upon Little Andelys.

As we passed Allériot, and for some time previously, the wind

---

[1] The lady alluded to in the text is Madame Boucicaut of the *Bon Marché*. Whilst these pages are in the press I hear of another of her good deeds. She has just given four millions of francs to the benefit fund of her employés, in addition to one million already given for the same purpose, and half a million for extra expenses. These large sums are talked of in the papers, but I have often heard, in conversation, of most efficacious help given by her quite unostentatiously to persons or institutions that she considered deserving. The best feature in her benevolence is not so much its vastness of scale as a thoughtful anxiety to produce the happiest results.

I add a line to this foot-note to say that since it was written Madame Boucicaut has undertaken to erect a bridge over the Saône at Verjux, which will cost her about £20,000.

had ceased, and the calm of evening had fallen upon the landscape. Poor Zoulou drew the *Boussemroum* with little difficulty, encouraged by Franki's cheery cry. Mr. Pennell and I sat on the deck with the distant view of Chalon before us, curiously reminding us of the approach to Paris by the Seine. The cathedral at Chalon has twin towers, which in the evening, and at a distance, may recall Notre Dame, and there are domes at Chalon as in the capital. With her many lights, and the

Allériot.

mystery of evening, Chalon had an appearance of vastness that impressed my fellow-traveller. There is no approach to a city that impresses one like coming slowly towards it on a broad and tranquil river in the late evening, when the stars are brightening in the sky, and the lamps show as little golden specks amidst the dark, uncountable houses, domes and towers rising in a stately way as landmarks above the confusion and the mystery. Then the lights brighten as we approach, they trail in long reflections upon the water, the houses seem taller and darker, the arches of the bridge become distinguishable, and the Pilot makes up his mind where he will moor his vessel.

It was not without mingled emotions of satisfaction and regret that we knew when the slow motion of the *Boussemroum* had ceased. Zoulou was brought on board, the Captain's tent was occupied by one of the new men, and Mr. Pennell used his for the last time. We were close to a band that played for dancers at the fair. It kept me awake in my hammock for a few minutes, during which I went through a short *examen de conscience*. "Have I done well," I asked myself, "to hire the *Boussemroum* for this voyage?" The answer was a decided "Yes, you have done wisely and well." The next question was, "Shall I ever hire a berrichon again?" and the answer came, with equal decision, "Never another berrichon!" I leave you to reconcile the contradiction if you can. For me it was soon reconciled in sleep.

LETTER XXXIV.

AUTUN, *July 10th*.

When the *Boussemroum* expedition had come to an end, the Mayor and Sub-Prefect of Chalon kindly gave Mr. Pennell a safe conduct, which made him independent of gendarmes within the limits of the *sous-préfecture*, and he was recommended to the Mayor of Tournus. At Mâcon he might consider himself safe also as the Prefect knew our history, but near Lyons the case was different, so we recommended him to take his safe conduct to the Préfecture there and try to get a *visa* with permission to sketch. This being refused, Mr. Pennell returned northwards and observed that, whether by accident or design, there was a gendarme in the same railway carriage. It had been believed by the authorities at Chalon that with their recommendation there could be no difficulty at Lyons. The result showed the extreme stringency with which the recent law is enforced.

Evidently, under the circumstances, Mr. Pennell could not work in that very interesting part of the Saône which is within a myriamètre (six miles and one-fifth) of the detached forts that are themselves far in advance of Lyons, in fact, it was not safe for him to work much below Mâcon. It was therefore impossible for Mr. Pennell to complete his task. The intense—almost intolerable—heat was another obstacle. Mr. Pennell had exposed himself to the full glare of the sun during a long walk between Tournus and Mâcon which had produced bad effects, and he returned to England to recruit.[1]

Franki had been engaged as Mr. Pennell's personal servant to accompany him down the river. The lad was better dressed than before, and his new master gave him a fine hat. Franki had also acquired the art of brushing his hair, and even of parting it, wherein he attained a temporary success by a plentiful application of pure water. As soon as the water dried the strong and vigorous crop resumed its ancient ways.

The Patron did *not* take Franki into permanent service as a donkey-driver, so after his short engagement with Mr. Pennell

---

[1] Mr. Pennell needed rest for another reason. He had worked too much on the Upper Saône. I never met with an artist who equalled him in industry, but, although I sometimes told him that he was doing more than his duty required, the Upper Saône had such an attraction for him that he was led to overwork himself by the pure artistic passion. An interval of rest was therefore necessary. He soon recovered in England.

the lad returned to his mother at Jonvelle, where no doubt he has narrated the voyage of the *Boussemroum* in terms more lively than these letters. I cannot give you any recent news of the Patron. When last I saw him he was in a rage, probably because I had submitted his pecuniary demands to arbitration. After the settlement of these he wanted to do a little business by selling me the *Boussemroum* for £24. It had originally cost £120, but the bargain tempted me not. Our expedition was the last of the Patron's voyages. He intends to pass the remnant of his days on land, somewhere in George Sand's country.

My last glimpse of Zoulou was when the *Boussemroum*, all my things having been removed, was taken back into the canal. Zoulou pushed the door of his stable open, according to his wont, and observed the scene that was familiar to him with an expression of tranquil satisfaction. After a minute of contemplation he allowed the door to close, and I beheld his intelligent countenance no more.

Zoulou's Farewell.

LETTER XXXV.

AUTUN, *August 24th.*

Since my last letter I have been endeavouring to obtain from the French authorities a kind of passport, giving permission to sketch, with the following result.

The authorities, from the French War Office downwards, have been uniformly most courteous, and I willingly acknowledge that I have been treated with the consideration due to the subject of a friendly Sovereign. Not one of my letters has been left without a reply, and in every instance the reply has been considerate. Nevertheless, whilst fully appreciating the form of these communications, I have, at the same time, had the opportunity of admiring the extreme skill with which the different French authorities parried all my attempts to procure, directly or indirectly, anything resembling a written permission to draw.

Let me admit at once that in my view the Government of a country has a right to forbid drawing if it pleases. An artist has no property in the landscapes of a country that he visits—certainly a foreign artist can have no claims whatever. A Frenchman might perhaps think it a hardship not to be permitted to draw the landscapes of his native land.

I have always been quite willing to obey any interdiction coming from the higher authorities. They had only to say, "Drawing from nature is not permitted to foreigners in France," and I was ready to go elsewhere.

They have, however, very carefully avoided any interdiction

of this kind, and they have taken equal care not to grant any explicit permission to draw. I therefore still remain exposed to the penalty of a year's imprisonment with a fine of a thousand francs if I draw within "un rayon d'un myriamètre autour d'une place forte, d'un poste, ou d'un établissement militaire ou maritime à partir des ouvrages avancés."[1]

Now it so happens that all the river Saône, from a point about two miles above Trévoux—in other words, all the most beautiful part of the Saône—is within a myriamètre[2] either of the fort on the *Mont d'Or*, or of the forts on the outskirts of Lyons. If I draw at all in that part of the river everything will depend upon the interpretation of my drawings. Are they *opérations de topographie?* Yes, and no. An artist's drawing is not really topographic, but it may easily be described as such, and he cannot prove that it is not. I do not see any legal issue from the difficulty.

In case of arrest, therefore, I have nothing to rely upon but the British ambassador's passport and a special recommendation from our *Chargé d'Affaires* written in the French language for the gendarmes. But the law of 1886 does not say that a passport is sufficient. On the contrary, it expressly requires an "autorisation de l'autorité militaire ou maritime."

There is, however, in the correspondence of different French authorities with me a kind of unexpressed permission. They will not give a licence to draw, but they know that I am going to draw, and they do not forbid it. The Minister of the Interior and the Prefect of Saône-et-Loire have recommended

---

[1] Loi du 18 Avril, 1886.
[2] Ten thousand mètres (about six miles and one fifth).

me to carry a passport. The *Chef de Cabinet* at the War Office has told me that the Prefect of the Lower Alps is empowered to facilitate my studies. The Prefect, however, will not venture to assume this responsibility outside of his own department, which is not traversed by the Saône.

My position is perfectly clear. I shall be liable to arrest, and legally liable to a year's imprisonment, but as I am known at the War Office and the Ministry of the Interior, and also to several Prefects, I shall, if arrested, be speedily released. To be arrested and detained for a day, as at Pontailler, is not a very terrible misfortune, but it is an annoyance. Even to have to answer a long interrogatory by a Justice of the Peace, as at Verdun, is a trial of patience and a waste of time. Worse than this, the gendarmes in a country place may take you with them to a town before your innocence is established.

LETTER XXXVI.

CHALON-SUR-SAÔNE,
August 25th.

You will remember that this is the place where the voyage of the *Boussemroum* came to an end. I am now making arrangements for the second voyage, that of my own boat, the *Arar*, which is to travel over the Lower Saône from Chalon to the Île Barbe, immediately above Lyons.

My former companions and crew are all dispersed. Captain Kornprobst is far in the north-east, in the department of the Meuse, where he is very busily occupied in fishing and boat-building.

Mr. Pennell is drawing English cathedrals, and the crew of the *Boussemroum* are scattered I know not where. Those who lived together on that vessel, so strangely associated with their different ages, different occupations, different nationalities, are separated never to meet again, and that voyage seems hardly real, even to me, who remember all the details of it so clearly, but I remember them like the details of a dream. To convince myself of its reality I have to refer to some place such as Chemilly or Port-sur-Saône and ask myself how I came to know that place so well. Even my presence at Chalon makes the voyage more difficult to realise. The *Boussemroum* is neither by the quay nor in the canal, not even the big Pilot is here to connect the present with the past.

The crew of the *Arar* is with me here. It is composed of my eldest son, Stephen, aged twenty-seven, and my nephew, Maurice Pelletier, aged eighteen. They are both very strong and active young men, excellent swimmers, and ready for any emergency on a boat. As they are well acquainted with the *Arar* and her peculiarities, they make a more efficient crew than two sailors of greater general experience. For this particular reason, although they are only amateurs, the voyage will go more smoothly with them than with any professional boatmen. After the noisy and rebellious disposition of the Patron, I look forward with pleasure to the silent alacrity with which everything is done on board our little schooner.

The *Arar* is not yet quite ready for sea—or river—she has been lying here for nearly a year, and has to be put in sailing order. New cordage is amongst her requirements, and whilst Stephen is splicing his ropes—for we have to do our own rigging here—I will give you some account of Chalon, which was left entirely and purposely undescribed during the voyage of the *Boussemroum*.

In its present condition Chalon strikes the visitor as being a very modern town with but few remnants of the Middle Ages, and nothing whatever of Roman times. There was, however, an important Gaulish town here before Cæsar came to the place. It cannot have presented any architectural splendours, as the architecture of the Gauls was limited to low houses with thatched roofs, in fact, it was scarcely more advanced than that

The Bridge from the North.

of the Central African tribes of to-day. But the Gauls knew how to erect very strong fortifications of a kind that is well known to us, composed of earthworks, stones without mortar, and logs of wood ingeniously placed and nailed together, a composite work that had really a formidable power of resistance. A Gaulish city, though poor in appearance, might be by no means despicable as a storing place for provisions, and we know that Cæsar made use of Chalon for this purpose.

As for the first beginnings of the Gaulish city nothing is known because the Gauls had no historians, but we may legitimately suppose that the embryo of a riverside city would be a pre-historic fishing village. There are two islands opposite Chalon, the Saône being divided into three channels here, or we might describe it as a broad basin in which two islands are situated. If these existed in pre-historic times it is probable that they determined the choice of the site, just as Paris is now situated where it is because there are islands in the Seine. When the insular habitations became crowded the town would extend to the mainland, and spread itself there.

After the Roman occupation the Gaulish town was replaced by the Gallo-Roman city of Cabillonum. The size of Cabillonum is well known, as the local architects have traced its walls, indeed a Roman wall existed still as the defence of the town so recently as the fifteenth century, though at that time it had become much dilapidated, and was replaced by a new fortification of a greater circumference. Some fragments of this wall are still in existence, hidden amongst the modern houses, but there are no visible Roman antiquities except in the museum; there is nothing at Chalon to compare with the long Roman wall and the gates still existing at Autun, or with the yet grander remains at Arles and Nîmes. We have some historical evidence that there were fine public buildings in Cabillonum, and there is good archæological evidence of Roman country houses in the neighbourhood, villas adorned with marbles and mosaics. Cabillonum was used as a quarry when the mediæval Chalon was substituted for it, and some of its adornments were carried to a distance, for example, M. Niepce tells us that in 1001 "the Abbot William collected, amongst the Roman remains at Chalon, a quantity of rare marbles, with which he built the rotunda of St. Bénigne at Dijon."

There is one tradition of classic times still preserved in the hearts of the Chalonese. They venerate the memory of the Emperor Probus, which may induce the reader to believe that probity, bravery, and moderation are particularly held in honour at Chalon. They may be so, but the especial reason why Probus, "vere probus," is honoured on the banks of the Saône is because by his encouragement the vine was first cultivated here. M. Niepce says that the Chalonese are not yet grateful enough to their Imperial benefactor, that they ought to rebuild the altars of Bacchus and sacrifice a white heifer, and set up a statue to Probus, whilst shattering that of Domitian, who uprooted the vines under pretext that the heads of the Chalon folks were hot enough by natural constitution.

Our railways lead us to undervalue the ancient arrangements for communication, but such a place as Cabillonum was almost as well situated in Roman times as it is to-day. It was the northern head of the river navigation extending to Arles; it was the seat of the river superintendent,[1] and for land traffic it was exactly at the intersection of two important roads.

I have already mentioned the interesting fact that two towns on the Saône, Auxonne and Trévoux, have been at one period of their history capitals of small independent States. A third town on the same river, Chalon, has also been a capital, but of a very great and important State. After Hlotair's death (A.D. 561) his empire was divided, and Burgundy was the share of his son, Gontran. The Burgundian kingdom of the sixth century was vastly more extensive than the Burgundian duchy of a later period. From north to south it included Sens and Avignon, if not Arles; on the west it included part of the Loire, and on the east

---

[1] Praefectus navium araricarum.

it embraced the lakes of Geneva and Neuchâtel and extended almost to the glacier of the Rhône. This kingdom was about the size of England, and Chalon was its capital. Augustin Thierry, in his delightful *Récits des Temps Mérovingiens*, tells us *à propos* of King Gontran one of the best stories that have come down to us from the Middle Ages. Haribert, King of Paris, and brother of Gontran, having died unexpectedly when away from home, his wife Theodehild consulted her own interests by laying hands on the royal treasure, and, recommending herself by so rich a dowry, offered herself in marriage to King Gontran, who seemed delighted by the charming proposal. "By all means," was the message he sent in answer; "let Queen Theodehild come to Chalon with her treasure, and on her arrival I will marry her, and she shall be a greater queen than ever." The august widow, on receiving this reply, set forth at once from Paris to Chalon with her well-stored baggage waggons, and when she arrived the contents were carefully inventoried and put in store. Then said the king to his councillors: "Would it not be better that this treasure should belong to *me* rather than to this woman who was unworthy to be my brother's wife?" Of course they were of the royal opinion, and Gontran forwarded the lady under escort all the way to a monastery at Arles, where she was quietly put in seclusion.

Many a fortune-hunter has said to himself, "Ah, if I could only have the fortune without the lady!" King Gontran realised this desire. Philosophers tell us that man is always endeavouring to sever the sweets from the bitters of life, and never succeeding. Did not Gontran succeed in this?

Whatever may have been the importance of Cabillonum, and of the early mediæval Chalon that was visited by Charlemagne, that city was entirely destroyed by Lothair a thousand years ago, and all its inhabitants massacred.

In the early history of mediæval Chalon we find it governed by Counts, who were first merely lieutenants of the kings, but afterwards raised themselves into petty sovereigns. William the Second, twelfth Count of Chalon, a cruel tyrant, was punished for his misdeeds in a terrible manner. Being seated at a high festival "with a luxury like that of Vitellius or Heliogabalus," he was appalled by the arrival of a supernatural visitant, having the appearance of a man riding a black horse with fiery eyes. At a sign from this unknown personage the Count left the daïs and mounted behind him, when the animal immediately rose in the air and rushed off into infinite space. One cry of despair from the victim, and he was never more heard or seen, but none believed that the swift steed had been sent to fetch him to Paradise.

It is probable that Chalon was never so richly and completely picturesque as in the fifteenth and sixteenth centuries. As one of the most important towns in the Duchy of Burgundy, it was fortified anew with walls and towers, the present cathedral was finished, and there were fourteen churches, whereas at the present day there are but two, and one of them is modern. There existed, also, an old Abbey on the highest ground, and there was a picturesque fortified bridge across the Saône. If only the Chalon of those days could have been preserved till the present, if only it could have been gently and tenderly repaired, and not destroyed by vandalism and revolution! By an effort of architectural science a city of that quality may almost be reconstructed. Viollet-le-Duc could have made a hard architectural drawing of some town built with equal richness of fifteenth-century invention, and then told us that Chalon was, if not that, at any rate similar to that. But the difference between all such resuscitations and the reality is that the sun does not shine upon them; the cloud-shadows do not fall upon them; they do not take their place in the life of the land and the river. The real Chalon of those days reflected her hundred towers in the gentle summer Saône, and in the winter the angry floods washed against her walls and made her seem like a great stronghold in the sea.

Chalon, the Bridge, A.D. 1600.

Our desire would be to live near such a city long enough to see her under a thousand aspects, clear in the splendour of hottest noon, with her gilded vanes bright against the blue, dark in the solemnity of the twilight, mysterious under the moon.

In the sixteenth century Chalon was fortified anew by royal command, to the intense dissatisfaction of the inhabitants, but the conditions of warfare had changed, and the art of fortification with them. After that, the beauty of the mediæval town appears to have been gradually more and more completely effaced till we come to the prosaic modern way of building. Nor has the Renaissance left any beautiful work as a compensation. There are old towns in France, such as Blois, for example, where the Renaissance artists have made it difficult to regret the destructive change of fashion that made room for them, but it is not so at Chalon.

Place du Châtelet, Chalon.

On the right hand, as you descend the river towards the bridge, stand the twin towers of the cathedral, substantial and, alas! likely to last as examples of modern Gothic. Unhappily a great material mistake of this kind is *never* rectified. All the vulgar would cry out if so much excellent masonry, worth so many francs the square mètre, were demolished for a mere question of art.[1]

[1] The old towers, according to M. Chevrier, were unlike each other and unworthy of the nave, yet still preferable to these which were erected between 1827 and 1851.

The interior of the cathedral has been restored, but not spoiled like the west front. Without deserving a place amongst the great French cathedrals, it is a fine church of the fifteenth century. The architecture is simple, and the arches do not impress the imagination by height, but the capitals are well carved, and the windows rich in stained glass.

The square before the cathedral which serves as the market-place must have been perfect with the old front and towers. Even yet the old gabled houses retain the character they had in the sixteenth century, and the square is delightful on a fine morning in summer when the market-women are selling fruit and vegetables, helping to make a picture full of colour, and rich in vigorous contrasts of light and dark.

During the last hundred years the destruction of old Chalon has been accelerated by modern improvements, yet there are still some relics for those who know where to look for them. At the back of the cathedral is a courtyard with the Deanery Tower of the fifteenth century, exquisitely elegant both in general design and in its details, and close to the base of this tower you enter two long Gothic galleries, or corridors, meeting at a right angle.

One of these is now a chapel, but they were formerly an open cloister looking on a garden or close.

The most remarkable of the mediæval courtyards is one in the Rue aux Prêtres, with open galleries and a turret. The galleries are on the first and second stories, and entirely constructed in massive oak with good architectural panelling. The inhabitants increase the beauty of the colour by flowering plants, and I have seen a delightful effect produced by coloured clothes that the women hung out to air. There is a tradition not sustained by any evidence, that Charles the Bold of Burgundy stayed in this house during his visits to Chalon.

Chalon, the Deanery Tower.

A few towers are still preserved at Chalon, independently of the churches. There is La Tour de Coco-Louvrier perched high on a hidden fragment of Roman wall near the river, and believed to have been originally a military observatory.[1] There is also

[1] Coco-Louvrier was an eccentric personage still living at the beginning of the present century, a money lender (said to have been also a gold-sweater), who dwelt in the narrow tower.

the old belfry tower, preserved when the Hôtel de Ville was destroyed.

Rue St. Vincent, Chalon.

St. Peter's Church, south of the bridge, is a specimen of ugly Renaissance built just at the beginning of the eighteenth century. For me Renaissance architecture roughly classes itself under

Chalon, Place de l'Hôtel de Ville, Flooded.

three heads. 1. The elegant. 2. The cold. 3. The ugly. The first I am never weary of admiring, the second chills and repels me like a stiff corpse, the third produces very mixed feelings, its ugliness being often made strangely tolerable by qualities of a merely picturesque order. I should hardly attempt to draw the elegant Renaissance, it is too beautiful in its delicate accuracy, nor would any artist care to draw the cold Renaissance, it is too dull and unrewarding, but the rough and ugly Renaissance is sometimes very tempting if you have a box of water-colours. This is the character of St. Pierre at Chalon. The lofty domed church is a good subject in its picturesque, irregular Place, with houses of all heights and of the most various character. In the greatest floods of the Saône, this Place is inundated and the people go about, not exactly in gondolas, but in flat-bottomed boats. If there were but gondolas at such times the Place de l'Hôtel de Ville would be a little Venice, and under fine effects it must present most striking and interesting pictures.

LETTER XXXVII.

CHALON-SUR-SAONE,
August 27th.

My boat, the *Arar*, wintered at Chalon last year in charge of the only sea-sailor in the place, who left her high and dry in a time of flood, and as river-floods do not occur with the punctuality of ocean-tides, we have been obliged to launch her, not an easy operation, for the boat was on very rough and irregular ground. However, being within the inclosure[1] of the Blanzy

---

[1] By the kind permission of M. Morin, who for many years has superintended the affairs of this important company at Chalon and on the river. Many boating men

Coal Company, which has a building-yard and a fleet of steam-tugs and barges, I had only to ask for seven or eight men to help us. Some of these were very powerful, fine-looking fellows, so the launch made quite a picture. I was greatly pleased with the careful and attentive manner in which the men followed my instructions, and also with their perfect good humour, but the difficulties only seemed to amuse them. After considerable effort we moored the boat to a place where the incline was more regular, and then it went briskly to the water on rollers.

I had occasion to admire the courage of my nephew Maurice. We found that wasps were numerous about the boat so he discovered a nest under a part of the deck that could be removed. He took up this part with the nest under it and walked coolly down to the river, his head in a yellow cloud of wasps. Then he deliberately plunged the nest in the water and escaped without one sting.

I need not trouble you with the details of what we had to do upon the boat. The evil of Chalon is that there are no professional builders of sailing boats. Steam-launches are built here, and even torpedo-boats, but if a little yacht has to be rigged the owner must do it himself. We are not afraid of the work, except as a cause of delay. A certain sympathy with material things is required for work on a boat; you must love cordage, and wood, and metal. I have this kind of instinct by nature, and so has my son Stephen. He has a peculiar affinity for cordage, and can pass a whole day quite happily in splicing

have had good reason to feel grateful to that gentleman for his unfailing urbanity and kindness. His thorough knowledge of the English language will make him one of the readers of this volume, and I am not sorry to have this opportunity for thanking him. We have never met with anything but civility and attention from the men in the building-yard, and all our things have been quite safe in their keeping.

ropes; he can make fishing nets, too, and hammocks, so that although I select and purchase cordage myself I leave its details to him. My specialty is more in planing and filing, in short, in fitting things, and in seeing that everything will act properly and conveniently when called upon. Maurice has the valuable quality of being always ready to lend a hand when required. This he does with the most cheerful alacrity, as if an order were a pleasure to him.

When you start from a port where there is a yacht-builder, and when you have professional sailors on board your craft you are above the necessity for manual labour, but in our case we must always be prepared for it. We really enjoy being hard at work in a building-yard in our shirt-sleeves; it is good for both body and mind. In my own case the manual labour connected with boating and boat-building has been a source of amusement and of health. I could not recommend it to every one, as the natural instinct must be there to give it the necessary zest, but for those who have the instinct there is no medicine comparable to it, especially when, as in my own case, the passion for field sports is wanting.

I value manual labour for another reason, which is that it gives us a sympathy with and an interest in so much of the common work that is done in the world. A building-yard is, for me, quite as interesting as a picture gallery. Here, for example, is still practised the old craft of building the great river barges. The construction of these barges is apparently very rude, yet in reality it is most skilful. A vast quantity of good oak timber goes into one of them, and it is used with clever economy, the irregularly shaped planks being made to fit each other with a minimum of loss. The work is so good of its kind that these boats are remarkably free from leakage. They are caulked with moss fixed between the planks by thin iron clamps of which millions must be used. I learned that it is impossible to make these clamps by machinery as every one of them has to be hammered in a particular manner on an anvil. An English critic might be tempted to despise such boat-building as out of date and unscientific, but it is in reality a survival of ruder times *which stands the test of science.* There is science enough at

Chalon from the Little Creusot.

Chalon, considering that torpedo-boats are on the stocks in the next yard, at the "Petit Creusot." As rough and cheap weight-carriers there are no boats superior to the old-fashioned Saône barges, but they may be eventually replaced by a new class of vessel now coming quickly into favour, the steam-barge, built of steel, and going four miles an hour when laden.

The overlooker and I had a conversation about the building of the smaller boats which are used as cock-boats for the barges. I argued (from experience on the *Boussemroum*) that they were needlessly heavy, and, in fact, their weight is enormous. He maintained the necessity for the great oaken knees in them and said that, on account of the rough work, such boats "*avaient besoin de quelquechose de confortable.*"

I found an ingenious joiner in the yard whom I knew personally already. He is a clever amateur sailor and was now occupied in building, during leisure hours only, a scientific sailing-boat for his own use in the Chalon regattas. You will at once infer that his vessel is made of wood. No, she is entirely of steel, which gives the builder all the relief of a change of work, and the pleasure of practical amateurship. I was much surprised to see how completely he had overcome the great technical difficulty of hammering the steel plates, so as to give them the proper curves, which are exceedingly complex. Happy and unhappy mortal! Enviable in the possession of the most delightful of all hobbies, pitiable in this, that the ideal of the amateur boat-builder is never, and can never be, attained![1]

When my boat was in the water I noticed that the men were preparing to launch a great barge, sideways, according to their custom. In answer to a question from me the overlooker said that there was no hurry to get the *Arar* out of the way; however, I thought differently and poled her to a safe place. No sooner was my boat in safety than the barge came rushing down exactly where she had been, and set up a great wave.

[1] I asked him why, being a joiner, he had not preferred wood to steel as more in his way. His answer is worth quoting, he said: "A joiner knows the defects of wood too intimately to think of using it for a boat." Steel is certainly preferable in places like Chalon where the summers are extremely hot. A beautiful little sailing yacht was in the yard at the same time with the *Arar*. She was of wood, the *Arar* is of steel. When the wooden boat was put on the water (though newly painted) she sank to the bottom. The *Arar*, which had been out of the water much longer, of course floated as usual.

There is now a whole fleet of steam-tugs and barges in that place, doing nothing, because the Saône is at its lowest, and the navigation is stopped whilst the sluices are all open, and the civil engineers are repairing the works all along the river. The commercial navigation is therefore suspended for the present. The crowd of boats near the building-yard is so dense that the *Arar* is completely imprisoned by them, and will not be able to get out unless the large boats make way for her.

Chalon, the Hospital.

Besides this the heat is so intense that it would not be safe to row on the shadeless river in the daytime—it would be deliberately courting sunstroke. Sailing is out of the question, as there is not a breath of wind. However, we cannot remain indefinitely at Chalon, so I have decided to do our travelling by night. There is no moon, but we have an intimate knowledge of the river, and there will be " the pale light of stars."

Before we leave, let us look at the island where the building-yard is situated. This yard is inclosed with high palings and is itself extremely picturesque in the interior, as such places often are, but beyond the palings there is a superb avenue under which there happens just at present to be a large military encampment of white bell tents, and the place is guarded by sentinels who challenge us every time we pass. Behind this avenue is the hospital, originally a very remarkable building of the sixteenth century. Only a small part of the old hospital remains, but the modern one that has replaced it is rather a fine structure with an elegant dome, that produces a pretty effect above the noble masses of trees. The rest of the island contains some streets but no building of any artistic or archæological interest. There is, however, a poetic interest in the road across the island, for it leads straight to St. Marcel, only a mile and a-half from here, and St. Marcel is the spot where Abélard was first buried. His bones now rest at Père-la-Chaise by the side of Héloïse.

During our work in the yard, we received a visit from a tall and powerfully built gentleman, who sat down on a log of wood and criticised the set of our sails. As a general rule, one pays little attention to critics, but here is one who knows all about his subject. There are now some thoroughly scientific amateur boat designers, and M. Vitteaut is one of them. Surely no man ever had the natural instincts and gifts of the ship-builder in greater strength. M. Vitteaut was as plainly intended by nature for a ship-builder, as a born artist is for painting, and being a rich man with abundant leisure he has gone into the whole subject scientifically and knows, perhaps, as much about it as any one, at least so far as small yachts are concerned. He is clever, too, with those brown, strong hands of his, and can plane a mast and rig a vessel and even sew her sails. His greatest happiness in life is first to design a sailing-boat, then have her built under his own eyes, not too rapidly, and finally to satisfy himself that she has good nautical qualities. After that he very seldom makes any further use of a boat, but being extremely good-natured he willingly lends, or even gives, his vessels to others, and in this way does much to promote a taste for boating on the Saône. His yacht, the *Falourde*, is both swift and commodious, but too large and heavy to be quite convenient on a river. She would be more at home on one of the great lakes.[1]

Before leaving Chalon, a few words are due to the remarkably open and courteous ways of the inhabitants towards strangers, These manners are traditional. In the sixteenth century Saint-Julien said they were "gracieux, de franc et bon cœur envers ceux qui abordent leur ville." In the eighteenth century, the historian Courtépée said that these manners had been preserved down to his own time. " Ils ont conservé cet aimable caractère de politesse et de générosité qui rend le séjour de leur ville délicieux aux étrangers." I gladly join my own testimony to these. Some years ago I was quite surprised by the remarkably open and pleasant nature of the Chalon people, and their happiness in making themselves agreeable or useful to a stranger, but now I am surprised no longer, because I know that this amenity is natural to them and in their blood.

[1] M. Vitteaut is deservedly President of the Chalon Regattas. He has done more than any one both for sailing and boat-building on the Saône. By always having his boats constructed on the spot he has encouraged and advanced the art there, and others have followed his example. M. Brunet-Meige, of Chalon, is now quite an accomplished builder of steam yachts, and also of sailing boats in steel so far as their hulls are concerned. I mention his name with the greater pleasure that it was he who built the *Arar* after my designs. At Chalon steel hulls are all the fashion.

LETTER XXXVIII.

Port d'Ouroux,
August 30th, Morning.

The *Arar* set out on her voyage from the quay near the statue of Niepce at Chalon. It is a very beautiful quay, with steps of immense width going down to the water, a stately, convenient place like the quays in the pictures of Claude. The Queen of Sheba might have embarked there with all her retinue. In this respect the modern town far excels the walled stronghold of the middle ages.

The starlight was at first so feeble that we could see nothing on the river. Some barges were moored along the shore and we were conscious of their existence as great, indefinite, dark objects, but we could not easily guess our real distance from them. We had to pass under a railway bridge and I could not see all the piers with the naked eye, but just made them out with the binocular. At this moment a flash of lightning showed one pier most distinctly, so I was able to take my bearings.

Stephen and Maurice were at the oars, there being not a breath of wind. I may tell you that the *Arar* was designed simply for convenience in river travelling, and is not at all a regatta boat. You will become familiarised with her different qualities as the voyage proceeds, but just now I ask you to notice three points. We start, as you see, to row the whole distance to the next port, so that although the *Arar* is a sailing boat, able to bear the stress of 260 square feet of canvas in a strong breeze and much more in a light one, she can be propelled with oars in a calm. I may add that the arrangements for rowing are convenient and have received especial attention. There is nothing to interfere with the oarsmen who have their full liberty of action unimpeded by the sailing gear.

Another convenience is that we are never obliged to lower a mast or even a gaff when passing under a bridge. The height of the masts is under nineteen feet, which in summer gives us the freedom of all the bridges on the Saône.

The third convenience is that we only draw fifteen inches of water, and are consequently not confined to the deep channels. Low masts and a light draught of water mean liberty in river navigation. I know that a tall mast may be lowered and formerly had a boat on which this was necessary, but it is troublesome to have to stop for that, and the sails, just at the very moment when you want them to sail through the bridge, are converted into a vexatious encumbrance.[1]

These prejudices of mine against deep keels and tall masts have reference to river navigation only. I should prefer a different type of boat if I had the great luxury of deep water and nothing between it and the stars.

After leaving Chalon and its lights behind us, we soon came into the open country, and the great curves of the river, which just here is very serpentine, made the town seem already remote. We were soon in complete silence and calm except that now and then we could hear some peasant driving a cart on a distant road, and singing as he went, the sounds coming to us with that strange distinctness combined with distance that they have in the night time when Nature is at rest.

The lightning which at the moment of starting seemed to

---

[1] Another objection is that the mast must be down when you are towed behind a steamer, and nothing can be more awkward than a mast all along a boat's deck.

promise a storm, had now entirely ceased and the clouds which had been so vividly illuminated by it had now all sunk beneath the southern horizon, so that the entire expanse of heaven was splendid with innumerable stars. Their light was certainly a great help to us as it enabled us to distinguish clearly between the star-studded water and the obscure shores, but the land was mere darkness with an indefinite edge and we could not make out anything even with the help of the binocular. The power of a night-glass in *lighting up* obscure detail is most evident in twilight.

The lantern we had on board (which I kept well behind me to accustom my eyes to the starlight) was a subject of wonder to the invisible inhabitants of a house on the right bank. From the distance we had travelled I knew this place to be Port Guillot which is close to the village of Lux, about half a mile inland, a place that I never pass without thinking of two very dissimilar personages.

The first is the Emperor Constantine. You know, of course, the legend about the apparition of the cross in heaven and the words "In hoc vince," or "In hoc signo vinces," indeed, I believe the original words are said to have been Greek. You know, also, that Constantine adopted the cross for his standard or "labarum," afterwards. Well, if the incident ever occurred, tradition, and history registering tradition, have fixed the scene precisely here on the right bank of the Saône in the land round the village of Lux. During our starlight voyage nothing appeared in the heavens but the familiar constellations that had shone exactly in the same way for the earliest of all earthly navigators, yet by a very slight effort of imagination, one might see with closed eyes the celestial cross of Constantine. Indeed the natural forms of clouds are so various that a bright cloud may easily have assumed for a moment some resemblance to a cross. This, however, is mere sceptical criticism. In the poetical mood we believe in all beautiful legends and this legend is incomparable in its grandeur. What magnificent elements! A Roman Emperor is riding with his host in battle array and suddenly there appears a miraculous sign in heaven that he takes for his victorious standard! Can anything be grander than that? Could any legend more ennoble this somewhat dull and commonplace scenery on the banks of the Saône at Lux?

The next association with Lux is quite of a different order. It has neither antiquity nor the rank of a great personage to recommend it, and yet there are good reasons for supposing that it will be remembered in the most distant ages. The father of photography, Nicéphore Niepce, made his experiments at Lux and there succeeded in fixing the photographic image. You will remember that the voyage of the *Arar* began from the quay at Chalon where the statue of Niepce now stands. I need not go into details about the origin of photography in this letter but may say briefly that the common opinion which attributes the invention to Daguerre is erroneous. Niepce was the inventive genius, Daguerre the commercial partner who brought the invention to the knowledge of the public and gave the Daguerrotype his name. Inventors have often aimed at marvellous results and attained them, but surely no quest could be more exciting than this eager hope that the image in a silvered mirror might be kept after the departure of the original! These banks of Saône have seen much that is memorable in the history of mankind, they have been visited by Julius Cæsar, by Augustus, by Constantine, Charlemagne, Napoleon, but which of all these conquerors ever made so *permanent* a conquest as this ? The Roman Empire is split into fragments, the Empire created by the sword of Napoleon is a tale that is told, but the results of those researches and experiments made at Lux are independent of all frontiers and will endure with the civilisation of the race.

How recent it all is! When the statue of Niepce was unveiled a little time since at Chalon his widow was living yet, in her old age.[1]

It is a strange coincidence that the name of the place where Niepce worked was Light (Lux), and one name of the triumphant worker was Nicéphore, the victorious, the bearer of the prize (νικηφόρος.)

It is time, however, to return to our voyage on the *Arar*, which, you will think, is getting forward very slowly. Yes, slowness is one of its principal characteristics, and one of its great superiorities over ordinary hurrying from place to place.

Some time after leaving Port Guillot we came to a dead stop with the intention of having our supper, as the preparations for departure had caused us to omit the ceremony of dining altogether.

---

[1] The statue is well situated in a place forming three sides of a square, the fourth being open towards the Saône. The face looks straight in the direction of Mont Blanc, sometimes clearly visible from thence. The inventor, with a gesture a little too emphatic, has brought his right arm across his breast to point to the camera at his left. The sculptor worked for nothing, animated by no motive more selfish than the desire to express in lasting bronze his respect for a great man's memory. If every human being who has had occasion to be grateful to the discoverer of photography had contributed to this work the sculptor might have been royally remunerated, and the statue instead of bronze, might have been of silver and gold.

There is a museum at Chalon for the preservation of antiquities and pictures, but it possesses one treasure that is absolutely unique, a glass case containing the apparatus with which Niepce made his immortal experiments, and some plates engraved by him which are the earliest specimens of heliogravure.

It is one of my rules always to have the materials for one meal in reserve on board the *Arar*, but never more. This meal is ready cooked to save trouble, and if it is not eaten I have it cleared out of the provision-box at the next inn, and replaced by a fresh one on departure. By following this rule we avoid spoilt food in this hot weather, though if we remain away from the inns twelve hours at a time we may be put on rather short rations.

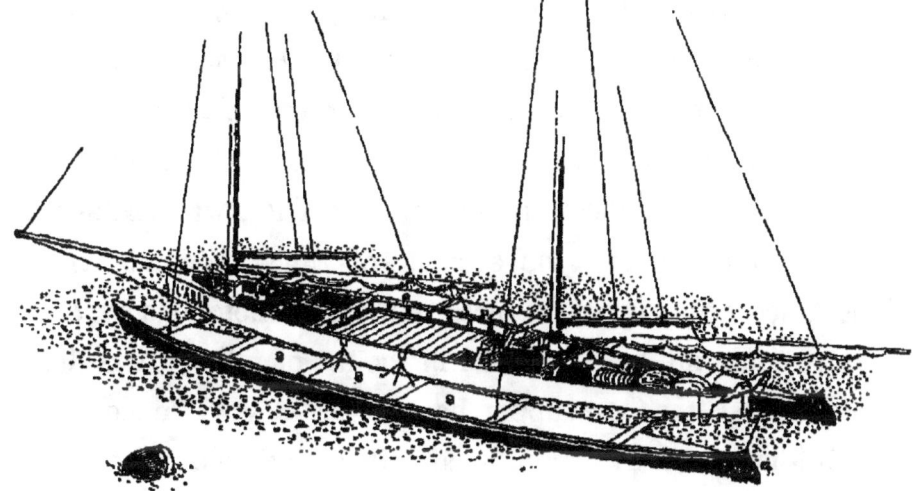

The Arar, Deck View.

I have been anxious to spare you details about boat-building, but some parts of our voyage would be unintelligible if I did not tell you that the *Arar* is a catamaran or double boat on the principle of the *Calais-Douvres*. She has consequently a flat, floor-like deck, and when she is run aground she remains steady without heeling to one side or the other, and requires no "crutches." You will therefore imagine us at supper on this flat deck with a lantern hanging above us from a piece of string that goes from one mast to the other. We possess very low, but very comfortable, chairs expressly devised for the boat, and I can assure you that on a fine night there are less pleasant supper-rooms than the "chamber," as we call it, of the *Arar*. How we manage in bad weather you will learn when that kind of weather comes.

As we are quite accustomed to living on board, our repasts are conducted with order. Without carrying anything superfluous we possess all the apparatus necessary for a civilised meal, and our out-door existence gives the appetite of a savage, which is a happy though a rare combination. Stephen and Maurice supply that gaiety which I am young enough to enjoy, but perhaps too old to originate. On this occasion the enjoyment of the night was enhanced by the intolerable heat of the burning day that had preceded it. The air was neither hot nor cold, but deliciously temperate. There was nothing to hurry us, and we took no account of time. We might row along quietly till sunrise on these tranquil, monotonous waters.

Burgundian inn-keepers excel in the art of filling a traveller's provision-basket. Our supper began with a great melon, ripe and full-flavoured, then continued with a fine cold roast *poulet de la Bresse*, a slice or two of Mayence ham, a little Gruyère cheese, and for dessert we had an abundance of fine peaches and grapes. Is it æsthetic to mention these details? I fear not, but Mr. Grant Allen admits that dessert may be poetical, if not dinner, and you may remember that Byron was enthusiastic about Lady Mary Wortley Montague's lines,—

> "And when the long hours of the public are past
> And we meet with champagne and a chicken at last."

Byron said "Is not her champagne and chicken worth a forest or two? Is it not poetry?" We had not champagne with our chicken, but we had sound red Burgundy, which is better though not alliterative.

It was hard to disturb the young men and tell them to resume their toil as galley slaves when the kettle was singing over the spirit-lamp and they had lighted their cigarettes, so we fell to talking about the constellations, deeply regretting that we had not some learned astronomer to lecture to us. Our ignorance did not proceed from any want of interest in the subject. We are the happy possessors of some excellent treatises on astronomy, and we know as much of the subject as my grandmother, being able to recognise the most popular constellations. I have humbly tried to fix the names of others without attaining to certainty. They do not really look like bears, lions, dragons and dogs, or, if they do, I cannot understand why others, that to my uneducated eye appear strikingly similar, should be compared to a lyre and a ship. These may be bold words, but I take courage from the reflection that the constellations existed some time before the unaccountable names that were applied to them.

In their presence is there really any time? How long is it since Cæsar crossed the Saône and tried to see which way the imperceptible current flowed? In a museum of Gallo-Roman antiquities the interval seems immense; here on the river at night, when not a habitation is to be seen, nothing but calm water, dim shores, and a starry heaven, the war in Gaul is an incident of yesterday.

After rowing some miles further in perfect solitude, and in a silence broken only by the leaping fish, one of whom jumped into the boat and was kindly restored to his native element, we came at length to a place where the dark silhouettes of houses were visible on the left bank, with a turret at the north end of them. This was our haven, and the inn was not difficult to find, being the last house at the southern extremity of the hamlet. The whole place was dark, silent, and asleep, nor was there any sound in the country except a flageolet played by an invisible swain away across the fields. The notes came to us very distinctly and with great purity, but it was always a repetition of one tune. Was the invisible musician a piping shepherd, or was he some rustic lover? That will never be known, but the tune did not seem plaintive enough for passion, it breathed a calm content.

I always feel a disinclination to disturb people in their sleep, but the hostess here recognised my voice and gave us a hearty welcome. Soon all our things were housed, and we saw the stars no more.

When I tell you that this inn is a poor, cheap little place you may infer that the rooms are wretched. That would be a great mistake. We have a very large room with three magnificent *armoires* (linen-presses) in old walnut, elaborately panelled and carved and adorned with most artistic iron-work about the locks and hinges. The beds, too, are handsome and comfortable, and have red curtains. Altogether it is one of the richest-looking peasant interiors I ever saw, and it would certainly produce an admirable effect in a picture if the details were carefully painted.

We made the discovery of this room on a previous voyage. We had been beating to windward in cold and rain, and after passing this place, as we were then sailing northwards, we had still some hours of tedious work before us in the dark. I began to feel symptoms of chill and thought it prudent to return here, when we discovered the qualities of this quiet inn and those of the good people who keep it.

LETTER XXXIX.

La Colonne,
August 30th, Afternoon.

Few scenes are more characteristic of the Lower Saône than the view from Port d'Ouroux early on a splendid morning. The place has no advantage of altitude, it is merely the river's bank, perhaps twenty feet above the level of the water, and yet there is a most open prospect in every direction. It is useless

Port d'Ouroux,   *North End.*

to attempt any minute description of scenery, but you may soon realise the character of this. To the east is a vast green prairie without a division, level for a long distance, then rising gently to a low eminence, which is crowned by a village. Westwards, across the river, is another green plain, quite flat, with a village in the middle of it and hills beyond, with white gleaming villages on these. To the north another stretch of plain and another village, to the south a straight reach of river four or five miles long interrupted only by a distant bridge. I have often heard this scenery described as dull, or even ugly, but it has character, and on a bright sunny morning the character is exhilarating. One would like to be a horse galloping in freedom over the soft green plain, or, better still, one of those sea-gulls that fly above the river, and have come up so far from the Mediterranean.[1]

The village of Marnay, just opposite the Port d'Ouroux, is situated on a river called the Grosne, which falls into the Saône a mile further to the south. The Grosne is a sluggish stream, only remarkable near Marnay for its many windings, but higher up it is remarkable for something else.

Port d'Ouroux,   *South End.*

On the banks of this little river Grosne stood at one time the largest and grandest church in Christendom. After the building of St. Peter's, at Rome, it was the second, and remained so. In other words, all such buildings as York Minster, Notre Dame, and the cathedrals of Cologne, Milan, Strasbourg, and the rest were its inferiors, at least in size. They were also very generally its inferiors in unity of design and in magnificence of plan. Of all the colossal churches in the world it was probably, except St. Peter's, the most harmonious and the

---

[1] Sea-gulls are very common below Chalon, but not on the Upper Saône, though we met with smaller marine birds there.

most complete. It was also one of the oldest, having been begun in 1089 and finished in 1131.

The great abbatial church of Cluny, with its many towers and chapels all built consistently in the same style, was the most magnificent example of Romanesque architecture in existence, and might have lasted like the Pyramids had it not been pulled down by the secular authorities of Cluny early in the present century, for no reason in the world but the devilish desire to commit an act of Vandalism. The loss is the more painful and provoking that the edifice had escaped the Revolution intact, and if it had only been left standing half a century longer it would have been classed as a *monument historique*, and preserved as long as civilisation lasted.[1]

The first question for travellers with a sailing-boat is, "Any wind to-day?" the second, "In what direction?" The faintest of faint breezes began to touch the surface of the river early in the morning. They came from all points of the compass, then died away and left a sullen calm with increasing heat. After eleven the south wind sprung up, and we determined to set sail and beat against it. We had at last the pleasure of seeing white canvas in the sunshine and the small waves dancing and glittering, and it was sweet to hear once more the merry noise they made as they dashed vainly against the twin steel hulls of the *Arar*.

---

[1] The act of the civil authorities was the more brutal that Cluny had been in the middle ages the home of learning and the light of Europe. "It is unquestionable," says Violet-le-Duc, "that Cluny supplied western Europe with architects as it furnished reforming scholars, professors for schools, painters, savants, physicians, ambassadors, bishops, sovereigns, and popes, for if Cluny were effaced from the eleventh century little would be left but darkness, ignorance, and monstrous abuses."

It is pleasant to know that when the Cluny Vandals presented themselves before Napoleon at Mâcon he reproached them as they deserved.

I had a fancy for making an experiment. I had found on the last voyage that the *Arar* would come round without her jib, and therefore tried to suppress it, but after a fair trial it was Stephen's opinion, and mine also, *that a jib must be considered an indispensable sail on a catamaran*. On canoes the case is different, and the suppression of the sail is wise.[1]

The Arar under sail.

This question being settled we restored the jib, and perhaps it was quite as well that we had done so when an unforeseen peril revealed itself. Just at the moment of tacking, when the *Arar* was in stays, I perceived that we were within a very few yards of

---

[1] "A jib in canoes is a troublesome snare, its driving power is comparatively small, and it is only in play when the wind is abeam or forward of the beam; yet it entails a lot of extra gear, requires constant watching, and in a really bad squall is suicidal to the boat."—DIXON KEMP.

one of those great subaqueous walls that are called *clayonnages*. These walls are built out in the river to protect the shore from erosion, but as they do not rise above the surface and are not marked, as they ought to be, by buoys, you have to learn where they are by actual experience. This *clayonnage* first came far out into the river from the left bank and then ran parallel with the shore for a long distance, after which it returned to the same bank, forming a vast inclosure. Where it came out the current (rather strong in this place) was carrying us rapidly upon it, and it was a question of seconds whether we were to strike or not. However, the *Arar* got way on her new tack just in time to take us clear. We were then within five or six yards of the wall, but of course cared nothing for it as soon as the sails began to draw.[1] What would have happened if we had missed stays? We should simply have been carried against the wall and *glued* to it by the steady pressure of the current. With the *Arar*, which has two insubmersible steel hulls divided into water-tight compartments, there would have been no danger either of sinking or upsetting, but the difficulty of getting out of such a situation might have been very great. Captain Kornprobst and I both retain a vivid recollection of an accident of this kind in which we got the boat over the wall twice, as a huntsman leaps into an inclosure on land and out again. This is the only

[1] A catamaran has two defects at the moment of tacking. She does not come round so quickly as an ordinary boat, neither does she shoot forward rapidly in stays. The first of these defects may, I think, be easily remedied by a special form of hull, but the second is due to the lightness of a catamaran and its consequent want of momentum. Lightness is, however, such a precious quality at all other times that one does not like to sacrifice it. Mr. J. Mackenzie, of Belfast, has overcome the difficulty by having a watertight chest under the deck. This chest was filled with about 6 cwt. of water for beating to windward, but kept empty at other times, the water being easily discharged by the opening of a valve.

danger in the navigation of the Saône. There are neither rocks, as in the Rhône, nor sand-banks like the shifting sand-banks of the Loire.

Beating to windward is the sure test of a vocation for boating. Young men like Stephen and Maurice, who have the true vocation, will go on working steadily against the wind for a whole day without complaining, and, if the weather is pleasant, with actual enjoyment, but any one who looks upon boating simply as a means of getting from one place to another, will always find the zig-zag method of progression exasperatingly tedious. For us, since we intended in any case to stop at La Colonne, a contrary wind was the best we could have had, for it gave us prolonged occupation on the water. When we came to the bridge of Thorey, above La Colonne, we managed to sail through one of the arches without tacking under it. This is always rather delicate work against the wind, as you must come close to the first pier in order to clear the second. At the weir of Gigny we found the lock closed and the sluice open, so we had to sail down the sluice. We had the current in our favour, but the wind was dead against us, so we had to tack in the sluice, which is narrow with a great wall on one side and the weir on the other, just a place for a strong current of air. After the weir was past we had to avoid the backwater, which ran back with a strong counter-current to the foot of the fall.

La Colonne is a small hamlet on the right bank of the Saône with a few picturesque cottages and an inn. The place takes its name from a Roman column which existed here and has since disappeared. The shaft of a great column was found in the bed of the river near this place some years ago, and is now at Tournus. This is believed to be, and probably is, the monolith which gave its name to the hamlet. It is also believed, with great appearance of probability but no exact certainty, that this is the place where Cæsar crossed the Saône with his legions when pursuing the Swiss, and that the column was erected as a memorial and as a guide to other Roman armies. One desires to fix the place of an event so important as the first Roman passage of the Saône, and here it is, accurately enough for belief though not for knowledge.

There is an inn at La Colonne and it is a favourite haven of ours. The host is a prosperous corn and hay merchant, very friendly to us but often away from home on business. This time he and his wife are both absent at a fair, and, strange to say, there is nothing to eat in the house, usually so well provided. The servants knew us and were distressed by the dearth of provisions. "Be not anxious on our account," I answered, "there is always food in reserve on board the *Arar*. Only fetch the provision box." So we ate our own *déjeuner* in the cool shade of the inn. This is a charming specimen of the Saône inns. The entrance hall is a great room trellised round three sides which can be closed with shutters against sun or wind, or open to the roof. There are half-a-dozen small tables at the sides, with one great round table in the middle. The door is open, and through the doorway we have an uninterrupted view of the river from our table, which is in a corner. You would think that I had enough of the river by this time, but the love of water is an insatiable passion, and I like to see it without stirring from my place at table. I remember on a former voyage sitting in this sheltered corner and seeing the moon just in that doorway, and the shore quite dark beyond under the clouds, and the silvered waves tossing restlessly under a strong south wind. To-night there will be no moon, and the wind has fallen, and the heat is like the heat of Africa. But the water is cool in the well, and the wine cools in the water-bucket on the floor. It is a cheap white wine that sparkles naturally, and though rather piquant is neither harsh nor acid. It is grown in the neighbouring vineyards, and its reputation is entirely local. The colour is a pale amber, and it is clear as the fountain of Bandusia. Nothing drinkable could be prettier than a goblet of it,

"With beaded bubbles winking at the brim."

LETTER XL.

TOURNUS, *September 1st.*

Our host and hostess at La Colonne returned before dinner-time with an abundance of provisions in their carriage. We dined in the trellised hall, and afterwards had a long talk with the innkeeper. Then came the keeper of the lock at Gigny, which is a few hundred yards up the river. He is a great friend of ours, not for any good we ever did to him, but because he once rendered a service to us, and whenever we pass this way he never fails to pay us a visit. On these occasions he particularly enjoys a long talk with my son. I wish you could see the interior where we met. I told you that it is a large room trellised on three sides and open to the roof, which is high. A large lamp hangs from the middle beam, and fishing-nets in picturesque festoons from others. We have dined, the peaches and grapes have disappeared, the cloth has been removed, and our host offers us chartreuse on the green table, which liqueur will not be included in the bill. Our host is a large, strong man with a rubicund face and a thick moustache. The heat has reduced his costume to a pair of white trousers and a shirt. Stephen and Maurice are almost as lightly clad, and enjoy this liberty after hot broadcloth in a town hotel. The young men contrast much more strongly in outward appearance than they do in character and tastes. Stephen looks entirely English and Maurice entirely French. Stephen, as you remember, has a light florid complexion with fair hair and a full beard; Maurice is dark, with a young, dark brown moustache. A painter would not wish for a better contrast, and it is repeated between our host and myself. Anybody would guess our nationality at once, but it is not so with the lockkeeper. No one meeting him out of France would say immediately, "That is a Frenchman." He is above the middle height, spare and active, and reminds me in his general appearance of an English gamekeeper. Altogether we made a diversified and picturesque group under the light of the high lamp.

"Ah, *Messieurs*," said our host, "I shall ever remember that night when I first made your acquaintance. I was sleeping quietly in my bed, about one o'clock in the morning, when I heard a loud noise at the door and opened it. I saw our friend here, the keeper, and he asked if I had beds for three poor shipwrecked mariners. And then you came in, sir, you and your sons, and I heard your story and we laughed over it merrily, and part of your wet cargo was spread out upon these tables, and the next morning we got out of the boat everything that remained in it."

"My recollection of that night," said the lockkeeper, "is as clear as if it were yesterday. Somebody came and awoke me before midnight, and I got up to let you through the lock. I did not see you as there was little moonlight and the sky was cloudy, and you down in the lock, too, where it was very dark; but when we had opened the lower gates I asked why you did not go forward, then you answered that you could not go on very fast as the boat was sinking."

"I remember," said Stephen, "that you were very much alarmed just then. You thought we were all going to be drowned and were kindly anxious to save us."

"Yes, I was more frightened than you, but you soon put me at ease by telling me that it would be a bath and mattered nothing."

"It was a double boat like that you have now," said our host, "but each hull was divided into three sections."

"That was done for portability, so that the boat might be readily put on board a steamer, and this division into sections was the cause of leakage. The builder had made a mistake, he ought to have given her a double skin with canvas between applied with marine glue, but he relied on thin single boards and they leaked at the angles. Every compartment was leaky more or less, but the starboard hull much more than the other as it filled first with a gurgling noise that my son called '*le sinistre glou-glou.*' I said it would be worse when the *glou-glou* ceased, and so it turned out, for then the starboard hull sank bodily and hung suspended from the other."

"I recollect," said the keeper, "that when I came to you with my boat you had somehow got out of the lock by using your oars as paddles whilst you stood up, but I could see nothing under you. You appeared to be standing on the water."

"One hull had sunk entirely and the other only just floated.

We were able to stand by putting one foot on the angle of the floating hull and the other on the bulwark of the deck. The most wonderful thing in this adventure was that we did not even get wet."

"If the things you had on you remained dry," said our host, "you cannot say the same for those in the coffers of the boat. What a fishing up of soaked and ship-wrecked goods we had the following morning:—clothes, books, provisions, what a cargo you carried with you!"

"We had started on a long voyage. Our plan was to go down the Rhône to Avignon and Arles, and it was a part of my scheme to make use of the interior of the hulls for storing things The hulls of the *Arar* are merely air-boxes containing nothing. All we have with us now is on the deck."

"I think that kind of portable boat would have been very practical if it had not leaked," said the innkeeper. "The day after your accident, when you took the steamer, the different parts of the boat were as readily put on board as common passengers' luggage."

"That was my first plan, to have a thing that would sail much better than a canoe, and yet be as readily put on a steamer or a railway train. I like a heavy, well-ballasted sailing-boat when there is a wind, but in dead calms she is a fixture on the water and keeps her owner a prisoner unless he abandons her."

The day after this conversation we ourselves experienced a kind of imprisonment not due to the immovableness of the *Arar*, which can be either rowed or towed, but to the excessive heat. I enjoyed my day in spite of it by observing my hot-weather rules, which are to rise very early and take advantage of the cool hours, to keep in shade as much as possible during the hot hours, and to travel in the evening. I worked hard from morning till night making two water-colour studies, and only tore up one of them. This is true self-denial, as there is no pleasure in the practice of art comparable to the savage joy of annihilating one's own works. Nature sets us an example in this respect; she never keeps her pictures. All her groups are immediately dispersed, all her sunsets obliterated.

In the afternoon, just at the hottest time, an astonishing incident occurred. On entering the trellised summer-house I beheld our host with the crew of the *Arar* seated before three glasses filled to the brim with what seemed to be pure water. "Can it be possible," I asked, "that the liquid before you is *water?*" "Certainly," our host answered, "it is nothing else;" but there was a humorous light in his eye, and after a pause he added, "There is an explanation for every wonder. The water is but to cool the glasses."

We quitted La Colonne just before sunset without a breath of wind. It was therefore decided that Stephen and Maurice should tow the boat as long as the twilight lasted, and after that we calculated that we should be near Tournus and might row into the town. The tow-rope for the *Arar* is merely a piece of good string eighty-five yards long, which is passed through a pulley on the foremast and brought down to a cleat on the deck. By this arrangement it can be continually lengthened or shortened on the boat without troubling the man who tows. It was my business to steer, Maurice took charge of the tow-rope, and Stephen walked on the somewhat irregular shore with a broad belt over his shoulder. I am not quite sure that towing is a good economy of power except because two men can take the work alternately. The toil itself is certainly heavier than that of reasonable rowing, but it is a change after a sitting posture, and Stephen, who is a pedestrian, enjoys it.

After the miserable experience of the *Boussemroum* it was a pleasure to be on the *Arar*, which answered to the helm as delicately when towed as if she had had a side wind in her sails. Her power of lateral resistance is so great that when I desired to keep off the shore she would travel forward steadily with the rope almost at a right angle with her course, and the rudders were so persuasive that Stephen could do nothing whatever against them, indeed he said that by simply steering I could almost have dragged him into the water.[1] It is in this variety of service that consists the merit of a travelling as distinguished from a regatta boat. The traveller does not want brilliant qualities, but he wants to go on steadily, whatever the motive power. Our first day's voyage was done with oars, our second by sailing against the wind, our third by towing. This adaptability to different uses is explained by the comparative lightness of the *Arar*, which does not carry a single pound of ballast, and by her shallow draught of water. For travelling on the Saône the oar and the tow-rope, though more prosaic than "white wings," are at least equally necessary.

The sun went down after we had been half an hour on the water, and just at that time we were opposite Ormes, a charmingly situated village on rising ground to the left. The view from this village, that we did not visit, must be one of the finest on

---

[1] A catamaran offers a far greater lateral resistance than any single boat can do if it has only the same draught of water. The inner sides of the hulls of the *Arar* are flat walls, which act as keels of a greater depth. These make her rather slow in stays, but are invaluable in towing. The centre-board is of course always raised in shallow water, and is only used in sailing.

the Saône, as it includes two long reaches of river, two great woods, and a distant view of Tournus. After sunset we crept along the edge of one of these woods, and then the towers and bridge of Tournus became visible far away, a dim grey picture over miles of water still to be traversed. After sunset the twilight deepened rapidly, and then Stephen became absolutely invisible on the darkening shore, so that we had the strange effect of being drawn by an unexplained force like the boat in Poe's "Domain of Arnheim" or the ship in "The Ancient Mariner." A very thin young crescent moon, only two days old, hung over the sombre forest on the right in a sky still warmed by the afterglow.

The Saône, as I told you from Chalon, is so low at present that the business navigation is suspended, and even the *Arar* could not make her way near shore without occasionally grounding. The rushes, often far out in the stream, prepared us for some shallow places, but we came upon others unawares. On these occasions we had good reason to congratulate ourselves upon the absence of ballast and on the steadiness given by the two keels when the *Arar* runs aground. She was always very easily set afloat again, either by forcing her over the shallow or by going back and seeking another channel. When poling we walk from end to end of the two hulls on their own special decks left free for the purpose, the middle deck being encumbered with sailing-gear and luggage and divided into compartments.

Maurice took his turn bravely enough at the tow-rope and we found that our rate of progression averaged four kilomètres an hour, or two and a half English miles. This is exactly the speed usually calculated for the horses that tow empty barges, so that there would have been no advantage in having a horse with us.

Sailing is rapid with a good wind, and even a light breeze

gives motion, but the *average* speed of sailing is often low. One of my friends who has an excellent sailing-boat built by a famous builder and the winner of many prizes, told me that on a long Saône voyage his average speed had been but half of that which we easily maintain with the tow-rope.

The moon set about eight o'clock, and after that we had nothing but stars and the distant yellow lights of Tournus. The bridge had now become invisible and its place could only be known by its lamps. It being now too dark for towing on an irregular path, the crew took to the oars and I steered for the central arch, as yet perfectly invisible. It became visible, however, on a nearer approach, in the shape of a great dark and dim shadow.

There is a most deceptive effect of perspective in approaching a bridge when your mast is *nearly* as high as the arch. The mast being close to you and the bridge still at a little distance it *always* seems that the mast is sure to strike. No reasoning, no recollection of measurements, can overcome the delusive testimony of the eye. You think "that mast was low enough for the other bridges, but certainly not for this," and you resign yourself to the inevitable accident. There is no accident, the mast passes easily, but the old illusion will recur at the next bright.

LETTER XLI.

Tournus, *September 2nd.*

The morning after our arrival here I rose early and enjoyed a walk about the place just after sunrise, whilst the air was still cool and refreshing.

This old town was very familiarly known to me already, but

Tournus, the Bridge.

no degree of familiarity can take away its one great and striking characteristic. All the towns and villages we have seen hitherto on the Saône visibly belong to northern or to central France. Even Chalon, the last of them, is not at all a southern city, it is not more distinctively southern than Dijon, but at Tournus you are really in the south, and might easily believe yourself in one of the old towns on the Rhône. This southern character begins exactly at Tournus itself. The village of Ormes, that we passed after leaving La Colonne has nothing of it, there is not a sign to warn you that the genuine south is at hand. Your boat touches ground at Tournus and you are in another country,

On the Quay at Tournus.

a country as distinct from central France as Middlesex is from Midlothian.

How shall I describe the effect of this sudden plunge into *the true South?* First, you have a vague general impression of change, like that after arriving in a foreign land, then you look about and notice one by one the many details which in their aggregate have produced the impression.

Some even declare that the sky at Tournus has the southern azure, and has it not yet at Chalon. It is difficult, in a matter so gradated as the depth of the sky, to determine where the veritable azure begins, but assuredly on the first of September the rosy towers of the old Romanesque abbatial church of St. Philibert caught the first rays of the eastern sun against a sky of such blue that it seemed Italian.[1]

The picturesque character of the streets here is quite the southern picturesque. The roofs are pitched at a very obtuse angle, and they project far out at the eaves; the tiles, too, are of the rounded, southern form, and more often of a pale ochrous yellow than of the comfortable northern red. The small degree of inclination in the roofs makes them generally invisible from below, you see only the projecting part that casts its dark shadow. The houses themselves are often roughly built, so that even when new they have a picturesque texture from the beginning. Occasionally the walls are supported on arcades.

Ruelle at Tournus.

---

[1] The stone of the highest story of these towers has a reddish tinge, which in early or late sunshine becomes rosy.

At one café there is a spacious arcade of this kind giving coolness that is much appreciated by the crew of the *Arar* at noon. Many of the streets are extremely narrow, as in the far south, in one of them you pass under low arches which reminded Stephen of Algiers. In this little street there is a long external

The Marketplace at Tournus.

balcony with a balustrade of turned oak; as I was admiring this a man came out upon it and said it was the greatest convenience in his house, being the sole means of communication between one room and another.

There is more colour in Tournus than in the northern towns. To look down one of the narrow streets when the buildings on one side are in strong sunshine, and those opposite in broad shadow is to incur a painter's temptation, so rich are the ochres and russets, so deep the glimpse of blue! Then there will be flowers and verdure at the windows, spots of pure bright colour amidst the yellows and browns.

The important streets are irregular, and there are two or three *places*, one opposite the Museum with a marble statue of Greuze. There is an old *tourelle* at the corner of this place and the market is held here. But no scene in Tournus is so impressive as the quieter place on the hill before the great church. It has no describable shape, but is narrow at the entrance, guarded by an old round tower, then the ground rises and the place widens with irregular and very picturesque buildings on each side, but it is impossible to pay any attention to these in the presence of the extraordinary church.

The west front looks on the place. It is a striking example of a certain kind of power in architecture, that is separate from beauty. You feel the power at once, and may account for it afterwards at your leisure. It is a strong assertion of military and ecclesiastical domination at the same time, fortress and church in one, and the effect on the mind is far stronger than that of more elegant and amiable architecture. This piece of rude eleventh century building goes up first to a great height like a precipice, with no openings but loopholes, and nothing to amuse you but the rough texture of the stones and their various warm or cool greys. Then the architect indulges in a military *mâchicoulis* and twin towers, one only being completed. They are good Romanesque towers with as much elegance as is compatible with the serious character of the style. Besides the finished tower at the west end there is another, also finished, but so much further eastwards, that from a distance it seems almost to belong to another edifice.

On entering, we do not find ourselves in the body of the church, but in a vast covered porch or narthex, with a low vaulted roof carried on eight huge round columns.[1] Above this narthex there is a hall or chapel, with lofty nave and low side aisles. The narthex is one of the peculiarities of the great monastic churches of the Cluny fraternity. At Vézelay it is rich with sculpture, here it is as plain as a prison, and as depressing. One feels a sense of relief on emerging from the low vault into the lofty church. The nave is very plain, too, with its tall unadorned columns, round arches, and wooden tie-beams from one column to another. Beauty is reserved for the choir and apse. The *pourtour* of the apse is delightful with its richly-carved capitals, the intricate perspective given by the intersection of the arches, and the charm of the small chapels that seem like refuges from the uncouth vastness of the rude monastic church. One of these chapels is dedicated to Saint Filomena and adorned with a series of illuminated pictures, each of which has under it one stanza of a quaint old poem that I transcribed. I give the original here for readers who relish old French, and a prose translation for others.

I

Al palais dou bon roy son pere Li Princesse Filumena Son cuer por sa vie entiere Deis onze ans al Jesus dona	In the palace of the good king her father the Princess Filomena dedicated herself to Jesus for all her life from the age of eleven years.

---

[1] Two of them are against the west wall, and partly sunk in it. The aisles have half columns.

2

Or l'aima l'Empereor de Rome
Cuidant quelle le volorat amer
Ains Filumena ne vvot home
Ne trone ne joiel amer

2

Now the Emperor of Rome loved her, thinking that she would love him, but Filomena would love no man, nor any throne or diadem.

3

Donc come Jesus despoliee
L'benoiste fille de roy
Mult grantement fust flagellee
Par les maugreeurs por sa foy

3

Wherefore, being stripped like Jesus this blessed daughter of a king was heavily scourged by blasphemers for her faith.

4

Lors dielx envoia bons Angeles
Saluer la saincte en son nom
Elx evatant bianches ailes
Pourterent doulce garison

4

Then God sent good angels to save her in His name, and beating the air with white wings, they brought her sweet relief.

5

Al ancre de nef attachee
Li dolente Filumena
Al Tiberis fust enfourchee
Ains dour Jesus li salua

5

Being fastened to the anchor of a ship, the suffering Filomena was cast into the Tiber. But kind Jesus preserved her.

6

Li prenant por magiciene
Mult fust mautraitee par bourels
Ains li tres bone Crestiene
Neust pour doulcurs tormens cruels

6

Taking her for a witch, the executioners mistreated her, so this good Christian had cruel torments instead of pleasures.

7

Oyant ce l'Empereor eust mult ire
Baillant ordre al ses archiers
Di ferir la poure martyre
Ains li cops vont al ses chiers

7

The Emperor heard of this with great wrath, and gave orders to his archers to strike the poor martyr so their arrows entered her flesh.

8

Lors de li saincte persone
Li biau chef fust taille
Ains par Dielx trone abe corone
Al Filumena fust baille.

8

Then from her holy body the beautiful head was severed. And thus God gave a throne and a crown to Filomena.

This seems to me a most able piece of poetical work. A tale had to be told in a very few words and I think it would be difficult to combine brevity more perfectly with grace. How decidedly the story is opened in the first stanza, how completely it is concluded in the last! The finish of the concluding lines in their reference to the last line of the second stanza is masterly. The sympathetic sentiment is pure and elevated and it is never overdone. There is pity, yet not too much, for what need had she of pity who was to be so rewarded? The poet has a sense of beauty, he thinks of the white wings of the angels,[1] and of Filomena's beautiful head, but he thinks more of what seems to him the religious beauty of her life.

In the chapel of St. Filomena, where these illuminated stanzas form an appropriate decoration, it was almost irritating to observe

---

[1] What can be more beautiful than these two lines in the fourth stanza, describing the descent of the healing angels?

Elx ebatant bianches ailes
Pourterent doulce garison.

The Towers of Tournus.

the readiness with which the priests had accepted the most trivial offerings. I believe they do this from a good motive, the desire to avoid hurting the feelings of the poor, the wish to make them understand that the Church cares for them, but this indulgence is disastrous to ecclesiastical edifices. A poor believer buys a bad coloured print in a sixpenny frame and the priest hangs it in a splendid chapel, as if he were destitute of all sense of the incongruous. In the south transept at Tournus there is a small collection of water-colours, copied by Creys, a miniature painter, from Poussin. These water-colours are framed and hung exactly as if they were in a gallery and nobody seems to perceive that they look nugatory where they are.

The whole church is interesting but the present crypt contains an edifice more interesting still, a small and very ancient church, one of the most ancient in Europe. A vault of the rudest masonry is supported by ten thin columns, some of which have been borrowed from a Roman building. Here is the tomb of St. Valerian, and also a sacred well. The water is still believed by some good people to have miraculous qualities. Round the ancient church is a *pourtour* which is comparatively modern, being of the eleventh century. There was a fascination in the gloom and silence of this relic of antiquity that made me linger in it long. The desire for historical continuity is gratified by the preservation of buildings for their original uses. The present Bishop of Autun has officiated in this church—at how wide an interval from those who first worshipped there!

LETTER XLII.

Tournus, *September 3rd.*

You will remember that in my letter from La Colonne I mentioned the Roman column which gave its name to the place. The shaft of it is now at Tournus, lying prostrate in a court-yard behind the *gendarmerie*. It is a monolith, about twenty feet long, of a pale, slightly reddish, colour. After fishing it up in the Saône, the authorities erected it at Tournus in the square of the *hôtel de ville*, and afterwards removed it. A thing of this kind loses half its interest when displaced. It ought to be re-erected at La Colonne.

The place opposite the *hôtel de ville* is at present occupied by a statue of Greuze in white marble. If you enter the museum you will find a letter bearing the signature of Greuze between the two windows that look out upon the square, and you may read the letter and see the statue at the same time. The two together point to a combination which is not rare in the history of men of genuis. The statue tells of established and enduring fame, the letter of lamentable and absolute penury in old age. It is a most painful letter, but only from sad circumstances, not from any lack of dignity. If the unfortunate writer could have received the present value of one of his pictures he would have been above anxiety in his declining years.[1]

Greuze was born at Tournus in 1725. The date is commemorated on a slab of marble placed outside the house. Besides this, and the statue, there are other memorials of him.

---

[1] The popularity of the engravings from his works had enabled Greuze to save money, but he lost it in the turmoil of the Revolution.

The museum contains a few very able sketches, besides one or two copies from his more famous works, including, of course, the inevitable *Cruche Cassée*. But nothing of his charmed me so much as a small picture of a girl's head, painted with that indescribable lightness and grace of execution that belong only to a master, and in fine colour too. The face of the girl is attractive without much beauty of feature. This led me to notice that the style of prettiness immortalised by Greuze in his paintings is still preserved by Nature herself in living faces at Tournus, and that the artist's inspiration came evidently from his native place. Whilst we sat at dinner a girl was sent to fetch cold water from a public fountain. When she came back she paused a moment in the doorway, and I said, "There is the *Cruche Cassée!*"—not because the pitcher was broken, but it was exactly the shape of that in the famous painting, even to the little spout, and the girl had the peculiar grace that inspired the artist.

Our inn at Tournus is an eccentric, yet pleasant house. The stairs, which are narrow, open directly on the street, but by turning aside you stumble somehow into the kitchen, and after that into a sort of large café-restaurant, at present rather encumbered with oars and other *impedimenta* from the *Arar*. The master of the house is a joiner, absent all day, and there is neither the usual male cook nor even a *garçon*, the work of the house being entirely done by women, but it is very well done. Cleanliness and good cookery are the great merits of the place. I wish you could see our hostess, so fat, so kind, and so maternally attentive to our wants!

A dead calm has reigned ever since our arrival until yesterday evening. As we were at dinner we were startled by a sudden roar and a great noise of shutters clattering violently, and lo! the town was enveloped in a great squall. We ran to secure the boat more effectually, and it was all we could do to reach her against such a furious blast. The river must have been rough, but the truth is that we could not see it. The Saône was entirely concealed from view by a cloud of dust like a sandstorm in the desert. Had we been out on the water in this brief hurricane,

Tournus, the Big Parasol.

we could only have scudded before it under bare poles; sailing and rowing would alike have been out of the question.

After the squall came a thunderstorm, very short and sharp, but hardly any rain, and to-day the sky is as clear as ever, and the sun like the sun of Africa. I have not thought it prudent to start before evening, so we shall travel at night. My time has been occupied in sketching a solitary house, above the bridge, that the people call "The Folly," because the builder ought to have known that it would be surrounded by every flood. Of course, he knew it, just as he must have known that his house would be exposed to the east wind, but he accepted these occasional evils for the enjoyment of a site generally delightful. There is now a fine group of trees for shade, and the front of the villa has an open prospect looking towards Mont Blanc. This does not imply that Mont Blanc is always or often visible. Would that it were so this evening, for that would be a sign of rain! The stately king of mountains only shows himself before a change of weather. It is almost incredible that he can be there really when we see the open sky to the east without a trace of the vanished Alps, yet clear as in a picture by Perugino. I cannot imagine any better example of the most perfect dissimulation. To hide things behind a visible cloud is what a clumsy person may accomplish; but only a master can hide them behind an appearance of perfect clearness, as Nature conceals her Alps.

LETTER XLIII.

Port of Fleurville,
September 4th.

We left Tournus an hour before sunset. There was not a breath of wind, so we rowed to Villars, which I sketched from the boat.

The day before, having occasion to make a purchase at a linen draper's, I had been amused by his extreme interest in the *Arar*. He had asked a dozen questions about her, all showing real nautical knowledge, and now when we were out on the river he came to us in his boat and examined ours. He was much interested in the Herreshoff rudders, which indeed are a scientific curiosity. There is a rudder to each hull, and the two are so connected that the one inside the intended curve always turns more than the other, though the action of the steersman is as

Villars.

simple as in ordinary steering. Either a tiller or cords may be used with this apparatus. I prefer cords as in a rowing boat, and steer without effort, though the rudders are large and heavy.

Villars is an uncommonly picturesque little village, perched on the top of a steep height, and crowned with a Romanesque church of the twelfth century. At a distance sufficient to explain the fine situation of Villars in a sketch, it is not possible to discern the picturesque detail which reveals itself only when you are under the steep. By the time we arrived there the sun had set, and as the calm continued Stephen went ashore with the tow-rope.

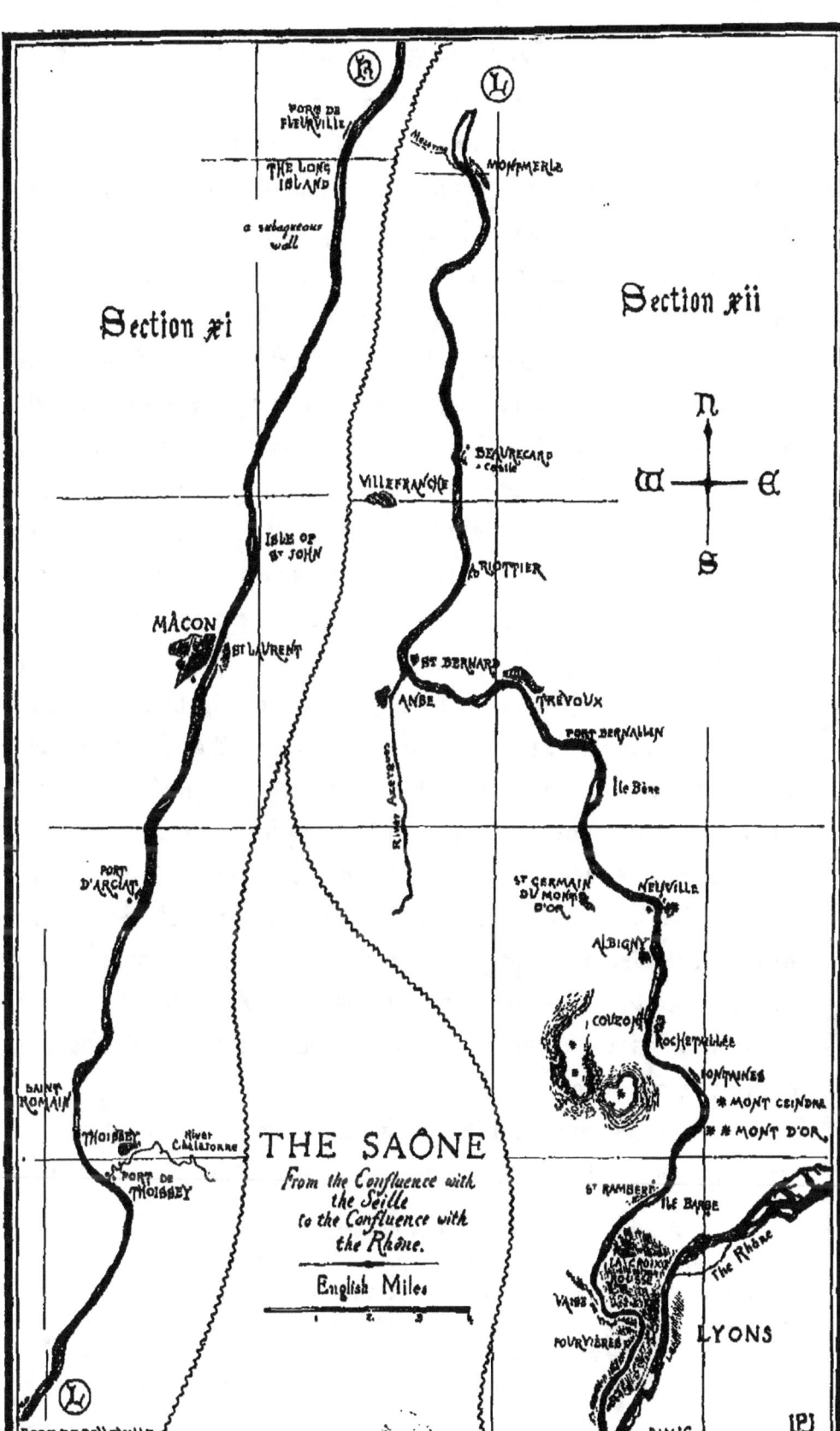

After some time we passed, on the left, the mouth of an important tributary, the Seille, which takes its rise in the Jura near Baume-les-Messieurs, in abounding springs. There cannot be a greater contrast in the life of a river than that between the early and the late existence of the Seille. It begins as a mountain torrent, rushing through the deep, rocky ravines of the Jura, then at Louhans it joins another such torrent, the Vallière, and after that they flow together in one peaceable stream till they end in "the gentle Saône." Had we not been pressed for time and impeded by the hot weather, we might have explored this river as far as Louhans, where it first becomes navigable. This is its great distinction, as the Saône has no other navigable tributary.[1]

After passing a place called Farges, on the right bank, we had a good example of the un-communicativeness that often marks the peasant. Stephen was still at the tow-rope, and he questioned some peasants, who allowed him to go on without warning till the *Arar* was engaged in a channel between an island and the mainland. This channel was an *impasse*, being closed at the lower extremity by an engineer's wall. We had consequently to row back and turn the point of the island.[2] After that we gave up towing as usual when the light is insufficient, and trusted entirely to our oars.

The departed sun had left only an orange glow in the clear western sky, and the moon was now bright enough to be of

---

[1] The Doubs, it will be remembered, is not navigable where it joins the Saône, though a part of its upper course has been canalised.

[2] The same thing happened afterwards on our return from Lyons. There is a very long island below Fontaines, and we rowed up the wrong channel, finding it barred by a *clayonnage*. There was a peasant on the island, but he did not warn us. It would, no doubt, be rather a pleasure to him to see two *bourgeois* labouring in vain.

great value to us. Nothing could exceed the perfect serenity of the night. Not a breath of air disturbed the broad surface of the river, and before us the distance seemed without limit except that a light and lofty bridge was just dimly discernible. I always profoundly enjoy these hours of nocturnal calm when we are alone on the great river under moon or stars, and hear no sound but that of our own leisurely rowing.

Stephen reminded me of an interesting ethnological tradition concerning a village to our right, not quite two miles from the river. When the Saracens invaded this part of France they left, it appears, a colony here which founded this village of Uchizy,

A Landing-stage.

and it is said that until quite recent times the difference of race between their descendants and the neighbouring French people was very strongly marked. We regret not to have visited this village, but we cannot leave the *Arar* except in safe keeping.

Passing under the bridge we remembered in time the existence of a subaqueous wall more than a mile long, and kept to the open channel. There was no sign of life but some dark houses on the right bank, with lights shining in their windows and a group of barges at anchor visible vaguely as a dark space with very dim outlines. Having left the *clayonnage* behind us we kept in mid-stream, and the river appeared to increase in width till it resembled a lake. Here Maurice began to talk about the opera, where he has been much more frequently than I, and he illustrated his discourse by singing various romantic songs. This animated Stephen who also favoured us. I was a little surprised by this sudden musical ardour, and the more so that the crew of the *Arar* never sing in drawing-rooms, but boating develops all kinds of latent ability.

The moon being low in the west we decided to sleep on the boat, being aware that lodgings were not to be had at the next "port," or for several miles after it. It is a fixed rule of mine, in this kind of travel, always to have the means of sleeping comfortably on board our little yacht. She has no cabins, that is to say, the six water-tight chambers in her hulls are too narrow for use as berths, and, in fact, are employed only as pontoons.[1] The arrangement of the *Arar* will be best understood if I describe what we did on the present occasion.

First we beach the boat, and as soon as her two hulls rest on the sand the deck presents a perfectly steady platform, with no risk of heeling over to one side or the other. The deck is divided by partitions, the large middle compartment being called the "chamber." We sling a long pole between the two masts by cords running in pulleys. The roof line of a tent being suspended to this pole we raise it by the pulleys, and then tie the bottom of the tent outside the central deck. An arrangement with oars and slender external side-poles helps to give more room inside and opposes more effective resistance to a wind.

---

[1] The hulls of a double boat made in Ireland contained four berths, but I have never wished to sleep in the hulls, because they are low in the night fog, and often contain a little bilge-water. Hammocks well above the upper deck are, in my opinion, much healthier.

No internal poles are necessary, as the masts replace them admirably. The tent is pitched in a few minutes, and is always handy when rain comes on, even in the daytime. In a heavy shower we beach the boat and encamp till it is over.

On the present occasion we used the tent first as a dining-room. It is of a warm, reddish-brown colour, and looks the

The Arar, with tents.

perfection of comfort with its flat wooden floor, like a room, and a lantern suspended from the roof. The height of the tent allows a man to stand up, so it appears lofty to us on our low chairs.

The moon set at 9-31 when we pitched the tent. Having eaten nothing since noon we appreciated the skill and foresight with which our good hostess of Tournus had anticipated all our wants. There are moments when the provision box is more interesting than the box of books, and when three very hungry men meet over a very good supper they may be merrier than dyspeptic philosophers think mortals have any right to be. I often admire the prowess of my young companions, but never more than on these occasions.

As we were eating our grapes and peaches Stephen reminded me that we had encamped exactly at this place last year under very peculiar circumstances. We were sailing up the river by moonlight when heavy rain came on, so we stopped to encamp and passed the night under a downpour. There is nothing remarkable in this, and it would not have been worth mentioning but before the rain we had been in a perfect storm of *ephemeræ*. You probably know those flies, but it is very unlikely that you can ever have met with them in such prodigious quantities. They have large white silky wings, and long, slender, pale-yellowish bodies, and are said to live only for a day. That night they were quite as numerous on the river as the flakes in a heavy snow-storm, and it is the simple truth that they pelted against my face in such quantities that I could scarcely see to steer. Whenever one of them touched the boat he remained on it helpless, and the consequence was that in about fifteen minutes the decks were entirely covered with their bodies, in some places to the depth of two or three inches.

To return to our encampment. We stretch hammocks for Stephen and myself in the chamber, and another for Maurice in the poop. Then we erect a small habitation for Maurice, whose berth is not too spacious. His tent is fastened to the mainmast at one end and to a short, upright pole at the other. It gives good shelter from wind and rain, but he cannot stand up in it as we can in ours. Nothing would be easier than to have a much wider tent in the middle with hammocks over the hulls, but this would occupy the gangways which we prefer to keep disengaged on each side in case of sudden alarm at night.

Our clothes, books, papers, and sketching materials are kept in japanned tin boxes with pill-box lids. These are not the most convenient lids to open, but the advantage of them is that everything remains dry inside, even in the heaviest rain. Leather and wooden boxes are never to be trusted, and it is better to reject them on an expedition of this kind.

And now you may fancy us fast asleep, as comfortable on board the *Arar* as Mr. Vanderbilt on his big steam-yacht, our one practical inferiority being that we cannot sleep and advance on our voyage at the same time, but the earth will carry us eastwards and bring us surely to the dawn.

LETTER XLIV.

MÂCON, *September 5th.*

I rose early the next morning and made a study. When the crew turned out of their hammocks they soon prepared for sailing. Everything has its place according to two systems, one called "night order" the other "day order," and each of us knows the place of each detail under the two. There is consequently no confusion, and I am spared the trouble of giving directions.

Those young men had dined so heartily that there was nothing in the provision-box for breakfast. Stephen found a piece of dry bread for me and a pear. He had not even a glass of ale to bestow on his aged parent.

The lack of food and drink decided our immediate departure, it being quite contrary to rule that the *Arar* should be destitute of provisions.

There being, as usual, no wind, we crossed the river for the towing-path, and as we rowed observed a pair of magnificent buzzards, the largest birds of prey except eagles which are found in this part of France. The coolness of these birds is amazing. When not much disposed for flight they settle on the bank of the river, and if you follow them in a boat they will rise and settle a little further, and so on, not taking the trouble to fly more than is necessary at a time. They are not exactly lazy, but they understand the economy of effort.[1] Their strength of wing is great. I know a sportsman who once saw a buzzard fly across the Saône carrying a hare in its claws. He fired, when the bird (having crossed the river) dropped the hare in a field. On examination it proved to have been already emptied, but the muscles remained intact.

Stephen towed the *Arar* vigorously enough till he came to an embankment with a glacis of masonry. He walked on the top of this, and as the water is low a herd of cattle had been driven down on the bare ground between the glacis and the water to drink. Our tow-rope passing above them kept clear of their horns, but the water was extremely shallow and we grounded. We found it most difficult to get off, as it was necessary to keep the tow-rope stretched, and it constantly pulled the *Arar* to shore before she could get way on her for steering. To add to our perplexities there was a formidable bull on the embankment

---

[1] On referring to Macgillivray (*Rapacious Birds of Great Britain*) I find this passage on buzzards: "The birds, in fact, are not fitted for such headlong flights as falcons, and are satisfied with a sufficiency of food, and when they have no curiosity to satisfy, nor any amusement to engage in, they naturally take their rest. Buzzards are generally in good condition, which proves that they are industrious." In France a very stupid person is often called "une buse," but this is unfair to the bird, which seems to be a practical philosopher. Why should he kill more game than he requires, or trouble himself to fly further than is essential to his safety?

which contemplated Stephen in an unfriendly manner; however, nothing came of these little dangers, and if a cow had entangled herself in the tow-rope I should have cut it at once.

At this time, wonderful to relate, there suddenly sprang up a strong breeze. It was contrary, of course, as we do not seem destined to have a favourable wind in the whole course of our voyage, but any wind is better than tiresome calm.

At length we approached the suspension bridge of Fleurville, and as Stephen towed the *Arar* sharply round the corner under the bridge my anxiety was not for the boat. I desired to see a certain person, and there she was, washing in the river! You may perhaps be curious to know the reason for my strong desire to meet with this particular washerwoman. The reason is that she is an excellent cook, and her husband keeps a little public-house. It is really wonderful how well you are served in some of these humble places on the Saône if only you know them. Our *déjeuner* was fit for a prince: a great ripe melon, a dish of perfectly fresh fish, then *poulet sauté*, excellent cheeses, and an abundance of pears, grapes, peaches for dessert, all served with irreproachable neatness and cleanliness.

There is a window in the room where we had our meal that looks out upon the Saône. On a former voyage we dined here, and had a perfect view of Mont Blanc all the time. Our host was not at all aware that Mont Blanc was visible from his window, he had always taken the mountain for a cloud. So we lent him our telescope and made him see the dome and the *aiguilles*. At first all the snowy parts were of a warm white, and the aiguilles dark by contrast, then the white became rosy at sunset, and after sunset the mountain remained visible for some time as a purple-grey silhouette, both snows and *aiguilles* dark against the sky. A cloud rose gradually behind it, exactly of the same hue, and after a while we could only distinguish the summit of the mountain by its well-known forms. The distance is a hundred miles.

This time Mont Blanc remained invisible though the day was brilliantly fine. The breeze increased and got up a sea, but

Island of Fleurville from the Inn.

it was still against us, and on continuing our voyage we had to beat to windward in a narrow channel the whole length of an interminable wooded island. We had a short, chopping sea, and the water was too shallow at the sides to permit the use of the centre-board; however, the *Arar* had sufficient lateral resistance to go to windward without it. On this occasion she was exactly in those circumstances which are most unfavourable to a catamaran—rough water and short tacks—but in course of time we got past the long island, and then the wind declined. After the island a long subaqueous wall has been continued by the engineers in the same southerly direction. Not knowing how far this extended we had a mistaken idea that it had come to an end, and ignorantly sailed straight at it. The keels struck simultaneously and rose upon the wall, bringing us to a dead stop.

This gave us an opportunity for examining the wall, which was of strong masonry with a rounded top. Neither the wall nor the ship seemed any the worse for the collision, and we ourselves were perfectly at ease, for the boat retained her usual stability. The deck sloped upwards, that was all.

Soon after this incident there was a dead calm again, and we had to row. We talked of another incident that happened to us in this part of the river in 1885. The heat was stifling, and the south wind so feeble that Stephen had rigged out the tent as a spinnaker to catch whatever there was of it. We were lolling here and there on hulls and deck, trying to keep ourselves in the shadow of the sails, when I happened to look to the southwest and saw that a tremendous thunder-squall was coming, dangerous shreds of cloud flying, as it seemed, straight at us, and all the sky rolling like sudden smoke. Stephen got in his tent and we had time to lower the mainsail, but the fore halyard was impeded in its action by a piece of string that my son had tied round the mast for his ingenious tent-spinnaker. In obedience to a word from me, Maurice whipped out his pocket-knife and severed the halyard just in time. Then the squall was upon us, a fifteen minutes' tempest of such fury that the white waves were up in an instant, and we ran for shelter under bare poles into the port of Fleurville.[1]

---

[1] The only danger to a catamaran in a squall of this kind is that if too much canvas is left upon her she may *dive* head foremost, not having great floating power in the

Having got the *Arar* off the wall we lowered our sails and rowed on deliberately till nightfall. It is sometimes necessary to stimulate industry by an edict, so I proclaimed that there should be no dining till we reached the island of St. John, exactly seven miles from the place where we struck the *clayonnage*.[1] We looked for this island down the long expanse of grey river and made it out at last like a dim cloud suspended between water and sky. This part of the Saône is as straight as the railway, and you often see ahead for miles.

Mâcon from St. Laurent.

The island of St. John is about five hundred yards long by one hundred in width, and is thinly wooded. We moored our vessel to the southern extremity, and dined quite at leisure, as we knew that Mâcon was easily within reach. On leaving the island we saw the lights of Mâcon miles away, brilliantly reflected in the straight reach of river, and they gradually seemed to brighten till we found ourselves amongst them.

We moored our boat at St. Laurent, a distinct town exactly

bows. If I had to design a new catamaran I would increase the floating power forward and have high prows as a precaution against squalls.

[1] A seven miles' pull is nothing in a light rowing-boat, but in a sailing-craft weighing eight hundred pounds it is more serious. The young men pulled nine miles that evening, which, in muscular exertion, is fully equal to twenty in a skiff.

opposite Mâcon. Here dwells Batafi close to the water-side. He was already sleeping, when I knocked loudly and announced the arrival of the *Arar*. As a fireman springs from his couch when he hears the electric signal, even so sprang Batafi from his bed, alert and ready. He knows the *Arar*, and surely the *Arar* must know him, and the spot where he brought her to her mooring, for Batafi is her guardian, and this is her permanent home.[1]

LETTER XLV.

MÂCON, *September 6th.*

The peculiarity of the present voyage is that we sleep in all kinds of places, one night in a little rustic inn, another on board the *Arar*, a third in a large hotel. We might, no doubt, have slept regularly on the boat, but I dislike being encumbered with bedding, so we have only rugs and hammocks, and do not undress on board. Our floating accommodation is therefore reserved for an emergency.

The hotel where we are staying at Mâcon is the *Sauvage*, which merits a brief description. In the last century it was a fine private residence belonging to one of the important families of the place, a sort of *palazzo*. My bedroom has an old oak *parquet* in squares. The door opens upon a vestibule, which is wainscoted with elegant old-fashioned taste; and another door in the same vestibule is that of my study, formerly a

---

[1] The *Arar* is kept at Mâcon when not in use, simply because Batafi is the most careful and orderly man I have been able to find upon the Saône.

private cabinet in the old house. Nothing in travelling is so agreeable to me as the occasional possession of a study, especially a quiet little old room like this where I am now writing. It seems like a sort of home, with my books on a shelf and a spacious table to spread my papers.

There is a fine staircase in this house with some good forged ironwork, and there is also good ironwork at the back of the house in the narrow street. Some of the rooms are stately both in size and decoration, with old-fashioned adornments of carving

Mâcon, the Hotel du Sauvage.

and painting and marble. One of them on the upper storey retains much of its old magnificence, but has been divided. It was probably a saloon put there for the view of the river. Another good room on the second storey contains a bed and an arm-chair which have some historical interest, as they were used by Napoleon on his return from Elba. They are still in service amongst the ordinary furniture of the hotel, but that their historical character may be preserved care has been taken to leave them exactly as they were in 1815. The bed has four slender fluted columns supporting a light iron framework, the whole painted a pale grey. The chair is of the same style and colour, with faded green upholstery. It has happened to me sometimes, as to many other travellers, to be lodged in this room. I dislike historical associations got up for the occasion, but you may readily believe that it is quite impossible to sleep in that bed without thinking of Napoleon. I have lain awake in it at night wondering what could be the real state of his mind at the beginning of the Hundred Days. His reception at Mâcon had been most enthusiastic; the people themselves had made a little local revolution in anticipation of his arrival, and that day had been a successful day for him, but so cool a head as Napoleon's was not likely to be intoxicated because Fortune smiled on him once more. He must have clearly foreseen the difficulties of the immediate future. One of his great superiorities was his clear sense of the value of time, but that tells both ways. One who knows the use of time also keenly feels the want of it, and the difficulty of Napoleon's position after his evasion from Elba was, that his enemies were not likely to give him the time necessary to organise a really effectual resistance. His anxiety would be far more about this want of time than about the restoration of the empire, which he looked upon as already achieved. The date of his stoppage at Mâcon was the 13th March, 1815; the next day he went on to Chalon, and afterwards rode forward quietly by way of Autun, Avallon, and Auxerre. Exactly a week after sleeping in that bed at Mâcon he rested in the Palace of Fontainebleau.[1]

---

[1] Though the bed and arm-chair in the hotel at Mâcon are those used by Napoleon the room is not the same. Napoleon's room has since been demolished along with others to make space for the present large dining-room of the hotel.

The most remarkable event in the history of Mâcon is not of a military nature. It is not the invasion of Attila who pillaged it in the fifth century, nor that of the Saracens in the eighth, or of Lothair in the ninth. There was a great and terrible famine here in the eleventh century, but there have been terrible famines elsewhere. There have been fearful religious wars at Mâcon between Protestants and Catholics, but there have been religious massacres in many other cities. The unique distinction of Mâcon amongst the cities of the world is, that a Council of the Church was held here in the year 585, during which learned ecclesiastics argued solemnly on the question whether a woman ought, or ought not, to be considered a human creature.

Like Tournus, Mâcon has a strongly southern character. A reason for this may be that it belonged to the Provençal kingdom of Arles after the division of the empire of Charlemagne.

Roman Mâcon (Matisco) was not close to the river, but on the height. In the Middle Ages the town was picturesque, as we know from the remains of mediæval fortifications still visible in old views of the place. The bridge was grandly fortified at both ends; the town itself was surrounded by a wall with towers. There were spires and towers of many churches, and a cathedral, whilst the height once occupied by the Romans was the seat of a mediæval castle. Every change since then has been a diminution of the picturesque, but the town has gained in convenience by the fine quays and by the modern French tendency to build handsomely near a river.

I have never seen Mâcon under a more favourable aspect than one August evening in 1885. A large and very complete military band was playing in a lighted kiosk in the broad open space between the houses south of the bridge and the river. The gardens and terrace there were occupied by a dense crowd sitting on chairs or sauntering on the gravel. The *cafés* along the river front were brilliantly lighted, and the tents opposite each of them, on the other side of the causeway, were crowded. The air was deliciously warm, not hot, but it had the kindly temperate warmth of a southern summer night. The whole sky was perfectly clear and serene, and in it, over the river, hung the full moon in her most perfect splendour. On such a night the air is not wholly stagnant; you feel it gently moving, and now and then a faint touch of it may silver the water under the moon, yet

> "If zephyrs come, so light they come,
> Nor leaf is stirred, nor wave is driven."

There is always some powerful reason why we remember a particular scene, a particular time, and the reason why that evening remains in my memory is this: Amidst the crowd and the music and the lights of the town, I had only to turn my head to see one of the calmest and most lonely landscapes in all France. There was the broad, tranquil river flowing slowly and quietly to the south. Beyond it dimly stretched the vast plain that ends only at the mountains of Savoy, a wide and open country in which the villages are but as little groups of fishing boats at sea. It was the strength of this contrast that fixed the evening in my memory. Here we were in the heart of city life, with the crowd and the music and the lights, and only a few yards from us began the silence of the great spaces of Nature.

The statue of Lamartine stands here by the Saône like that of Niepce at Chalon. It might have been more appropriate to place it near his birthplace in the upper town, but here it is visible to all who pass on the river. Unfortunately the statue is a little ridiculous from its total absence of repose. The well-booted poet is clothed in a mantle, the mantle of inspiration, and this is blown about him in such a way that he seems, in the serenest weather, to be inconvenienced by an unpleasantly high wind. Of all the arts that of the sculptor most requires tranquillity. A work of this nature ought to have been dignified and monumental.

The house that is shown as the birthplace of Lamartine does not answer to the grandeur of the description in his memoirs, and there may be some confusion about it. The one I know is old, but neither large nor stately, and it is in a narrow street. The difficulty may be explicable in this way. Lamartine may have been born, as he says, in the great house, but whilst still a young child he went to live with his mother in a small one because the family mansion was sequestrated. Both the description and the situation of the smaller house answer to that which has always been shown me as the birthplace of Lamartine. He describes the street as "a gloomy lane, narrow and silent as a street of Genoa." If he lived there as a child, the inhabitants of the street may easily have supposed that he was born there. It was from this humbler house that his mother shot arrows carrying letters across to the prison where his father was detained, and also a file with which he filed a window-bar, and a thread that served to draw up a rope that he used as a bridge for nocturnal visits to his wife. If the narrative in the memoirs is trustworthy he returned to his prison cell by the same means before morning.

Lamartine is the great man of Mâcon, and was certainly one of the most gifted among mortals. Besides his poetical genius, which is indisputable, he had the gift of the most persuasive eloquence and an attractively handsome person. The kind fairies gave him the qualities that command admiration, but not the wisdom that leads to happiness. He was an idealist out of place in the world of reality, yet bearing himself with fine courage when he came into contact with it.

LETTER XLVI.

MÂCON, *September 6th.*

Before leaving this historical town I must give you some account of its present state. The Middle Age fortifications have entirely disappeared. The bridge is still the old bridge, but so much repaired and modernised that its age is revealed chiefly by a certain pleasant irregularity. Some of the arches towards the Mâcon side are either new or re-cased; those towards St. Laurent are the old arches. The bridge does not go straight across the river, it is not level, and it has not a uniform width. These are great merits in the eyes of an artist. We might have preferred the stone parapet, which must have existed in the Middle Ages, but it has been replaced by an incongruously light iron railing. Still, it is the finest bridge upon the Saône; more than that, it is all that is left of the old bridges, and after the numerous modern festoons of wire carrying a road of planks, it is a pleasure to see arches of massive masonry, and piers wedge-shaped and iron-armed to meet the wintry ice. We may well regret the loss of the castles at each end, but they have very rarely been preserved, that of Cahors being almost a solitary example. The modern passion for convenience demolishes everything that even seems to be in the way. The bridge of Mâcon has a very fine tone of colour. It is neither chilly nor dingy, but of a warm yellowish tone that is singularly favourable to the best effects. On a moonless night

The Bridge at Mâcon.

it can be as gloomy as Hood's "Bridge of Sighs," when the arches are dark over the black flowing river, but nothing can exceed the mellowness of its colouring in the warm-toned August moonlight, and in the most brilliant sunshine it is light but never glaring.

Our first feeling about the churches at Mâcon is a grievous

sense of loss. The place is an ancient bishopric. In the Middle Ages there was a cathedral which existed down to the Revolution, when it was almost entirely destroyed. Nothing remains of it now but its two towers, which have been lowered, and its narthex of the twelfth century which is converted into a coarsely decorated chapel. One of the most melancholy sights on the banks of the Saône is a sort of lapidary museum of the cathedral that once existed, kept in a little garden close by. It

Mâcon, St. Laurent.

is astonishing what a destruction of old churches there has been. Chalon in the Middle Ages had fourteen, it has now three if you include the Protestant chapel; Mâcon had twelve, it has now three if you include the poor remnant of the cathedral. With this exception the Mâcon churches are modern, an unmeaning structure opposite the hospital, and a Romanesque edifice with twin spires not far from the river. The exterior seems a little meagre, it appears to lack the solid substance of the true Romanesque, but the interior is effective and interesting, with the usual round apse and chapels of the style. There has been a determined attempt at mural painting in this church, with good effect in parts but a lack of *ensemble*. Mural painting is always a dangerous experiment. It ought to be strictly subordinated to the architecture and carried through in one consistent spirit. If many different artists are employed the church becomes a sort of

Mâcon, Towers of St. Vincent and Prefecture.

picture exhibition, with the inconvenience that the pictures are not afterwards dispersed.

I did not speak of the picture gallery at Chalon, and pass this at Mâcon for the same reason. These little provincial collections contain a few good examples of modern painting, generally by men unknown in England, but they are lost amidst a quantity of mediocre or bad work. The scientific and archæological museums, and the public libraries, are not open to this objection, as in them we find interest for the mind without offence to the eye. Of course there is an imposing portrait of Lamartine in the gallery here.

The prettiest modern building in Mâcon is the Prefecture. It is in that recent French Renaissance style which gives great importance and elegance to the roof, and as the Prefecture is situated on a steep which has been planted with massive trees and adorned with terraces and stairs, it has a romantic aspect like a palace in an opera. Beautiful as it is, it suggests something more beautiful still. The river ought to have washed the very foot of the steep and reflected the terrace and foliage instead of being separated from it by a space of flat land with houses, and there ought to have been a stately landing-place with stairs going down into the water.

I took my English passport to the Prefecture to get a *visa*, which was given at once and most courteously. The Chef de Cabinet told me that the Prefect, who was absent, had left instructions that a special French passport was to be prepared for me, and that this would be forwarded to me *en route*. Here is a new move easily traceable to the influence of the British Embassy in Paris, as the Prefect would not have ordered this passport to be delivered without instructions from the Ministry of the Interior.[1]

[1] Since the Prefect had said that it was impossible for him to authorise sketching, I had not applied for any further countenance from the Prefecture, and was surprised to learn that there had subsequently been a move in my favour there.

LETTER XLVI.

Port d'Arciat,
September 7th.

Before leaving Mâcon we were invited to *déjeuner* by an old officer, a friend of ours, who has earned his leisure by nineteen campaigns, his only regret being that the Crimea was not amongst them. We tried to console him by remarking that he might possibly, like so many others, have left his bones at Sebastopol, but military men do not take this much into consideration, either in prospect or retrospect.

He is a humorous old gentleman and he entertained us with some excellent stories, especially one about an unexpected meeting with a lion. In our friend's younger days lions were numerous in Algeria, and sometimes approached the outposts. One moonlight evening he and some other officers, quite unarmed, had gone outside a fort to the banks of a little stream, where they suddenly perceived a very handsome lion on the opposite bank within a very few yards of them. The humour of the story lies in the skilful strategic movement of the officers, which our friend describes without the least pretence to useless bravery. His name is not Tartarin, and he is not of Tarascon.

What a pleasure it is to have to do with competent, quiet people! What a difference between Batafi and the Patron of the *Boussemroum !* Batafi does what is to be done and vexes not my soul with verbosity. Stephen and Maurice know their work on the *Arar,* so I have simply to fix the hour of departure and then step on board to find everything in its place. A push with the boat-hook and the voyage is resumed.

Will there be any wind to-night? The answer is ever the same, calm and the toilsome oar, calm and the straining tow-rope! There is, no doubt, a profound poetry in wide expanses of tranquil water, especially under moonlight, but it is like always reading the same line from Moore :—

> " All hushed—there's not a breeze in motion ; "

or this from Byron :—

> "No breath of air to break the wave ; "

or Tennyson's :—

> " Calm, and still light on yon great plain."

The note, you see, is the same, the expression only is different. But the poetry that we should just now prefer to read in nature, would, if we had the choice, be more of this quality :—

> "A wet sheet and a flowing sea,
> A wind that follows fast
> And fills the white and rustling sail
> And bends the gallant mast ;
> And bends the gallant mast, my boys,"—

and so on—not quite to the point of carrying all the gear overboard, but enough for lively motion and just a little anxiety.

There being, however, not a breath of wind, the young men rowed through the bridge, and as it fell behind us I turned round and saw Mâcon under a rarely beautiful effect. The moon was high in heaven, but the light was hardly moonlight yet; it was that indescribable yet exquisitely tender and delicate illumination when what remains of the afterglow is mingled with a *beginning* of moonlight. The old bridge assumed a kind of pale golden brown, so mellow, so entirely opposed to all coldness or crudity of colour that it harmonised exquisitely both with sky and water, and seemed as fair as they. As the *Arar* continued to descend the stream the long quay was foreshortened and reflected with all its lights. Even the white spires of the new church seemed poetical in the magic light. The last sound that reached us was from a chorus of singers, whose voices came to us softly rising and falling over the water. Then we met a dark boat with rowers, and some women in the boat sang also, not without sweetness.

After that I turned my back definitively on Mâcon and paid more attention to my steering. Having passed under the railway bridge (the line to Geneva) we had nothing before

Mâcon from the Railway Bridge.

us but what seemed in the moonlight a long, calm, silent lake. There was an island in this lake a mile or two below the bridge. When we had left this island behind us, the scene became one of the most perfect in its absolute unity that I had ever beheld.

The moon had now gained strength, giving real moonlight, and there was just enough mist to convey the impression of vastness without concealing very much. Amongst the hills to the right were plainly visible the pale silhouettes of two remarkable cliffs, one of which is Solutré, close to the cave where such prodigious quantities of pre-historic remains have been discovered. These cliffs present a very striking profile, the land rises in a gradual slope up to the edge of them, and then there is a sheer precipice as if the hill had been blasted away, but it is natural in both.

As we were now quite clear of the town, the young men began to use the tow rope and I had good reason to congratulate myself on the small draught of water of the *Arar*, and also on her lightness, for the river was extremely shallow near the shore, and she grounded repeatedly. Whenever she does this, a man walks on each of her hulls and poles her

Cliffs of Solutré.

off easily, thanks to the entire absence of ballast and the stability of the double construction.

Whilst Stephen was towing he found a great number of quails, as many, he thought, as fifty in one place. They are in season now, wonderfully plump birds, and as good to eat as partridges.

At length the absolute solitude of this most tranquil and peaceful scene was enlivened by a sign of human habitation. Far to the south-west we could make out a dark spot on the right bank more square in shape than a clump of trees, and in the midst of this burned one brilliant star of golden light reflected in the river.

What an advantage it is to know a river well already and be your own pilot! Stranger tourists would have seen nothing in that dark spot but a lonely peasant's cottage. Stephen and I knew better. We shouted to Maurice, who was laboriously doing his duty at the tow-rope.—" Maurice, do you see that light? It is the Palace of the Vatican!"

" I understand. You mean the residence of the Pope."

The Pope is a fisherman, not a fisher of souls like the representative of St. Peter. Everybody here has his *sobriquet*. Batafi is not Batafi on the register, and there is nothing Papal in the real name of the Saône Pope. How he came by his Papal title I know not, but he has it for life, quite as securely as Leo XIII, the fisherman by the Tiber.

As I have said that the light is in the window of a fisherman's cottage you will imagine some very poor and perhaps dirty little place. We, however, intend to spend the night there, so as soon as we get opposite we take Maurice on board and pull straight across.

The fisherman has nothing quite ready for supper, therefore the provision box of the *Arar* supplies our repast, which is served in the cottage. Then Maurice and Stephen play at billiards. A billiard-table in a fisherman's hut? Yes, and more surprising things than that, an external staircase leading to a pretty balcony, both staircase and balcony adorned with a luxuriant *vigne vierge*. The door of my bedroom opens upon this, and I lean upon the rail and contemplate the peaceful scene. First a broad space gravelled, with a summer-house in it, then a garden, then the river-shore and the Saône itself, broad and tranquil, asleep in the moonlight. My bedroom is exquisitely clean, the woodwork all painted white, and there is a light paper on the wall. I have not the luxury of a carpet, but the deal boards are spotless and dustless, and the furniture good and sufficient. There is a prevalent good taste about this little inn that is a constant pleasure. You ask to wash your hands and are shown a little grotto with a fountain trickling behind green leaves.

I remember sleeping in this room before and awaking in the night with the vague idea that I was not alone. The door that opens on the balcony certainly began to move, I could see it distinctly in the moonlight. Then a ghost ought to have entered but it was only a large dog, my friend Pataud, the Pope's dog, a black and tan colley of the rarest size and beauty. To-day I inquired after him and was shown his skin, now used as a *descente de lit*, with a red cloth border round it. Alas, poor Pataud! He loved a comfortable rug and has become the thing he loved.

A peculiarity of this place is that in summer the people seem to live entirely in the open air. I have never seen the Pope eating in the house, or even taking his glass in the house, but always on a table outside under a great canvas awning, which is a permanent institution in summer. The Pope is a very short, thickset man, of most muscular build, and his summer costume invariably consists of light blue trousers with a white shirt (both so clean that they look fresh from the laundress), and a broad-brimmed straw hat with a scarlet riband round it. The Pope is a man of substance. He has erected this pretty inn himself with its commodious outbuildings. He rents this great reach of the Saône, and goes down to Lyons from time to time with the *vivier* in his boat full of living fish. His trade is far larger than a stranger would ever imagine;

sometimes he will take fish to Lyons to the value of several thousand francs. His nets are hung in perfect order under a shed, they are of enormous size, and very valuable. The success of his inn is explained by the moderate distance from Mâcon, whence parties come in summer as Londoners go to Richmond or Greenwich. A wedding party came in five carriages during our stay and had a fish repast. The Pope himself could not understand how these folks were able to eat. "They have just had a big wedding

A House at Port d'Arciat.

breakfast," he said, "at Mâcon, and they are going back to a great dinner, yet this does not prevent them from eating plenty of fish in the interval, and they have taken no exercise except sitting in a carriage." The Pope has kiosks in the garden for these parties. His success has been so marked that a rival inn has been set up close by. I would rather be this Pope than the one at Rome. See what a pleasant life he leads! His wife and servants do all the work except the fishing, and that is an amusing occupation for those who like it.

These little inns have often some celebrity for a particular dish. Here we do not fail to order the traditional *matelote*, the masterpiece of the Saône fisherfolks. A *matelote* contains many kinds of fish cut into pieces and served in an abundant sauce with red wine and toasts of bread therein. Its excellence depends on the quality of the fish and the genius of the sauce-maker, but when at its best it is indubitably a great invention, enough to convert Lent itself into a festival. It may be a cheap or an expensive dish. A *matelote* was once ordered of a Saône innkeeper famous for his culinary talents, and *carte blanche* was given as to outlay, so he compounded a *chef d'œuvre* and charged sixty francs for it. As I said at Verdun the *matelote, pauchouse,* and *bouille-abaisse* are kindred dishes invented originally by poor ingenious fishermen to make a good meal out of such heterogeneous materials as they possessed.

They served us here at another meal a large bream that did not look at all promising. Its first aspect was that of a dried fish served with hay instead of a sauce. Further acquaintance only proved how wrong had been our first impression. The hay was herbs dry only on the top, and beneath lay a depth of savoury sauce which with the green things made a succulent bog, or marsh, in the bottom of the deep dish. As to gudgeons the art of frying them is practised to perfection all along the Saône, but only a Frenchman can love a *friture* with such constancy as to enjoy one every day.

The scenery at Port d'Arciat merits a word of description. From the inn to Mâcon, between four and five miles, there is a vast green plain uninterrupted by hedges, like the plain near

Ray on the Upper Saône, but more extensive and greener. There is nothing to be seen on this great space but cattle browsing here and there, as in the polders of Holland. To the west, at a distance of between two and three miles from the river, the land rises suddenly in a hilly region with the cliff of Solutré and another like it in the distance. The rising ground is enlivened by villages and *châteaux*. To the south there is also a plain extending for some miles, and the hills beyond it are more mountainous in character. We have now reached a part of the Saône where we shall be constantly accompanied by mountain scenery at a distance of a few miles from the right bank. On the left there is a great plain with very distant mountains sometimes visible beyond it.

It is wonderful how the simple fact of having made a voyage together draws men to one another. In the evening came the engineer and some of the crew of the boat that towed the *Boussemroum* to Corre. The engineer greeted me heartily He talked about our present voyage and offered to tow the *Arar* southwards. Unfortunately towing and sketching are almost incompatible. He said that for our purposes the right boat would be one with spacious cabins and a small engine steaming five miles an hour. This would be practical but still expensive, and there would be none of the pleasures of boating. It would be the *Boussemroum* with steadier travelling power, paid for in dirt and vibration.

LETTER XLVIII.

Port de Thoissey,
September 9th.

The pleasant inn at Port d'Arciat, and the want of wind, detained us till yesterday afternoon, when a light breeze sprang up and we continued our voyage. The liveliness of the *Arar* makes her move sweetly in light breezes, and it is pleasant to feel her free motion over rippling water. The wind not being quite directly against us, we got along by taking what sailors call a long leg and a short one. This was almost the perfection of *mild* catamaran sailing in the pleasant sunshine on the broad river, with beautiful mountains slowly altering position as we advanced. At St. Romain the breeze fell and we drifted, though by the force of the current only. There was an angler sitting on the islet of the central pier, and he must have thought that he had discovered three aquatic amateurs at least as indolent as himself.

It became a moral necessity that somebody should make an effort to clear us of this imputation, so Stephen shouldered the tow-rope and we entered a pool about two miles long and of exceptional width. This pool is situated between the two suspension-bridges of St. Romain and Thoissey. Calm as it was now, we remembered the second of September, 1883, the day of a great gale, that raised waves comparable to those of a Highland lake. We were out here with the *Arar* in that gale under double reefs, going before the wind from Thoissey to St.

Romain and beating all the way back. This we did at Stephen's request as a crucial test of the *Arar*. We found her perfectly safe, and our central deck remained dry though the water flowed freely over the hulls, but it is well known that wave water is unfavourable to catamarans. Notwithstanding their remarkable speed on mere ripples they become sluggish in high waves, to which their structure and their lightness are equally ill-adapted. However, on that occasion the *Arar* was handier than I expected

The Beaujolais Hills from Thoissey.

her to be, and we returned to port at Thoissey without the slightest accident or disorder.[1]

Now, in this smooth lake, the *Arar* was moving lightly when she disturbed the solitude of a group of girls bathing. They hid themselves in the water, and let the tow-rope go over their

---

[1] This is understated in the letter. Having returned as far as Thoissey, we continued in another reach of the river against the wind, and then returned with it. An experiment of this kind is of the greatest value, as it leaves you entirely without apprehension in all winds of inferior strength. The only danger that day was the tendency to run nose under in going before the wind, which is a well-known defect of catamarans.

heads. They were able to swim, but not with confidence or style. Three hundred yards lower down we came upon a numerous group of boys. All these were skilled swimmers, and two of them came out at a great pace to the boat. As they seemed breathless I told them to rest on the port hull, so they sat upon it for a minute and then plunged again. Those nearer the shore, rivalling their comrades, swam out vigorously to the *Arar*, and, one after another, would sit for a second or two on the hull, then plunge again with much laughter and splashing. Can any momentary happiness be more complete than theirs? Wisdom herself might wish to be fourteen years old, swimming about with merry comrades in a beautiful broad river, on a sunny afternoon, without a thought of winter that will freeze the stream, or of age that will chill the blood! It is the perfection of physical enjoyment, of mere *living* without a thought or a care.

Thoissey itself is a village about a mile from the river. Port de Thoissey consists of an inn and a few houses, and is connected with Thoissey by one of the most beautiful avenues of plane-trees I have ever seen. The inn at the port has the charm of a delightful situation. It is well above the water, and just by the garden flows a tributary of the Saône, the Chalaronne, which offers here a delightfully safe little harbour for small boats. The *Arar* could not use it on account of her masts, too tall for the bridge on this river. Before the inn is a large square terrace shaded by a flat thick roof of green, the foliage of many oriental plane trees whose pale grey peeling trunks stand like columns in a church. The art of cutting these trees to produce this result is well understood in this part of France, but I have never seen it practised with such complete success. The roof of green is impenetrable by direct sunshine. After a blaze of sunshine on the exposed river this terrace seems a paradise.

The peculiarity of our life at this inn is that we do not live in it at all. We have our meals in the open air, on the terrace, and we sleep in a large room in another building, quite rough in comparison with our pleasant lodgings at Port d'Arciat. Everything here is rough, yet the meals are served neatly on the

Where we slept at Port de Thoissey.

terrace, with all correct observances, down to cooling the wine. There is a tendency in the *déjeuner* to repeat itself during the present voyage—melon, *matelote*, grapes, and peaches reappeared at Thoissey under the shade of the much-spreading oriental planes. Peaches are almost as plentiful here as apples in Normandy.

The most expensive restaurant in Paris would be less to my taste than this terrace, with the broad Saône below, the slender masts of the *Arar* peeping up between the trees, and the hills of the Beaujolais beyond. It is perhaps most charming to dine here late in a summer evening and enjoy the delicious coolness an hour after sunset when the sky is still crimson in the west, and the evening star is brightening over the obscure western shore.

Near Thoissey.

LETTER XLIX.

PORT DE BELLEVILLE,
September 10*th*.

We quitted Thoissey immediately after *déjeuner*, and having a favourable wind soon came to the lock. There was a steam-tug in it but I saw that the gate was still open, and when we got within hailing distance asked if we could go through at the same time. "We are waiting for you," said the lockkeeper very politely. Had he not waited we might have been detained there for hours as there is no obligation to open the locks for pleasure-boats, and at present the keepers do not willingly *spend* the water of the river, which is very low. When the water is superabundant they will pass a pleasure-boat even if it is alone.

Soon after leaving this lock a trifling accident occurred. A block had been insufficiently fastened to the foremast at Chalon, so it now came down suddenly, and the gaff and foresail with it. This was a matter of small consequence, as Stephen immediately climbed the mast and fixed the block more securely, but it reminded us of an accident that once happened near the same place. The crew was then composed of Captain Kornprobst, Stephen, and myself, and we were on another boat rigged as a sloop with one very heavy and tall mast. This mast had wire shrouds, and the foot of it was fixed in what is called a tabernacle.[1] Owing to a little piece of lazy negligence on the part of the workman who made the tabernacle[2] it was not strong enough to resist the enormous leverage of the mast without the help of the shrouds. There came a sudden squall, the shrouds snapped, the tabernacle gave way under the sudden strain, and over went mast and sails and all their gear into the Saône with a magnificent splash! Being luckily quite unhurt, we soon got the wreckage on board, after which we immediately rigged up the boom as a jury-mast, turned the jib into a shoulder-of-mutton mainsail, and sailed on to our destination which was thirteen miles away.

Yesterday we had nothing but the west wind blowing kindly.

---

[1] A sort of case for the foot of the mast that allows it to be lowered when passing under bridges.

[2] I could not explain this properly without the help of a diagram, but may say that the workman's negligence was from the nature of the case, quite undiscoverable by any one before the accident revealed it.

It was the pleasantest sailing and yet we were all melancholy, the cause of our sadness being the knowledge, of which we spoke very little, that our dear companion, Maurice, was to part from us the next morning. He has to prepare for an examination in which boating, though a most profound science, is not of the slightest value. The examiners have not included it in their list of subjects, probably because they themselves could not tell the difference between a *vrisse*[1] and a *drisse*,[2] between a *drisse* and a *drosse*[3] between an *écoute*[4] and an *écoutille*.[5] And yet without this elementary knowledge all learning is but vanity!

It was hard for Maurice, perhaps, that this last afternoon was so agreeable. The *Arar* sped so smoothly over rippling water with all her canvas set that we had not a care except that this stealthy swiftness was taking us too quickly over the little distance that remained to us. It had been sagely but reluctantly decided in council at Thoissey that we were not to go beyond Belleville, because Maurice must sleep near a railway station to take the earliest train in the morning.

There are three considerable islands above Belleville, and also a long *clayonnage*, the top of which was just above water as we passed, with a fisherman perched on the end of it like an aquatic bird. The current here is reputed to be very rapid. I have been told that it is equal to the Rhône, but am sceptical about currents. No stream is rapid that can be ascended by a tug with a train of heavily-laden barges.[6]

We like the personal freedom we have on board the *Arar*. It is not like being cramped in a rowing-boat or a canoe. You

---

[1] Tow-rope.   [2] Halyard.   [3] Tiller-rope.
[4] The rope called a sheet in nautical English.   [5] Hatchway.
[6] The speed of such trains seldom exceeds three miles an hour on the Saône.

may stand up, sit down, lie down, if you like, or take walking exercise on the windward hull. With a favourable wind I leave the navigation to the young men and sometimes read, often looking up from the page to the passing scenery. It is delicious to read poetry under such circumstances, especially if it tells of aquatic travel in passages like the following :—

> " in the night
> They by the moon past the high cliff and white
> Ceased not to sail, and lost the other shore
> When the day broke, nor saw it any more,
> As the first land they coasted, that changed oft
> From those high cliffs to meadows green and soft."

or this :—

> " And the next day the long oars down they laid,
> For at their back the steady south-west blew
> And low anigh their heads the rain-clouds flew ;
> Therefore they hoisted up their sail to it
> And idle by the useless oars did sit."

This last line exactly describes our own indolence, but wherefore toil when Zephyrus was taking us along too rapidly? Too soon we came in sight of the bridge where Maurice was to end his voyage.

After landing, we found ourselves in a street thronged with noisy peasants and neighing, excited horses returning from the fair at Montmerle. The inns were so full that it was hardly possible to enter them, and a hundred people were dining on tables set outside. However, the Port of Belleville is only a passage, people do not stay there, and we got bedrooms high up in a lofty, ill-kept house.

There was nothing of interest in the place except one old house with a turret. This is inhabited by a gentlemanly old man with a long white beard, a red Arab *chéchia* (a kind of fez) and very good manners. I learned that before the Revolution the turreted house had been the depository for salt. You are aware that the withholding of salt from the people and the heavy taxation of it were amongst the most hated abuses of the old *régime*. The turret is the monument of a past tyranny, exactly like the pigeon-turrets still often met with where the *grand seigneur* kept pigeons to feed on the peasants' crops.

Neither painter nor novelist could have found a better suggestion for tale or picture than this old white-bearded gentleman

Montmerle from Port de Belleville.

living alone in his antiquated house. I felt a curiosity about him, and had ample opportunity for gratifying it as he passed a long time at our inn, or rather, in the open space before it where we were dining. There was a certain Philistinism about the house itself, but the scene in front of it was far from commonplace. I sat at dinner looking towards one of the finest reaches of the Saône, now in brilliant moonlight with an island in the distance, and near the island a height on the left bank, and on the height the towers of an old castle and church. In the foreground sat the white-bearded gentleman talking with animation, his fine countenance and red fez splendid in the glowing lamplight. After a busy life in Algeria he had settled here to spend the evening of his days by the Saône, angling from dawn to dusk. We discovered another angling philosopher of the same kind, perfectly solitary, who had no reason for living at the Port of Belleville, except that he happened to be there. The nooks and corners about the islands here may have a strong attraction for these brethren of the rod.

LETTER L.

BEAUREGARD, *September 11th.*

Maurice has left us, greatly to our regret and to his own. His disposition is lively and merry, which does not prevent him from bearing the delays and annoyances of a voyage with the most exemplary patience. Every such voyage has its drawbacks. This time the drawbacks have been dead calms and terrible heat, and our slow travelling, naturally tiresome to young people, has been made slower still by my sketching, but Maurice takes it all as it comes. Prompt in obedience,[1] cool in emergencies,[2] equally ready to enjoy a pleasure or put up with a

---

[1] For example, on one occasion, when beaching the boat in a strong wind, I was afraid that some large stones might injure the rudders. Maurice was over the side in an instant, working up to his chest in the water to get the stones out of the way.

[2] After swimming in the middle of the river for a considerable distance with Stephen against rather a strong current, Maurice suddenly felt exhausted. Stephen said, "Put your hands on my shoulders." Maurice did this, and after some time Stephen asked him to take them off, which he did instantly, not touching the stronger swimmer again till invited to do so. It is scarcely possible to imagine a severer trial of self-control.

hardship, always willing to help with his hands to the utmost of his ability, he is exactly suited to an expedition of this kind, and it is useless to think of replacing him.

Stephen and I resumed our voyage yesterday afternoon against a head wind, and for a second time had to beat to windward in a narrow channel between a long island and the mainland. This island is one of the largest on the Saône, but is noticeable only for its size. After passing it we came to Montmerle, a long village close to the river with the too much modernised remains

Montmerle from the South.

of a castle and a church, on a height that Turner would have elevated to sublimity.

The wind had now entirely fallen, and the boat ran aground which saved the trouble of anchoring, and enabled me to make a sketch of Montmerle. I was cheered at work by the music of a band in the fair. The hills to the west in the department of the Rhône made a beautiful picture here with the mouth of the little river Mezerine which loses itself in the Saône at this place. It was one of those rare moments when Nature herself produces her most lovely harmonies of colour, this time in her tenderest greys.

We pursued our voyage by rowing alternately at a slow pace, there being nothing to hurry us. The scenery below Montmerle is very rich in wood and meadow, and the river broad, with an imperceptible current. Though a breeze was denied to us the voyage was still enjoyable, indeed Stephen remarked, at the very time when he was labouring at the oar, that there was no travelling comparable to this, with the beauty of the river all to ourselves, and our indifference about arriving at any destination.

After an hour of solitude, I heard the footsteps of a man on the left bank but could see nothing, as he was in the gloom of the trees. However, I called to him and asked a question. Then a voice came to us from the shades with friendly advice about a *clayonnage* lower down. We never saw the speaker, or any sign of him. It was really, for us, a case of *Vox et præterea nihil.*

The moonlight now brightened, the river seemed still wider (the result of a slight haze), and after some time there sprang up an almost imperceptible breeze, so faint, so faint, that it just silvered the water under the moon. It was dead against us, but we spread all our canvas and began beating to windward. "Well," said Stephen, "if the *Arar* will come round in this she will do it out of pure good will." As he spoke, she came round very prettily, to please us.

Sailing with so faint a breeze is idleness, as we can row more rapidly, but we deeply enjoy the solitude of the broad river, so beautiful in the moonlight. Stephen declared that one such night is worth ten years of the life of a *proviseur.*[1] Our pleasure was simply in the beauty of nature, as we had no luxuries on board, there being nothing but bread and cheese in the provision-

---

[1] Head of a *lycée.*

box. On this we supped contentedly without regretting the flesh-pots of Belleville and the crowd of noisy horse-dealers from Montmerle.

After an hour of this lazy sailing the wind fell completely, so that there was a moon in the water as perfect as the other in the sky. Stephen resumed the oar, and I made out the distant bridge of Beauregard with the binocular.

The people at Beauregard being all asleep we took the *Arar* to a sheltered corner and speedily established "night order"— not too speedily, for we were hardly under the tent when it began to rain.

Our berth was near the bridge, and next morning we heard a long procession of waggons crossing from Beauregard to Villefranche. As each waggon came near the end of the bridge the driver uttered an exclamation, and all the drivers said nearly the same thing. There is not much curiosity about the boat itself; it is the tent that awakens interest, because travellers are supposed to be inside it.

We crossed over to the inn, and being at once recognised were very cordially received. Not only was the master the same that we had known several years ago, but the servants had not been changed. The master is an old Saône pilot with a brown skin, clean blue clothes and gold earrings, his wife is a lady who understands the tastes and feelings of the better class. Perfect order and the most scrupulous cleanliness give one the impression of being on a visit in some well-kept private house. Immediately in front of the inn there is a courtyard shaded with a canopy of oriental plane-trees, as at Thoissey. Beyond this courtyard is a garden with five summer-houses or pavilions in it. The garden is in the same state of order as the house, not a fallen leaf upon the walks. There is a shady terrace at the end of the garden by the Saône, well above the level of the water, and on this terrace are tables and lounging chairs, where one may rest deliciously in the heat of the day and enjoy that famous view which has won for the place the well-deserved name of Beauregard.

This view is a panorama of the hills of the Beaujolais, from nowhere better seen than from this terrace. The mountain outline extends for sixty or seventy miles, and is extremely varied in character. Far in the folds of the pale grey-purple hills you see innumerable white villages and many isolated farms. The detail is without end, especially if you explore it with a telescope. That small speck on the knoll is shown by the telescope to be a chapel, a place of pilgrimage. That other speck is a farm, so high and lonely that the farmer must hear no voices but those of the four winds. *Châteaux* and towers are in the pleasanter situations. The background of mountains rises to the height of those in the north of England. St. Rigaud, the highest summit, measures 3,319 English feet. These mountains are generally bare of trees, but beautiful in their changes of pale aërial colouring of greys, purples, and greens.

I wrote all morning in the garden, seated in one of the excellent lounging chairs and with this remarkable view before me. The servant came naturally to lay the cloth for us out of doors. It seems to be taken for granted that every one prefers a repast in the open air.

The village of Beauregard contains some picturesque houses, quite of a southern character, with projecting eaves and a predominance of brown or ochrous colouring enlivened with the green of their vines. Behind the village there is a gorge in the hills, and just to the south of this the castle is situated very grandly on one of the finest sites near the Saône. The present castle is modern but one or two of the old towers have been preserved. The design of the modern building shows in one thing an appreciation of artistic possibilities. The castle is in two principal masses connected by a central structure on three large open arches, and from the garden behind you see the Beaujolais panorama framed in these arches like a triptych, a most successful combination of architecture and landscape.

Beauregard from the South.

The rich scenery about Beauregard, the hills, the woods, the avenues on the left bank of the river and the open country on the right, make it a charming place for walking, and we spent the whole evening in the bright moonlight according to the custom established on the *Boussemroum.* The beauty of this place made Stephen give me a long and enthusiastic description of the beauty of Algiers. All who know Algiers intimately have the same enthusiasm, the same longing to go there once again.

LETTER LI.

TRÉVOUX, *September 12th.*

Our voyage from Beauregard to Trévoux was an enchantment. The scenery is lovely, the weather was perfectly beautiful, and we had just enough wind to speed the *Arar* as fast as we care to travel. With all our canvas set, and never either a spurt or a stoppage we kept the pace of a good walker, and so steadily that I was able to make several slight yet not unfaithful sketches of the shore.

Beauregard from the West.

After Beauregard the left bank takes a more broken character, with steep and strongly formed natural buttresses. Riottier is a charming little village with picturesque brown buildings and green vines and a clean-looking inn quite close to the river. Above the village rises a steep *mamelon* clad with vines and crowned by a little tower. The view on the opposite side of the river is much more extensive, there you have a vast range of elevated country interesting to explore with the binocular. It is dotted all over with hamlets, farms, or *châteaux*, new and old. We noticed one very large modern house in its own luxuriant woods. Costly residences begin on the Saône a little above Mâcon, and increase in number after Thoissey, becoming gradually more frequent as the river approaches Lyons. We

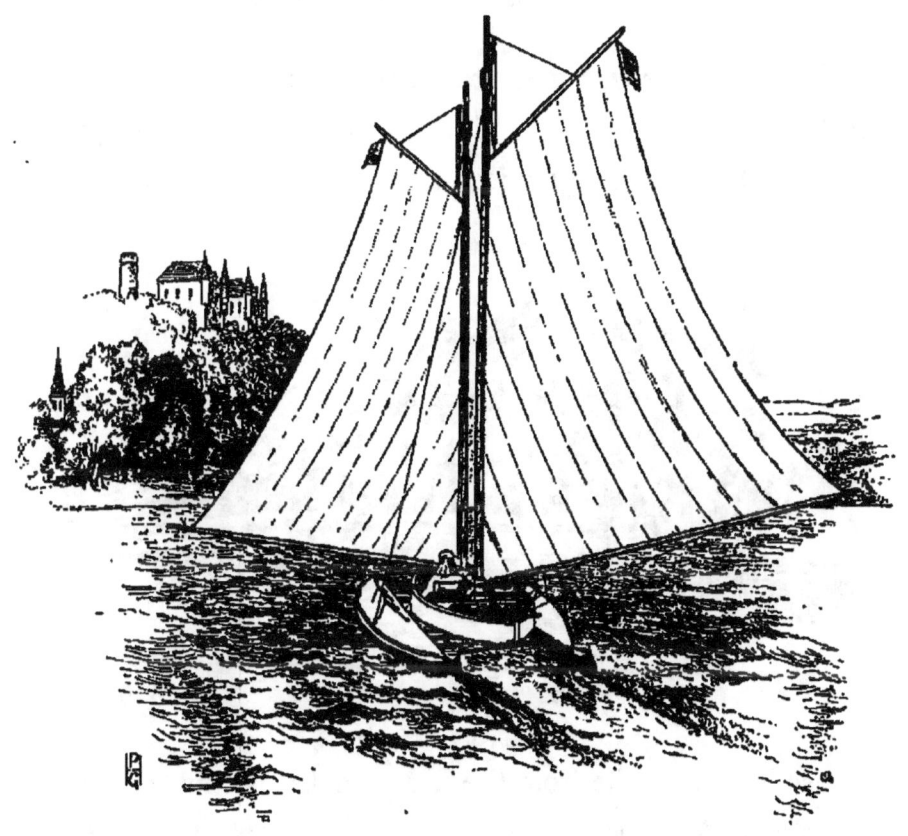

The Arar with a fair wind.

observed that at Beauregard it was already quite possible to guess (if we had not known from the map) that we were approaching a wealthy city. There is a small château near the water to the south of Beauregard, that has all the finish of Parisian building. It looks like a rich Parisian's dwelling at Passy or Auteuil placed on a smooth green lawn in the fairer landscape of the south.

Here we find ourselves between Villefranche and Anse, a region celebrated for its beauty even in a popular proverb:

> "De Villefranche à Anse,
> La plus belle lieue de France."

The rural poet who made this rhyme had perhaps not visited all the leagues in France, and his praise is certainly exaggerated, but it is honest exaggeration, due to love of the native land.

Riottier from the North.

Anse is half a mile from the Saône, but it is connected with it by the river Azergues. I have not explored this stream (fit only for a canoe), but think it not impossible that it may be the most beautiful tributary of the Saône, except, of course, the Doubs, which is an ally rather than a tributary. The Azergues is scarcely more than forty miles long and flows entirely through picturesque valleys. Anse was an important Roman station and there are still remains of Roman walls. Augustus had a palace here which has long since disappeared, but some remains of it were used to build a chapel that afterwards became a warehouse, the last state of an imperial dwelling.

Being anxious to reach Trévoux, where my correspondence was awaiting me, I did not, to my regret, take the opportunity of visiting Anse to see the great mosaics which once adorned a Gallo-Roman mansion, and, having been preserved and protected in their place, are now classed as historical monuments. There is also a mediæval castle at Anse, or the remains of one.

It is probable that the Romans liked Anse because it is so well supplied with water. One of the fountains has the ex-

Riottier from the South.

tremely convenient property of flowing most abundantly in times of drought, like the most opportune charity.

Opposite the mouth of the Azergues is the château of St. Bernard, which has the look of new masonry in old forms, but who can look at St. Bernard, or anything else, when Trévoux comes in sight?

The approach to Trévoux from the north is made into a more complete picture than common, by the presence of some beautifully wooded islands and islets on the right hand exactly where they are wanted. The first thing visible is the old castle of

Trévoux on its commanding height, an octagonal keep, two or three other towers, and some massive fragments of the connecting walls. The keep is built in bands of differently coloured stone, but grey is the predominant colour of the ruins. As you approach, the town itself becomes more distinctly visible. It rises on a very steep slope from the river to a point below the castle, and is composed of a most picturesque medley of houses

Trévoux from the North.

with a number of little towers. Many of the houses are capriciously coloured in a southern, almost Italian taste, but these pinks and ochres give no worse effect at a distance than a general impression of warmth. I remember seeing them glow in the red light of a sunset, when the city turned perfectly crimson.

As we were landing our things on the slope near the quay, a coal merchant kindly offered the use of his little boat if I desired to anchor the *Arar* at a distance. The navigation on the lower Saône being now resumed, it is necessary to keep our boat away from the towing path. We therefore anchor her systematically in the river nearer to the opposite shore. Our new friend was most obliging, and brought us away from our ship when she was anchored. During our stay at Trévoux he kindly placed his boat at our service.

Being within a *myriamètre* of a fort (that on the Mont d'Or) I am liable to imprisonment for sketching, so I was glad to find at the post the expected French passport with a personal recommendation. Having also a special recommendation in the French language from the British Embassy I may escape any lengthened detention, and yet these passports are not what the law requires, which is a permission from the military authorities, and that, in any producible form, I shall certainly never obtain.

The finest sight in Trévoux is the famous view from the terrace. This we did not fail to see at the best time, a little after sunset. It naturally suggests a comparison with the well-known view from Richmond Hill. It is not any recent passion for the Saône that leads me to prefer the view from the terrace here. It is grander for two or three reasons, but especially because it includes mountains. The Mont d'Or is hardly a mountain, being only two thousand feet high, but it has picturesque forms, it rises conspicuously from a low country, and it is near enough to be imposing. This is to the south-west. The view on the north-west is bounded by the hills of the Beaujolais that we saw from Beauregard, and immediately in front, in the west, is a remote mountainous distance extremely graceful in form, as seen from here range behind range to the crests of the Tarare Mountains, as high as Skiddaw or Helvellyn.

The Quay at Trévoux.

These hills divide the Saône from the Loire, the two rivers being here only thirty miles from each other as the crow flies. This description is not intended to convey the idea that the view from Trévoux is a grand mountain panorama. It is not that, but a lowland scene of the most exquisite beauty, with the added charm and poetry of remote mountainous distances. The perfection of the scene from Trévoux consists in the presence of different elements in sufficient but not overpowering strength. The river sweeps in one magnificent curve from north to south, calm as the tranquil sky that it reflects, its breadth spanned only in one place by the thin festoons of the suspension bridge. There are the well-wooded islands above the bridge, and graceful groups of trees on the rich green banks below. Beyond the river a fertile plain stretches far away to the foot of the Mont d'Or, and the more distant mountains of Tarare. Those of the Beaujolais rise in pale azure beyond the darkening woods.

"Stephen," I said, as we were gazing together in silence on all this, "I think that in the way of beauty—not grandeur or sublimity, but beauty only—this is the most perfect scene I have ever beheld, and we are here at its own hour. It can never have been more beautiful than now. There is enough, but not too much, of light, the colouring is as harmonious as a Titian and nothing is too sharply defined. The moon is brightening, the red in the western horizon is lingering still, but not for long. Let us go before it changes more!"

So we buried ourselves in the thick shade of the pathway that goes down to the river-side, carrying away in memory the fairest landscape on the Saône, perhaps the fairest scene in France.

LETTER LII.

Trévoux, *September 14th.*

There is such a glamour in romantic history that a place like Trévoux gains infinitely in interest when we know that it is not only very old and picturesque, but that it was once the seat of a

Trévoux, Rue du Port.

line of sovereigns, though they were but princes and had not a very extensive territory.

Trévoux has a history as romantic as its situation. It was the capital of the Principality called to this day "Les Dombes."

One of its princes was made prisoner at Agincourt. After fighting against the Counts of Savoy and the Dukes of Burgundy, the Principality was recognised and respected, and long retained a degree of independence that is very surprising in the case of a state neither large enough to be really powerful nor little enough to escape attention. The later princes of the Dombes lived at Paris, but retained almost complete sovereign powers. They could create nobles, coin money, levy taxes, and condemn to death. They had a Privy Council of their own at Paris and a Parliament sitting at Trévoux. The final annexation of Trévoux to the French crown only took place about the middle of the eighteenth century.

The Principality of Les Dombes was remarkable for the prodigious number of its fish-ponds. In the Middle Ages these were less numerous, but in the eighteenth century there were more than a thousand of them. They have since been reduced to about half that number, for sanitary reasons. Since their diminution, marsh fever has become much less prevalent. Some of these ponds are of considerable size; that of the Grand Birieux covers about eight hundred acres. This land of ponds would still be a most curious region to explore with a tent and a canoe, and I have not a doubt that it contains many strange landscapes highly interesting from an artist's point of view, but the dread of marsh fever keeps me out of it.

The upper town of Trévoux is now little more than a single street, and there is an ascent to it for pedestrians by a stone pathway winding in a curiously Italian little street of its own, with immensely tall gaunt houses on one side, whose lofty windows command the river and the plain. The lower town is not much more than a line of houses by the Saône.

Seen from the bridges, Trévoux abounds in curious details, remnants of mediæval times. The steep street that comes down to the bridge has one or two fine tall mediæval houses, and close to the quay there is an old oriel window.

A false bed of the Saône above the hospital remains a marshy pond when the river is low, and with its rich trees and aquatic vegetation presents some beautiful pictures. After we had visited this on the evening of the 13th, we dined as usual out of doors, when there came a sudden squall with thunder and

Trévoux, the Bridge.

rain. The diners passed all that was on the tables with surprising rapidity into the hotel through the windows, a very amusing scene. Amongst the company was a gentleman about twenty-two years old, weighing twenty-six stone. He is healthy, good-looking, has very animated and pleasant manners, and is wonderfully active, being a good walker and a lively dancer. He is built in proportions like those of Raphael's baby-angels. I saw him quite in the stern of a small boat whilst another man rowed. He seemed in great peril as the stern almost foundered under him whilst the prow rose high in the air, but he only enjoyed the humour of the situation. It was exactly that of "The Wee Man" in Hood's comic sketch.[1]

After the thunderstorm we took a moonlight walk, and when we looked for the *Arar* there was not a boat to be seen. Could she have foundered in a squall? Impossible, with six water-tight compartments; but whither had she gone? Following the direction of the wind, we presently discovered her serenely anchored in another place. Fairy sailors had navigated her, and chosen a safer anchorage. She had dragged her anchor during the squall and passed under the bridge. Here was a fresh reason for moderation in the height of her masts.

LETTER LIII.

NEUVILLE,
September 16th, Morning.

We quitted Trévoux in the evening of the 14th. Immediately below the town the river is not wider than the Upper Saône, which it closely resembles, but it expands afterwards. The moon was now high in heaven, and we had a fine disengaged view of the Mont d'Or, so that the effect in the bright moonlight was quite that of a lake. In this lake were several small islands, and Stephen at once drew my attention to them for a particular reason. The earth of these islands was quite invisible, their place being indicated only by their trees, the trunks of which were partly under water, exactly as if the country were inundated. In fact, it was a misnomer to call them islands at

---

[1] See Hood's *Whims and Oddities.*

all, since they were not surrounded by water, but submerged. We then rowed to the right bank to examine the state of the shore, and found there also the inexplicable appearance of inundation. The ground, it is true, was more elevated and therefore out of water, but the belt of trees stood in it as cattle do on a hot day. "Can there be a flood?" we asked, "or are we the victims of some extraordinary delusion?" A moment's reflection set aside the notion of a flood, as the river was low at Trévoux, and could not have risen since we left, and as for delusion, the *Arar* roosted like a bird amongst the upper branches. The difficulty was explained to us afterwards. A weir and lock had been established at Port Bernallin, below the islets, since the trees had grown, and these works, aided by a dyke on the left shore, had formed a reservoir of water, which had, in fact, flooded the islands and produced a purely local inundation.

In the midst of this pool the weir was not visible by moonlight, and we could have imagined ourselves on some broad river of America.

With the great mass of the Mont d'Or rising pale in the south and looking far vaster and more distant than it really is, the scene was the grandest, so far, on our voyage, though unfit for pictorial representation of any kind. We quitted it reluctantly to set up the tent on the *Arar* and have our supper, after which we enjoyed such an excellent night's rest that when we began to stir in our hammocks the sun of a new day was already warm upon our habitation.

"I notice, Papa," said Stephen, "that whenever we sleep on the boat you seem more refreshed the next morning and have a much finer appetite than after a night passed in an hotel."

The reason may be that there are no smells on a catamaran, not even bilge-water. In fact, the arrangements are sanitary, except that we are near the water, but we are raised far better above the surface mist than in the cabin of an ordinary boat. I have never, hitherto, got anything but benefit from sleeping on a catamaran. There is a prudent and a reckless way of doing everything, even gipsying.

We arrived at the lock just in time to see the public steamer *Parisien*, a pale green vessel, 245 feet long, her decks crowded with passengers and luggage.[1] The *Arar* was moored against the glacis to let the great ship pass, when, lo! in the opposite direction and quite close to the same glacis came a steam-tug with its train of boats. Apparently these must crush the *Arar*, but I had confidence in the steersman's skill and in the usual Saône civility. He managed his train beautifully and, of course, spared us. When the tug stopped I was amused to see a fat pilot lightly leap ashore without a gangway, other men repeating the same exploit, and the women laughing at their agility. I made their (the men's) acquaintance, and asked to be towed. They readily consented, and we went through the lock together. When the water had descended to its lower level, Stephen was still on the quay, but he let himself down with a rope, hand over hand, and very soon the *Arar* was going by steam.

[1] Not long after our voyage this vessel foundered in consequence of striking against the spur of the Vaise bridge (just above Lyons) in a fog. The captain, M. Meynier, behaved with remarkable presence of mind. He got his sinking boat alongside a barge, counted all the passengers carefully as they left his vessel, perceived that one was missing, and went himself to seek through the cabins up to his chest in water, and with the probability that before he could get out again the sinking ship would make her final plunge. A last he found a woman paralysed with fear standing on a table and carrying a child. The captain took both in his arms and brought them safe to the barge, the *Parisien* foundering immediately afterwards.

I have never seen anything in the way of locks so magnificent as these great locks on the Lower Saône. They are, in fact, more like docks than locks, and can contain a great train of enormous barges with one or two steamers all at the same time. In passing a lock along with very heavy boats on a comparatively delicate thing like the *Arar*, it is best to keep behind and

St. Germain au Mont d'Or.

contrive to be the last, so that when the steamer begins to tug its train out of the lock you may not get crushed between the oaken side of some huge rude barge and the granite wall of the basin.

Going by steam was quite exciting after our usual lack of motion, but I object to being pulled along through beautiful scenery without permission to stop and sketch it. We were in the finest reaches of the Saône, with a view of the Mont d'Or directly in front of us.

This basin, between the lock at Port Bernallin and Neuville, is the seat of the most refined boating on the river. It is the Solent of the Saône.

As the *Arar* went rather speedily behind the steam-tug (the train being light) we passed two or three rowing boats of delicate Parisian build. One of these was rowed by a gentleman in grey, with three charming little boys all dressed exactly alike in dark blue jerseys with soft hats of scarlet felt. He looked at our boat with evident interest, and made an attempt to follow, but the steamer was going too fast for him. We landed at Neuville and found, not an inn, but a pleasant little café restaurant close to the water, so I persuaded the people to lodge us. This being settled, we took the things out of the *Arar*, when the gentleman with the three little boys came alongside. In the kindest and most gracious way he offered to do all in his power to be of use to us. He was the owner of a pretty sloop, moored to a chain in the river, and he helped us to moor the *Arar* to the same chain. Then he took us to see his *garage*, a long building near the river full of boating things, all kept in the most perfect order. Like many amateurs of boating, our new friend likes to work with his own hands. He showed us a portable canvas boat that he had made himself, and there was another sloop in the *garage*, keel uppermost, that he was engaged in caulking. He had a Canadian canoe, bought in London, and other interesting things. "But this is nothing," said M. Vibert, "there is another *garage* close by which is far superior to this. I must take you to it now." He then guided us past the bridge where another yacht was at her moorings, and introduced us to his friend

M. Zipfel, who has a pretty house and garden close to the riverside. In the garden is a very long, well-lighted building that might serve for an infant school. This is the *garage*. It is a sort of museum of the prettiest boating toys and, in fact, is kept as neatly as any museum can be. M. Zipfel works with his hands, too; but few amateur boat-builders could compete with him in delicacy and finish.

Petite Amie in a Light Breeze.

There are several small yachts in the Port of Neuville, all of the same type, namely, the centre-board sloop, which is found most convenient for the river. We visited two of these, M. Vibert's *Petite Amie* and M. Zipfel's *Croquemitaine*. Every place soon acquires its own boating character. At Chalon this is scientific, but rather rough, and the local building is done in steel; at Neuville both the boats themselves and all their belongings are kept with a perfection of care and order that cannot be excelled anywhere. They are of Parisian build, and of wood. M. Zipfel has a light centre-board boat for rowing and sailing that he lent us for an excursion to the Albigny Islands. M. Vibert and a friend of his offered to row us, the little cardinal-hatted boys accompanied us, and in a few minutes our voyage had assumed quite an unexpected character. It was no longer the Saône, for the long channel to the right of the islands was like a narrow, but exquisitely beautiful river, hitherto utterly unknown to us.[1] It was no longer our own voyage since we had completely lost sight of the *Arar*. Here were friends treating us with the utmost kindness whom we had only known an hour. We were so completely disconnected from the past of the day before, and even of that very morning, that the present did not seem real. If a dream, it was a pleasant dream! Nothing could be more beautiful than this channel, completely hidden from the main river by densely wooded islands, whilst the mainland is hilly and picturesque, with a finely situated tower. The islands are six in number, in a chain a mile and a half long. They take their name from Albinus, the rival Emperor to Severus, who had a splendid villa with fine gardens on the right bank opposite the isles, one of the prettiest sites upon the Saône, afterwards occupied by a feudal castle.

---

[1] I had never explored this channel, knowing this part of the Saône only by voyages on the public steamer, and without our new friends it would have remained unknown to us, as we naturally avoid such passages for fear of obstructions.

LETTER LIV.

ST. RAMBERT, *September 17th.*

The *Arar* has reached her destination at the *Île Barbe*, just above Lyons. I have no intention of taking her through the city to the Rhône. The Saône in Lyons is so protected by high embankments and tall houses, and precipitous hills above them, that sailing is quite out of the question, and I dislike rowing a heavy[1] boat, short-handed, in a crowded water thoroughfare with fast little steamers flitting every five minutes through the bridges.

Sailing boats require something in the nature of a lake. Chalon possesses this in the quiet and well-exposed reaches between that city and Verdun on the Doubs. Neuville has its lake in a beautiful basin as long as Derwentwater. This basin has all the characteristics of lake scenery. The Mont d'Or rules over it as Skiddaw over Derwentwater or Ben Cruachan over Loch Awe, besides which the whole of the right bank is grandly precipitous and richly wooded, whilst the shore is as green as that of Windermere with weeping willows drooping their branches over the water.

As there happened to be a light breeze M. Vibert invited us to sail on this basin in his yacht, *Petite Amie*. She is the fastest boat of her class on the river, and as she stands for the best French building for river work, I was glad to have an opportunity of steering her. I found her easy to handle against the

---

[1] It may seem contradictory to call the *Arar* sometimes heavy and sometimes light. She is light for sailing, heavy for a rowing boat.

wind and very quick in stays, but so sensitive to the helm as to require incessant attention, in consequence of which these boats are not so easily managed when the wind is strong and fair.

Petite Amie in a Gust.

The clever Parisian builders, who work chiefly for the Seine, attach the greatest importance to rapidity of evolution which is of less consequence in more open waters. I should have liked to try the *Arar* in company with this boat, but her comparative slowness in stays would only have put us out of temper. The next day I invited the owner of *Petite Amie* and a friend of his [1] to sail on the *Arar* as they seemed curious to try her. We were six on board, counting two little boys who were certainly the ornaments of the boat. The boys were stowed away safely in the small fore-deck on rugs, very happy to be in this strange new kind of vessel. We had first to go to windward up the river and then return with a fair wind. Our guests took a keen scientific interest in the catamaran, and seemed to find her both

In the Basin above Neuville.

handier and faster than they had imagined. I believe they had inwardly suspected that we should be obliged to use the oar in coming about.

Catamaran sailing gives quite a peculiar sensation, which for our guests had the charm of novelty. The wonder is to see a boat getting up her speed without heeling, in fact, you may sail through a gust of wind without spilling a drop from a wineglass, I mean on protected water. On a catamaran, too, your relations with the water, though not dangerous, are very close and intimate. You see the emerald stream rushing faster than

[1] M. L'Eplattenier, also a member of the Neuville Yacht Club.

the Rhône under the suspended deck which is only a light bridge, and even small waves may splash harmlessly over the hulls. "I feel," said M. Vibert, "as if I were sailing on a plank."

Immediately after this trial of the *Arar* we bade adieu to Neuville. How marvellously the significance of a name changes with changed experience! "Neuville" once meant for me simply the least beautiful town upon the Saône with an ugly church, a long promenade, and a shot tower; to-day it means the place where the flower of French amiability grows fairest.

A good breeze soon took us past the islands of Albigny and down to the lock at Couzon, the last lock in the voyage.

Cliff of Quarry at Couzon.

The situation of Couzon is in the highest degree picturesque, indeed for valley scenery it is the finest site on the river. Couzon is on the right bank of the Saône, in a space of flat or gently rising ground bounded on all sides except the river by fine steep hills with much grandeur and variety of form. To the north, the hill has been extensively quarried for building Lyons, the result being a great precipice. To the south the hills are green and wooded, to the west wilder.[1]

---

[1] The southern hills include the Mont Ceindre, and the western the Mont d'Or.

The near neighbourhood of such an important quarry has had its effect on the village itself which is entirely of stone, and for the most part roughly built in the southern fashion that does not wait for age to be picturesque. The Byzantine church, which is new and very effective in the distance, has nothing glaring about it externally, being built of a stone almost the colour of yellow ochre. Internally, it is decorated throughout with gold, colour, and stained glass. Stephen protested against the glare of colour, but this may be endured if it is consistently and thoroughly carried

Couzon Church and Hills.

out. It is better than the common mistake of leaving a church quite bare in one part and richly decorated in another, making the decoration seem overdone and the nudity chilly and miserable. It is strange to find such a church as this in a country village; its place would be in the heart of Lyons.

Close to the shore at Couzon we found the finest willow we had ever seen, a tree as tall and strong as a well-grown elm, a most graceful tree with its delicate foliage.

Works were being carried forward on the opposite side of the river to fill up a "losne" or false bed covered only in floods. The treatment of rivers by engineers leaves these false beds generally dry but barren. In a natural state they often remain stagnant marshy ponds. Opposite Couzon a large stone dyke separates the false bed from the present river, but to the east of this is a wide stony desert at a low level. Beyond it rises a steep hill with the village of Rochetaillée and the remains of its castle. This village has some importance in the arts as the place first chosen by M. Guimet of Lyons for the manufacture of French ultramarine.

After the lock at Couzon the character of the Saône is completely changed. It is no longer the river of great spaces and great distances, no longer the best river for sailing in the world. It has suddenly been transformed into a curving narrow river of short reaches, shaded on both sides by richly wooded hills. To the right is the range that includes the Mont Ceindre and the Mont d'Or, to the left a wooded steep that rises to about eight hundred feet.

This part of our voyage was of a very peculiar interest. Inclosed, as we were, by the hills, it seemed useless to think of sailing, yet there was just air enough to keep the sails out like wings, and with the help of the current we maintained an unfailing motion. The daylight now deserted us; the moon had not risen, and we dined in complete tranquillity, broken only by the sound of invisible carriages on the road close to the water, suggesting the neighbourhood of a great city. In this way we passed through a long narrow channel where are two thickly wooded islands, the faint breeze being just strong enough to make steering possible.

This being a part of the river that we had not before visited with our boat, it was rather disquieting to explore it in total darkness. At such times Stephen takes the tiller-ropes and I stand in front of the foremast trying to see in the dark with a binocular. We passed under a bridge and near a dredger, then we suddenly found ourselves close to some intricate scaffolding rising out of the water, and veered to the right just in time to avoid being entangled amongst it.[1] Having escaped this danger by a few inches I concluded that it might be wiser to land and wait till the moon looked over the brow of the hill, so we beached the *Arar* on the right bank.

For some time previously we had heard a French horn advancing toward us. On landing I walked along the shore and met the performer. His instrument was slung over his shoulder and he had replaced it at his lips by a tall-bowled German pipe. He was young, and had a pale, melancholy countenance, which, with the doleful music, led me to conclude that he had the misfortune to be in love. I asked if he knew the river down to the Île Barbe. Yes, he knew it, but he gave a pessimist account. It was full of rocks, the navigation was difficult, we had better not attempt it with the sails. Under these circumstances of quite imaginary peril we turned to literature with a lantern as a resource against the tedium of waiting for the moon. In half an hour she rose above the brow of the dark wooded hill and began to silver the water. Stephen said, "Who could believe that we were on a river and near a populous city? Surely this is a little woodland lake in some unfrequented country." I answered that, for the moment, it was exactly like one of the quiet wooded inlets on Loch Awe.

---

[1] I learned afterwards that these were preparations for building a new bridge. Such a scaffolding is a nice thing to run your bowsprit into on a dark night.

Having now light enough to continue our voyage we rowed with needless prudence till we came to the rocky end of the Île Barbe. All we saw of the famous island by moonlight was a rocky shore, one or two dimly defined towers, and a great obscure mass of dense, dark, and apparently impenetrable foliage. We

Île Barbe, North End.

entered the western channel according to sailing directions given to us at Neuville. Here I landed and went to seek for the restaurant Des Tonnes which had been recommended to us. The polite restaurateur put a lantern on his private landing place. Guided by this beacon, the *Arar* accomplished the two last furlongs of her voyage.

LETTER LV.

St. Rambert, *September 19th.*

When you want to have a thing done, some competent person ought always to present himself and beg to be permitted to do it for nothing. Acting on this excellent principle, a very skilful amateur photographer came and requested permission to take a portrait of the *Arar*. It had been my intention to do this honour to our ship, and lo! it is done without cost.

The photographer took his station first on the Île Barbe, the *Arar* being at anchor with all sails set, and he afterwards, from St. Rambert, made an instantaneous picture of the boat in motion. The breeze was moderate and the channel narrow, but we sailed in circles before the photographer till he had taken his bearings.[1] At last, on passing before him, we heard the rapid opening and shutting of the apparatus, the time of exposure being the eightieth part of a second.

As we were preparing to be photographed a racing skiff passed us, and the occupant rested on his sculls to examine our vessel, after which a single powerful stroke carried him away. I observed his long brawny brown arms, and then it occurred to me that he was not of common mortal stature. The *Arar* had been

[1] The ordnance map gives the width of the channel here as about eighty yards. An eyewitness on the shore said that we had not occupied more than half this width in describing our circles. This is good evidence that a catamaran may be handy enough for river work, and it would be easy to build a catamaran much superior to the *Arar* in facility of evolution if the designer's study and attention were specially directed to that quality.

inspected by the gigantic Champion of France. Here, too, was a piece of good fortune, as we had particularly desired to meet with this very remarkable Frenchman on his own river.

He is about seven feet high and has all his life been fond of manly exercises. Rowing is but one of his accomplishments. He has had a bicycle specially built for him which looks as if intended for a superhuman cyclist. He is also fond of sailing, and of nautical travel as well as racing. The current anecdotes of his prowess are very numerous, and are likely to be preserved for generations in popular tradition like the legends about the heroes of antiquity.[1]

This place seems to be remarkable for one quality. I have only to wish for a person and here he is! First, it was the photographer, then the champion, afterwards I expressed a desire to know the address of some clever mechanic. "Restaurant des Tonnes," was the answer, where we are staying. The mechanic is a brother of our host's, and he has a workshop at the top of the house with a lathe and other delightful things. He did some good work for the *Arar*, and being a practical electrician expressed the opinion that she might readily be converted into an electric vessel. "What!" you will exclaim, "can a lover of sailing be hankering after a prosaic machine?" Dull calms have rather calmed our enthusiasm for white canvas.

We are lodged in a very peculiar sort of place that can only be made intelligible by a description. It is neither inn nor hotel, but a restaurant in front with a café behind it, and behind

---

[1] M. Bidault did not succeed in retaining the championship to the end of the year 1886, being defeated in the annual sculling contest on the Seine, but considering his various kinds of activity and his gigantic frame it is likely that on the whole he is physically the first of Frenchmen.

the café are a few rooms occasionally let to visitors, the restaurant is a summer-house open in front with a view of the Île Barbe, but our rooms look on a quiet street in the village. Without having hoped for such a luxury, I am in possession of a private study, furnished simply with a quiet artistic taste, and there are some interesting old engravings on the walls. In Stephen's room there is a painting of the Muse seated on clouds, a ray of light issuing from her forehead, and her left hand reposing on an open book with the legend "*non nisi grandia canto.*" I regret to say that Stephen is able to read *Pickwick* in this imposing presence, instead of *Paradise Lost*.

I have discovered who has given that artistic touch which pleased me in this house. It is the mechanic. He showed me a reduced cast of the frieze of the Parthenon, and a marvellous copy in pen and ink of an etching by Boissieu, a deceptive piece of imitation, but a waste of talent and time.

LETTER LVI.

St. Rambert,
September 19th, Evening.

The Île Barbe is six hundred yards long with a width of about a hundred and forty. The southern end is arranged as a public promenade easily accessible from both banks of the Saône by a suspension bridge. The buildings begin about the middle of the island and continue to the northern extremity, where there is a barrack occupied by one or two companies of soldiers. The southern part of the island has no character except that given by its fine trees; the northern extremity is rocky and rises to a

Ile Barbe from the East.

certain height which gives a fine position for the buildings upon it. On the eastern side is a Romanesque church tower in excellent preservation.

Stephen and I took a small rowing-boat and circumnavigated the island at our leisure whilst I sketched it from different points. It is certainly one of the most beautiful islands in Europe. From the north, the combination of rock and foliage with picturesque buildings is delightful, reminding one of the most perfect lake islands. I remember seeing it on a former voyage under an effect of warm, hazy afternoon sunshine so perfectly adapted to its character that it was impossible to believe it real. It seemed to be a painter's invention.

During our present visit we have seen this island under beautiful aspects also. There are three or four important views of it, from the two banks of the Saône, above and below, and also from the water. It has hitherto not been spoiled [1] but it had a narrow escape when the Government intended to build a fort on the north end, a project which, I believe, is now happily abandoned. There is nothing offensive in the present buildings which are picturesque and crown the natural forms of the island satisfactorily. By good luck, even their colour is mellow and agreeable. The strong northern end is still called the "*Chastelard*," *castellum arduum*, Castle Difficult. The name "Ile Barbe" is said to be corruptly derived from *Insula Barbara*, Wilderness Island, which was given before the monks built upon it.

The ecclesiastical establishments on this island are of great antiquity, but as it is not my business to write history in these letters I need not trace them from the fifth century downwards

---

[1] The promenade and suspension bridge have done less to spoil the island than might have been expected, as they are at the less interesting extremity.

The one astonishing fact is that in the twelfth century, when the Île Barbe was at the height of its power, the superior of the monastery there had a hundred and thirty-seven ecclesiastical establishments under him, and was himself a mighty feudal lord, treating with Savoy and France on the footing of an independent sovereign. The monastery itself was like a town, fortified and defended by its Chastelard, and full of accumulated riches. The Chastelard itself contained the library given by Charlemagne, the treasury of the Abbey, and one relic of surpassing heroic and poetic interest—the banner of Roland the brave, the paladin who fell at Roncevaux.

The monks of the Île Barbe deserve to be remembered for ever as examples of almost superhuman candour. First they became immensely rich and powerful, then their wealth made them self-indulgent, the severity of their rule was relaxed, and their idleness led to vice, so at last they themselves petitioned to the King to be disestablished. "We are so bad," they honestly said, "so sunk in turpitude and vice, so delivered over to iniquity, that we might be able to work out our salvation better if our monastery were dissolved, and if we abandoned our monkish dress, associated as it is with such a vile, licentious life." The King referred their petition to the Pope, Paul III., who admitted the validity of the reason assigned, and disestablished the monastery in 1549. The monks have left a reputation for many vices and one virtue. At least they told the truth.

In the present condition of the island we have to regret the disappearance of the monastery. A fragment of the monastic church is partially preserved. We visited the interior. All that remains of any value is a few rich romanesque capitals.

The north end of the island belongs to the State for military

Ile Barbe to the Right.

purposes, having been purchased for the intended fortress. A rocky and steep road leads past the barrack down to the water's edge on the west side, and we followed along the rocky shore till stopped by natural obstacles. The bank is here supported on strong arches.

The middle part of the island is owned entirely by private proprietors, who have houses upon it, not of a very dignified style of architecture, but picturesque and half concealed in beautiful foliage.

All the southern third is occupied by the public promenade with the usual fine trees and benches under them. From this promenade you have good views of both shores of the Saône. The eastern is occupied by a line of lofty houses between the fortress-crowned hill of Caluire and the rocky side of the river, leaving only space for a road cut in the rock. The western shore is covered by the village of St. Rambert, built on the side of a steep hill with its gardens in terraces supported by arched walls that leave the rock visible. The buildings are pretty and picturesque, with many turrets, and there are masses of foliage amongst them as well as beautiful separate trees and long "tonnelles de verdure," arched corridors of trellis-work entirely covered with creepers. It is a pretty village, but we feel that it is suburban, and that it has not the truly rustic character of the villages on the Upper Saône.

Above and below St. Rambert the ground is almost entirely occupied by a succession of parks with magnificent foliage and stately private residences. The one objection to these is their high walls. Those to the north leave only a narrow path on the rock between the wall and the river; to the south there is a broad public road that follows the river to Lyons. We readily understand the charm of this part of the Saône for the rich Lyonnese. It is delightfully beautiful and most charming to visit, but for permanent residence I should object to being down in a dell. I should prefer an open prospect, even with far inferior beauty.

The air, again, of the valley at Île Barbe is exactly the air of Lyons, which is so like that of London with its fog and coal smoke that with the help of a little imagination we could fancy ourselves in Kensington Gardens.

LETTER LVII.

Lyons, *September 20th.*

The natural beauty of the Saône ends now at Île Barbe, though it is easily seen that the river must have been beautiful down to the Rhône in Gaulish and Roman times.

There is, however, in the modern city of Lyons an artificial grandeur that is more impressive than anything in the *approaches* to London or Paris. For nearly two miles (to Vaise) the Saône keeps nearly straight, with but a slight bend to the left, but after that it takes a sudden turn towards the Rhône, coming to within six hundred yards of it; then it runs nearly parallel with the swift river for two miles and a half, and finally meets it at La Mulatière. At the turn after Vaise the Saône is in a deep gully between the heights of La Croix Rousse and Fourvières, but after that the tongue of land between the Saône and the Rhône is perfectly level, and entirely occupied by the better part of Lyons. La Croix Rousse reminds one strongly of Edinburgh by the dizzy height of its houses, and their grim unhomelike appearance. The opposite height is covered by a new and costly chapel (more costly than beautiful), whither the votaries go in pilgrimage to seek the aid of Our Lady of Fourvières. This part of the river is remarkable for its tall buildings against the steep rock that rises immediately behind them; the grim forts, too, are there on right and left to command the river and threaten the turbulent citizens.

The quays of the Saône in its course through Lyons had at one time the reputation of being the finest in the world, but since then Paris has exceeded them in extent and the Thames Embankment in architectural beauty. Still, the quays of Lyons are a magnificent work, not unworthy of the second city in France and her most navigable river; and if the Saône has been denuded of her natural beauty during the last league of her existence, it must be admitted that she ends her course with all the dignity of human wealth and civilisation.

The old cathedral of Lyons is near the river, on the right bank, at the foot of the height of Fourvières. The last of the great churches on the Saône has a gloomier aspect and sootier colour than the grand abbatial edifice at Tournus, but the architecture is richer. The west front, of course, is turned away from the river towards the steep. It has triple portals, like those of Amiens on a smaller scale, but all the statues are gone. The insignificant towers at this end remind one also of the stunted towers at Amiens, but at Lyons there are two others, more important, to the east. The apse, towards the Saône, has no *pourtour* with small chapels like that which gives such charm to the apse at Tournus. Down to the last century there was an ecclesiastical peculiarity about this cathedral—the situation of the episcopal throne. It was behind the high altar, and in the middle of the apse. This came from early Christian times, when the altar was a table only, without an altar-screen.[1] Though the apse is without *pourtour* there are fine fourteenth-century chapels on the south side of the cathedral. Altogether it is an interesting church, but not grand enough in scale for so important a city as Lyons.

The smaller church called L'Eglise d'Ainay, two hundred yards from the bridge of Ainay on the Saône (south of the cathedral), is an interesting and ancient little church. Viollet le Duc mentions the apse amongst the remarkable apses of France. There are some decorative mural paintings by Flandrin in the small apsidal chapels.[2]

After passing under thirteen bridges in the city of Lyons, the Saône joins the Rhône at La Mulatière. At the point of junction, the Saône has but one-third the breadth of the great river, but higher up they are equal in this respect, the Pont du Palais de Justice on the Saône being as long as the Pont de l'Hôtel Dieu on the Rhône. Nevertheless, although the width and depth of the two rivers may be nearly equal, the swift stream discharges more than twice as much water as the slow one. They also differ remarkably in colour. The Saône is emerald green when clear (its clearness is never more than relative); the Rhône is a blue-green, very like crystals of sulphate of copper.

[1] In a modern Roman Catholic church a bishop seated in the apse and looking westwards would have his face to the back of a stone wall.

[2] The reader may possibly not be aware that there is a very curious kind of quasi-independence in ecclesiastical matters at Lyons. The ritual differs considerably from the Roman, and is called the Lyonnese ritual habitually. Thus "*le rite Romain*" and "*le rite Lyonnais*" are spoken of just as Englishmen talk of the Roman and Anglican rituals. A Roman Catholic lady who passed a Sunday at Lyons told me that she had been embarrassed by the difference.

The point of junction is not so impressive as a lover of the two rivers might desire. It is spoiled by the mechanical perfection of the engineering works, including the railway bridge The distance is more noble. On the side of the Saône you have the imposing height of Fourvières, and on that of the Rhône a view of the broad river up to the first bridge, and beyond it the eastern faubourg of Lyons.

The peculiarity of this confluence is that the minor river immediately loses not only its name, but also its very nature. By a strange fate, the slowest stream in Europe is wedded to the most rapid, the most navigable of the great rivers to the least navigable. No, marriage it is not, but an absorption, a swallowing up by a creature of a different species. Beyond Lyons there is no Saône. *Flumen Araris* is no more—swift and pitiless *Rhodanus* tears his way, solitary, to the sea.

Confluence of Saône and Rhône.

EPILOGUE.

THE southward voyage narrated in the preceding letters terminated at the Île Barbe; but we brought the *Arar* back to Mâcon, which is her home. We rowed from St. Rambert to Couzon, then had a wind for five or six miles, and after that reverted to the old *Boussemroum* expedient of putting ourselves behind a steam-tug. We never had wind enough to get up the real speed of the *Arar*, that wild rush through the water which is the excitement and delight of catamaran sailing.

This persistent lack of wind has been a disappointment, but our only one. We have passed many delightful hours on a noble river, and have acquired that detailed knowledge of it which is the reward not of the rapid but of the patient traveller.

The result, for all of us, was an increase of admiration and affection for the Saône, of all rivers friendliest to man; so willing, as it were, to be tamed for his service that only a little art was necessary for its perfect conquest.

There is hardly anything deserving to be called sublimity on the Saône, but there are three distinct orders of beauty, that of the Upper Saône from Corre to Pontailler, that of the river of the plains, and lastly the beauty of the rich southern river, which is more and more hemmed in between precipitous banks till it flows past the fortress-crowned heights of Lyons.

Most of the principal islands have been described in the narrative of the voyage, but one was omitted because we were dragged past it quickly behind a steamer. This is the Île Bène, three miles above Neuville. We stayed upon it some hours on our return. It is remarkable for its beautiful sands, quite extensive and firm, and also for its picturesque old willows and a noble view of the Mont d'Or. Whilst we remained there the hill and the lake-like river showed themselves under precisely

Mont d'Or from Île Bène.

the same changing effects of rain which are familiar to us in the Highlands of Scotland.[1]

We slept at Trévoux, and left that place uncomfortably at five o'clock on a rainy morning. The tent made us a little saloon, and we tossed about for eleven hours in the eddies behind a great barge very deeply laden with copper ore. Any person

---

[1] Heavy showers came to the island itself during our stay, but having the ever-precious resource of the tent, we erected it on their approach and remained well sheltered till a return of fine weather. The tent is a good friend in these expeditions.

liable to sea-sickness would have preferred a different means of travelling, but we were interested in the behaviour of the boat amidst the swirling eddies, and concluded that she might be safely taken over the numerous cross currents and whirlpools of the Rhône.

We arrived at Mâcon on the 23rd of September at four in the afternoon, when the *Arar* was delivered into the hands of Batafi to be taken to pieces for the winter. The next day, from the deck of the passenger-steamer, we saw our own ship still quietly at anchor, unconscious of the temporary dissolution that awaited her, and we bade adieu to her with a regret all the more poignant that there was a glorious wind that day, precisely because we did not want it any longer.

[1] I made an experiment that is worth recording. On drawing the *Arar* close to the barge I found the motion less fatiguing, but the curious thing was this: *the* Arar *now followed without a hawser*. There was, in fact, no necessity whatever for a rope, as our boat was propelled by the back-water behind the barge. The *Arar* kept the noses of her two hulls at a distance of about three inches from the stern of the boat before her, and that with marvellous steadiness. For some time the two hawsers hung idly in festoons, but they were entirely detached before we came to the bridge at Mâcon, yet the *Arar* followed under the arch against the general current of the river, though, in reality, on the rapid counter-current of the back-water. How can a steamer tug a small boat without either increase of power expended or diminution of speed? The question appears insoluble, yet here is a solution of it: the steamer's motion may create a back-water behind a flat-sterned barge that she is towing, and the small boat may follow on the back-water without imposing the slightest extra tax upon the tug.

APPENDICES.

THE SAÔNE ABOVE CORRE.

I SHOULD have liked to follow the Saône from the source, on foot, of course, at first, and afterwards in a canoe to Corre, but the length of time occupied in the voyage of the *Boussemroum* compelled me to confine my exploration to the navigable part of the river. I have, however, for the sake of completeness, given the whole river in the maps, and a little information may be added here with regard to its character above the confluence with the Coney. The source is at Vioménil, in the department of the Vosges, a village of rather more than 500 inhabitants. Thence the Saône flows in a westerly direction to the village of Bonvillet, which is rather smaller than Vioménil, and here the river turns suddenly southwards. It soon passes Darney, a place of some relative importance (1600 inhabitants), with some remains of Roman and mediæval times. The next place is Monthureux-sur-Saône (1500 inhabitants), where there are the remains of a castle erected by Henri II. At Châtillon-sur-Saône (500 inhabitants) there are the remains of a Roman wall. The river now flows in a south-easterly direction towards Corre, passing by Jonvelle and Bourbevelle. Jonvelle is an ancient lordship of great historical interest. The history of it has been written by the Abbé Coudriet and the Abbé Chatelet in a volume of nearly six hundred pages. The Saône flows past Jonvelle in a curve, defending the place on two sides, and on the third it was strongly fortified. The fortifications have for the most part disappeared, though there are traces of them, useless to the artist but interesting to the archæologist. The following extract from the preface to the "History of Jonvelle," will give an idea of its past importance and of its present insignificance:

"The place was defended against external violence by the deep bed of the Saône and by a belt of good walls. A citadel and some detached forts protected the north side which was not covered by the river. Placed as an advanced sentinel on the frontiers of France and Lorraine, this fortress commanded the great roads from the Franche-Comté to Lorraine and Champagne. It was the key of the country on this point, and consequently one of the places most exposed to the attacks of the enemy and most burdened with the duties of national defence. It was a post of honour and danger. Twenty times in each century hostile armies presented themselves vainly before its ramparts. At last, after having long been the terror of the enemy, Jonvelle fell in 1641, given up to a French army by its cowardly Governor. The town was burnt, its walls, its forts, and its castle rased to the ground, and at the present day Jonvelle is nothing more than a commonplace village, where our curiosity, strongly excited by historical records, seeks in vain for some remains of a vanished strength and splendour. *Etiam periere ruinæ.*"

So far as I have been able to ascertain, the scenery between Vioménil and Corre is likely to be pretty and interesting, but not grand. The river winds between hills of moderate elevation and passes many woods. Its course from Vioménil to Bonvillet lies through a valley in the Forest of Darney, and probably offers nothing but close woodland views with a little stream running under the branches. After Darney the scenery is more open, but the reaches of the river are still short.

ROMAN REMAINS AT CORRE.

REMAINS of altars and fragments of architecture have been found abundantly in the plain called *le Parge*, situated between the present village and the confluence of the Saône and the Coney. Many rude Roman monuments have been taken from the antique cemetery. Several statues have been found at Corre, amongst them a fine colossal statue of Venus in white marble. This was in good preservation, but it was broken up from an objection to its nudity, and the abdomen was converted into the basin for holy water now at the entrance of the church, a strange vicissitude in the history of a piece of marble. It is to be regretted that this statue was not sent at once to Besançon, where many less valuable antiquities from Corre are preserved in the public museum.

THE DEFENCE OF ST. JEAN DE LOSNE.

THIS important incident in the history of the river Saône deserves more than the passing allusion in the text. The following account of it is abridged from the *Lyon Républicain* of October 24, 1886, where it was published with reference to the then intended festival.

"In 1636, at the beginning of the French period of the Thirty Years' War, the town of St. Jean de Losne was on the frontier (as Franche-Comté then belonged to the Empire), and it was considered to be the key of Burgundy. In the month of October of that year an army of eighty thousand men, composed of soldiers belonging to the Empire, with Hungarians, Croatians, and Spaniards, invaded Burgundy under the command of the celebrated General Gallas along with Edward of Braganza, the Marquis of Grana, the Duke of Lorraine, and others."

"Before Gallas attacked Dijon he was anxious to protect his rear by establishing himself at St. Jean de Losne, which he believed to be incapable of resistance. He came on October 25 to invest the little town, which had no defenders but four hundred citizens able to bear arms, and a hundred and fifty soldiers under the orders of the brave Rochefort d'Ailly de Saint Point, who was unfortunately smitten with the plague two nights before the blockade. There were eight guns on the ramparts."

"On October 26 the enemy summoned the town to surrender. The brave defenders knew the strategic importance of their town, and boldly replied that the enemy would never enter the place so long as they were alive to defend it. Gallas was irritated by this answer, and gave orders to begin the siege."

"This siege was endured with an ardour and an intrepidity that never languished for a moment. Women and young girls went upon the walls and encouraged their husbands and brothers taking their place when they fell. On October 30 the defenders took a flag from the enemy which confirmed their resolution."

"Meanwhile Gallas, astonished that so weak a place should resist him, renewed his attacks on October 31 and November 1. His artillery made a breach thirty feet long. The first assault was made on November 1, and repelled with great energy. On November 2, the enemy, before making a last and supreme effort, summoned the defenders of the place to yield, telling them that a longer resistance could add nothing to their honour, and that they should have whatever terms they desired."

"It was then that occurred an act of self-devotion worthy of the heroes of Leonidas and the sublime defenders of Numantia. Being called together by the two *échevins*, Pierre Desgranges and Pierre Lapre, some brave citizens, amongst whom was Claude Martène, who had paid the soldiers with his own money met in the guard-chamber of the Saône gate on the place now called 'La Place de la Délibération,' and there by common agreement composed and signed without delay that immorta, deliberation in which they declared that they would all courageously expose their lives to the efforts of the enemy, and even were resolved, in case of overpowering force, to set fire each of them to his own house and to the ammunition in the town-hall, so that the enemy might reap no advantage, and, after that, to die all of them sword in hand, and at the last extremity, where they had any means of retreat, to retire by the Saône bridge and destroy one of its arches behind them."

The original words are worth preserving. The inhabitants declare that they

"*Mesme sont résolus, au cas que par malheur ils vinssent a estre forcez, de mettre le feu chacun en leurs maisons et aux poudres et munitions de guerre estant en la maison de ville affin que les ennemis nen reçoipvent aulcun avantage, et ensuitte de ce, mourir tous l'espée à la main, et à toute extrémites ou ils auraient moyen de retraicte de la faire par le pont de soone et brusler en sortant un arcade d'iceluy."*

"This decision was then presented to the defenders of the Tour Truchot and of the breach, who signed it. The houses were then filled with inflammable materials, and it was decided that if the enemy succeeded in entering by the breach all the streets of the town should burn at the same time. All the defenders met at the breach; the brave Saint Point had himself carried thither, almost dying, to encourage the soldiers, and soon the attack began, impetuous, terrible. At one moment the shock was so violent that the breach appeared to be carried, and the watchman was on the point of giving the alarm signal; but at the height of the struggle twelve valiant men from Auxonne entered by the Saône gate, and going at once to the breach, encouraged the defenders by announcing the arrival of reinforcements. They took their share of the fight, and one of them, named Boillaud, was killed."

"The sublime sacrifice of the townsmen was not to be consummated. The Imperialists, having lost 800 men, suspended their attack. During the night the brave Rantzau entered the town, and the enemy alarmed by the noise of his cavalry, began to retreat. The next morning the defenders of the valiant town joyfully saw Gallas in retreat."

Surely this is as fine an example of courage in a little town as any in history, and it is well that amidst the petty political disputes of the day, St. Jean de Losne should keep in mind the noblest page in all its annals.[1]

---

[1] The name of the Imperialist General is written in three ways, Galas, Gallas, and Gallass. He himself used the last form in his signature.

GERGY.

At the time when we passed the village of Gergy, one of its inhabitants, Count de Chardonnet, was engaged in some interesting experiments for the production of artificial silk. By some chemical process, which is his secret, he dissolves fibrous materials (rags, paper, sawdust) so as to produce a viscous solution that he forces into a tube by hydraulic pressure, out of which it issues by minute orifices in threads like a spider's web, which are wound off rapidly on a reel. The material so obtained is indistinguishable from the silk of the worm. It is as glossy and as strong, and can be woven like the usual fabrics and made into velvet. It has not yet been produced on any but an experimental scale, as the patents are not all taken out yet (July 1887), but unless some unforeseen difficulty should prevent its commercial use, we have here a discovery rivalling in importance the artificial ultramarine of Guimet, also first produced on the banks of the Saône.

I may add that the three earliest of the silk-making machines have been constructed by M. Brunet-Meige, of Chalon, who built the hulls of the *Arar*. The silk from them that I have examined was made from some old newspapers. It deceived a manufacturer at Lyons who, after weaving some of it, believed it to be real silk dyed by a new and excellent process. In fact, the artificial silk is dyed in the solution before being drawn out into filaments. Sixty or seventy filaments can be drawn from the tube and wound off upon the reel at the same time. When the solution has not been dyed the silk resembles that of a worm in colour.

M. CHABAS, THE EGYPTOLOGIST.

I KNEW the late M. Chabas personally, and he was an intimate friend of my brother-in-law.[1] He was good enough to place his valuable library entirely at my disposal, but my lines of study had nothing to do with Egypt, so I made little or no use of it. M. Chabas himself was more interesting to me than his collections. He was a most genuine student, as is well known to those who are competent to appreciate his labours. In some respects he worked under a disadvantage, living in a provincial town like Chalon and in absolute isolation, so far as his special pursuit was concerned. He had a private fortune, but it was not large enough to enable him both to travel and collect, so he preferred collecting as the best way of getting materials for his studies. But this laid him open to the depreciation of the ignorant, who could not understand how a man could live at Chalon and study ancient Egypt. The truth was that photography, and the labours of draughtsmen and other students in Egypt, brought abundant materials to M. Chabas, and the extreme acuteness of his intellect enabled him to make the most of them. Besides that, he had a fire of enthusiasm which never failed. It is probable, however, that the closeness of his application shortened his life. The last time I met him was at the house of M. Jules Chevrier, a well-known antiquary and skilful amateur artist, and the conversation turned on the question whether the power of intellectual acquisition was limited by the nature of our faculties or only by want of time. I maintained that our faculties themselves were very limited, and that our receptive capacity was, at the best, but small, so that it was wise to learn only those things that were most useful to us. M.

[1] M. Charles Gindriez, who kindly aided me in the arrangements for the voyage with the *Boussemroum*.

Chabas strongly supported me, saying that he himself had found by experience that his brain could only receive a limited quantity of knowledge, having tried its capacity to the utmost. Some time after that he was speaking in public, and suddenly found himself unable to proceed, after which the worst symptoms of cerebral exhaustion supervened, unhappily with a fatal termination. He was a most kind and amiable man, and remained to the last entirely modest, notwithstanding the extent of his learning.

I have mentioned M. Jules Chevrier. He was a well-informed archæologist and an artist of by no means despicable ability. His volume of illustrations of Chalon-sur-Saône, in etching and aquatint, will remain as a record of old Chalon. My pen sketch of the *Rue St. Vincent* is from a clever aquatint by M. Chevrier, and the sketch of the Bridge in the year 1600 is from an etching that he had made on the authority of an old picture. He had considerable skill as a painter.

CORRESPONDENCE WITH THE FRENCH AUTHORITIES.

The following notes of my correspondence with the French authorities may be of interest to artists and amateurs who desire to sketch in France.

At the time of our detention at Pontailler, the Prefect of the Lower Alps, M. Gilliot, telegraphed at my request to the Minister of War. General Boulanger replied at once by telegram authorising M. Gilliot to take such measures as he thought fit. I have not seen the telegram, but I know its purport through a French officer of rank who kindly took the trouble to call at the War Office.

The measure that M. Gilliot intended to take was to write on my behalf to the Prefect of the department where the arrest took place. Unfortunately his letter, which inclosed the Minister's telegram, was addressed by his secretary to the Prefect of the Doubs instead of the Prefect of the Côte d'Or. The recipient caused a minute search for the three travellers to be made in all the prisons of his department whilst we were in our floating home upon the Saône. The strangest circumstance about this mistake is that two telegrams were at the same time *correctly* addressed to me at Pontailler, Côte d'Or, from the Prefecture of the Lower Alps.

The mistake arose from a confusion between Pontailler which is in the Côte d'Or, and Pontarlier which is in the Doubs. The *Temps* committed it shortly afterwards in an article headed in capital letters "*M. Ph. Hamerton et les Gendarmes de Pontarlier.*" And yet the contributor wrote with my letter to the *Pall Mall Gazette* before him, in which Pontailler was correctly printed.

I then asked M. Gilliot to give me some written document

that might be shown to a gendarme, stating that I had been protected by the Minister of War, but the Prefect of the Lower Alps felt some delicacy, with regard to other Prefects, his colleagues, in giving me anything that might seem like an authorisation to travel and work in departments other than his own. He therefore recommended me to apply to the Prefects of those departments which are traversed by the Saône.

I began by applying to the Prefect of Saône-et-Loire, as the Saône runs more than seventy miles in that department. This Prefect, M. Le Mailler, had from the first acted kindly on my behalf. He had written to the Prefect of the Côte d'Or asking him to protect me. This would have been of the greatest service to me if any intercession with General Tricoche had been necessary. That General, however, facilitated our work instead of hindering it.

My request to the Prefect of Saône-et-Loire was confined to a single point. I asked for permission to sketch upon that part of the Saône which traverses or touches the department of Saône-et-Loire. Such a request seemed the more admissible that there are no fortifications on that part of the river. The Prefect's answer, though very courteous, said that it was impossible for him to grant permission to draw freely, and that he did not think I should succeed in obtaining such a permission from the Minister of War. There was, however, a kind of hint in this Prefect's letter that was evidently intended to be of use. He did not by any means *forbid* me to make sketches, but he recommended me, during my artistic excursions, to provide myself with papers giving evidence of my identity. This was as much as to say that, on showing who I was, I should not be disquieted in the department of Saône-et-Loire.

I now decided to make another application at the War Office, not to the Minister himself, but to his *Chef de Cabinet*. I had no new favour to request, and begged for nothing more than a short note admitting me to be right in the belief that the Minister's protection had been accorded to me—a note that I could show to a gendarme. Colonel Jung, the *Chef de Cabinet*, replied with the very greatest courtesy and at some length. The gist of his letter was that the Prefect of the Lower Alps was now alone authorised to protect me, either by giving me the Minister's communication, if he thought fit to do so, or by recommending me to other Prefects.

I then wrote once more to the Prefect of the Lower Alps, but he did not remember the terms of the Minister's despatch.

There are no functionaries in France more observant of etiquette amongst themselves than the Prefects. They are careful to avoid, not only the reality, but the slightest appearance, of intrusion on each other's territories. There is, consequently, a peculiar difficulty in obtaining anything from a Prefect that is likely to have an effect outside of his own borders.

The Minister of the Interior is in a different situation. The limits of *his* prefecture are the frontiers of France. I therefore found means, through a friend, of applying to M. Sarrien, the Minister of the Interior. My case did not go through the usual channel of the bureaux, but was stated clearly to the Minister himself in a conversation. His reply was that he could not grant the desired permission to draw, that it was not within his competence, but he added that if I carried a passport no one could say anything to me. As this opinion was given in writing, not by the Minister, but by his acquaintance, who himself occupies an official position, and as it was written, by good luck, on official paper, I thought it might be valuable, and kept the letter. Still, I confess that I have not found in the law of the 18th of April, 1886, any article to the effect that the possession of a passport implies the right to draw.

Mr. Egerton, the British *Chargé d'Affaires*, gave me the Ambassador's passport and his own personal recommendation, written in his autograph and in the French language. He also kindly promised to communicate with the French authorities in Paris. This promise was fulfilled, with the result that the Prefect of Saône-et-Loire (evidently in consequence of a communication from the Ministry of the Interior) caused a French passport-certificate to be prepared for me, available for all France. Even this passport, however, though it contains a strong personal recommendation, *makes no mention of drawing*.

The conclusion I naturally arrived at after these varied experiences was that it was useless to ask any one in authority for permission to draw, as that would never be granted. The authorities would *tolerate* drawing in my own case—wink at it, as we say in English—but no amount of diplomacy could ever induce them to *authorise* it.

By never granting a written permission to draw, the French Government retains its hold on German spies, who might present themselves as artists. It also avoids the troublesome and invidious task of making a selection.

English artists may work in France if they are provided with a Foreign Office passport having a French *visa*. A good *visa* to procure is that of the Prefecture of the department in which the artist desires to work: if that is too remote, the *visa* of a sous-Prefecture or even a Mairie might answer the purpose; but local authorities are only respected in their own localities, as Mr. Pennell found when the recommendations of the Mayor and sub-Prefect of Chalon were treated as valueless at Lyons. An artist must, however, in all cases make up his mind to be interrogated, and perhaps occasionally arrested and detained for a short time. He should remember, also, that, at the best, he can only draw on sufferance, seeing that a formal licence to draw is never granted.

BOAT TRAVELLING ON RIVERS.

THE results of this expedition on the Saône may be given in a few words, for those readers who take a practical interest in the art of independent travel.

Let me define, first, what I mean by independent travel. I mean that which allows the traveller to stop wherever he pleases, in day-time or night-time, to observe, to sketch, or to rest. All modes of locomotion that drag the traveller past places where he would like to stay, were it but for a few minutes, are, in my opinion, only varieties of what the French call *assujettissement*.

A house-boat realises this condition admirably. It is most convenient as a solution of the problem how to devise a lodging that shall be spacious and yet movable. Unfortunately, travelling in a house-boat is at the same time the dullest of all the varieties of navigation, and, in fact, does not deserve to be considered "boating" at all. There is neither amusement nor exercise in being dragged over the water in a kind of Noah's Ark.

I set aside all ballasted sailing-boats without hesitation, I mean for travelling purposes on rivers. They are charming toys for little regattas between two bridges; and that, in fact, is almost the only use that is ever made of them. In travelling, when you have a glassy calm for a week together, what can you do with a floating castle that has a ton or two of lead in its foundations? A friend of mine, under such circumstances, leaves his heavy boat at anchor and goes home by railway. If you cling to your vessel a steam-tug is the only resource, and that deprives you of all liberty of stoppage. Mr. MacGregor had a yawl constructed for travelling, the *Rob Roy*. At first she carried thirty hundred-weight of ballast, afterwards reduced. One man was to row this, in calms, and there were oars for the purpose. What could the owner do with his ballasted vessel on the Seine? He ascended behind a tug, all the way from Havre to Paris, a distance of three hundred miles. The return voyage was begun under sail, but before reaching Poissy sailing was abandoned and the tug was resorted to again. The oars do not appear to have been used. I need scarcely observe that a houseboat would have been quite as amusing and incomparably more comfortable. The Saône is a better river than the Seine, but a friend of mine at Chalon who has an excellent little river yacht, told me that on a voyage to Neuville his speed had averaged little more than a mile an hour, and he returned behind a steamer.

The open boat for rowing, with *auxiliary* sails and little ballast, is a practical thing for river travel, but either the sails must be small or the boat is dangerous. The light boat for rowing only is far superior to the ballasted sailing-boat for *average* speed on a river, but it affords no lodgings on board and little room for luggage.

I like a catamaran because it is a safe sailing-boat that bears a good spread of canvas without an ounce of ballast. A Windermere yacht [1] carries at the utmost *one* hundred and forty square feet of canvas per ton of displacement, the *Arar* carries at the rate of *five* hundred and forty feet per ton, which might be safely increased to eight hundred in all ordinary weather.

Other reasons for liking a catamaran are because it affords comfortable lodging in a tent on the roomy flat floor of its deck, and also because it can be rowed easily (having no drag of ballast), whilst its great lateral resistance *in combination with a shallow draught of water* makes it incomparably superior to all other boats for towing. No other boat offers equal lateral resistance with so little depth.

[1] The Windermere yacht is selected as a type of boat that carries very large sails. Small yachts often carry half as much in proportion, or less.

Mr. Herreshoff's American catamarans are far superior to mine in speed, but their weight is a serious objection. A Herreshoff catamaran weighs four times as much as the *Arar*, which I consider too heavy already. An extremely light catamaran, that could be easily rowed yet at the same time would be able to carry about two hundred feet of canvas, seems the desideratum for river travelling.

I need not enter into minute details which would interest few readers, but may say that the *Arar* is twenty-four feet long and has a beam, over all, of seven feet three inches; this beam is much smaller in proportion, than that of the American catamarans (usually about one-half the length) but it is quite sufficient for the canvas I desire to carry, as big sails require proportionate spars, and the narrower beam gives greater rigidity to the fabric, besides its convenience in passing amongst other boats, and in locks.

INDEX.

ABÉLARD, 223
Ainay, church of, at Lyons, 342
Albigny Islands, 325
Allériot, 198
Amance, river, 66
Anse, 311
Apremont, 135
Arar, the author's sailing-boat, 1, 3, 205
    her crew, 206
    described, 225, 226, 230, 364
    her behaviour when towed, 246
    how she is arranged for the night, 265
    in a squall, 272
    personal freedom on board, 300
    towed without a hawser, 347
Arrest, probability of, foreseen, 114
    at Pontailler, 142
Athée, 155
Authorities, the French, 203, 358
Auxonne, approach to, 155
    fortifications of, 156
    historical associations, 157
Azergues, river, 311

BARGEMEN, their civility, 69, 131
Barges, the building of, 219
Batafi, 274, 285
Baulay, 76, 77
Belgian, a, 181
Belleville, port de, 301
Berrichon, a kind of boat, 5
    engaged, 7
    its instability, 80
    the last of the, 200
Beaujeux, 117
Beaujolais, mountains of, 298, 307, 314
Beauregard, 306, 307

Boat-travelling, 362
Bonvillet, 349
Boucicaut, Madame, 198
Bourbevelle, 349
Boussemroum, the, described, 10
    bad for towing when lightly laden, 56
    instability of, 80
    her behaviour between Verdun and Chalon, 194
Boxes, kind of, preferred for aquatic travel, 267
"Brick," in French, 33
Bridges, old, their rarity, 81
Burgundy, the plain of, 160
Buzzards, 269

CALUIRE, fortress of, 339
Canal, the Burgundy, 172
    from the Saône to the Meuse, 44
    du centre, 9, 202
Canals, beauty of, 91
    on the Upper Saône, 35
Catamaran, lateral resistance of, 246
    circumstances most unfavourable to a, 271
    sailing, 328
    reasons for liking a, 363
Cendrecourt, 64, 67
Chabas, the Egyptologist, 42, 356
Chalon from a distance, 199
    its origin, 207
    formerly capital of the Burgundian kingdom, 209
    the counts of, 211
    in the sixteenth century, 212
    the deanery tower, 214
    church of St. Peter, 217
    manners of the inhabitants, 224

Champion, the, of France, 335
Charnay-les-Chalon, 178
Chastelard, the, on Île Barbe, 337
Châtelet, Le, 176
Châtillon-sur-Saône, 349
Chemilly, 85, 86, 88
Chevrier, Jules, 357
Clayonnages, 238
Clergy at Verdun, 193
Cluny, the abbatial church at, 235, 236
Colonne, La, 239
    inn at, 240
Coney, the river, 42
Conflandey, 77
Conflans, 77
Constantine, the Emperor, 227
Constellations, the, 232
Corre, the canal, 41
    the church at, 44
    described, 50
    Roman remains at, 351
Côte d'Or, the, 160
Coursi, a kind of river-boat, 5
Couzon, 329
Croix Rousse, Lyons, 340
Crusaders on the Saône, 162, 163

DAGUERRE, 228
Darney, 349
Discipline, 27
Dombes, Les, the Principality of, 316
Doubs, the river, 183
Durgeon, the river, 87

ENCAMPMENT, on the Arar, 267

FARGES, 263
Filomena, St., an old poem about, 254
Flandrin, mural paintings by, 342
Fleurville, bridge and port, 270
Forest below Apremont, 137
Fouchécourt, 75, 76
Fourvières, 340, 341, 343
Franki presents himself, 51
    his separation from his mother, 54
    his berth, 113
    parties for and against him, 113
    his imprudence, 158
    the close of his engagement, 201

GALLAS, General, 169, 352
Garibaldians at St. Jean de Losne, 170
Gendarmes at Pontailler, 143
    at St. Jean de Losne, 165
    at Verdun, 190
Gergy, 197, 355
Gipsies at Corre, 45, 46
Gray, 30, 124, 125
    approach to, 123
Grosne, the river, 235
Greuze, 258

HERRESHOFF, his rudders, 262
    his catamarans, 364

ÎLE BARBE described, 336
Île Bène, 346

JIB, on a catamaran, 237
Joiner, at Corre, 45
Joinville, Sire de, 163
Jonvelle, 349, 350
Jussey, 66

KINGDOM, the Burgundian, 209, 210
Kornprobst, Captain, 15, 22
    his discretion and duties on the *Boussemroum*, 29

LAMARTINE, his statue at Mâcon, 278
    his birthplace at Mâcon, 279
    his gifts, 279, 280
Lanterne, the river, 77
Locks, on the Lower Saône, 322
Lothair, 211
Lux, 227
Lyons, modern city of, 340
    cathedral, 341

MÂCON, 273
    Hôtel du Sauvage, 274, 275
    the Council of, 277
    a summer evening at, 278
    the bridge, 280
    churches at, 282
    the Prefecture, 284
    under an evening effect, 286
Mailly-le-Port, 162
Mantoche, 131, 132

Marche, La, 155
Marnay, 235
Matelote, 292, 297
Mercey, 115
Mezerine, river, 304
Mont Blanc, 229, 261, 270
Mont Ceindre, 331
Mont d'Or, 314, 320, 331, 346
Montmerle, 304
Monthureux-sur-Saône, 349
Montureux-les-Baulay, 75

NAPOLEON, his bed and chair at Mâcon, 275
    after his evasion from Elba, 276
Neuville, its basin for sailing, 326
Niepce, 228
    his statue, 229

ORMES, 246
Ormoy, 59
Ognon, confluence with, 139
Otay, 117
Ovanches, 99

"PATRON" of the *Boussemroum*, 18, 21
    his personal appearance, 9, 10
    a good cook, 18
    his one lesson in rowing, 37
    and Pilot, their quarrels, 121
    the last of him, 202
Parisien, the steamer, 321
Pauchouse, a dish, 185
Paul III., Pope, 338
Péniche, a kind of boat, 70
Pennell, Mr., 31
    his difficulties about sketching, 200, 201
Petite Amie, a Saône yacht, 324, 326
Pilot, the, of the *Boussemroum*, 10
    he takes the command, 14
    his quarrels with Patron, 48
    his magnificent energy, 58, 80
    his wife on the Rhône, 122
Police of the river, 136
Poncey les Athée, 155
Pontailler, 140
Pope, the, 289, 290
Port d'Arciat, 289
    scenery at, 292

Port d'Ouroux, inn at, 233
    view from, 234
Port sur Saône, 79, 81
    the church, 82
Prantigny, 118
Princes, expulsion of, 152
Probus, the Emperor, 209

QUAILS, 288
Quays at Lyons, 341
Quitteur, 117

RANZEVELLE, 58
Ray, 106, 107, 108, 109
Recologne, 114
Rhône and Rhine canal, 162
Rhône, colour of, 342
Richecourt, 61, 62
Rigny, 120
Riottier, 309
Roland, Mount, 153
Roland, his banner, 338
Rupt, 103, 104, 105

SAILING, average speed of, 247, 248
Saône, colour of its banks, 155
    the Lower, its character, vii, viii, 159
    between Charnay and Verdun, 180
    colour of, 342
    friendly to man, 345
    and Rhône, confluence of, 343
    the Upper, vii, 345
Saracens, the, at Uchizy, 264
Savoyeux, canal near, 114
Scey, the basin near, 93
    the town, 95
Seille, the river, 263
Seurre, 177
Solutré, 287
Spy mania, the, 83
Squall, at Tournus, 260
St. Jean de Losne, 26, 164
    church at, 166
    defence of, 169, 352
St. John, island of, 273
St. Laurent-lès-Mâcon, 273
St. Marcel, 223
St. Rambert, the author's lodging at, 335
    parks at, 339
St. Romain, 294

TARARE, mountains, 314
Thoissey, 294, 295, 296
Tournus, 249
    southern character of, 249, 250
    the church, 253
Towing, 245
Trévoux, 313, 346
    the view from the terrace, 314
Trugny canal, incident in, 23
Tugs, their speed, 153
    their slowness, 174
Tunnel, effect of, 34
    passing through one in bed, 36
    below Scey, 97

UCHIZY, 264

VERDUN, 183
Verjux, 197

Vernet, Horace, 38
Vibert, M., his yacht *Petite Amie*, 323
Villars, 262
Villefranche, 311
Vioménil, 349
Vitteaut, M., and his yacht *Falourde*, 223, 224

YACHTS at Neuville, 324

ZIPFEL, M., his yacht *Croquemitaine*, 324
Zoulou, the donkey, 11
    his way of kicking, 55
    his difficulties on the river, 80
    good on a canal, 134
    slow on the Saône, 153
    the last sight of, 202

www.ingramcontent.com/pod-product-compliance
Lightning Source LLC
Chambersburg PA
CBHW071911230426
43671CB00010B/1558

5

ac
87 Seelen

30-